Criminal Typologies

Criminal Typologies

Exploring Crime and Criminal Behavior

First Edition

Aida Hass-Wisecup and Christopher Jerome Moloney

Missouri State University

Bassim Hamadeh, CEO and Publisher
Angela Schultz, Senior Field Acquisitions Editor
Carrie Baarns, Manager, Revisions and Author Care
Susana Christie, Senior Developmental Editor
Casey Hands, Production Editor
Jordan Krikorian, Editorial Assistant
Jess Estrella, Senior Graphic Designer
Alexa Lucido, Licensing Manager
Natalie Piccotti, Director of Marketing
Kassie Graves, Senior Vice President, Editorial
Jamie Giganti, Director of Academic Publishing

Copyright © 2023 by Cognella, Inc. All rights reserved. No part of this publication may be reprinted, reproduced, transmitted, or utilized in any form or by any electronic, mechanical, or other means, now known or hereafter invented, including photocopying, microfilming, and recording, or in any information retrieval system without the written permission of Cognella, Inc. For inquiries regarding permissions, translations, foreign rights, audio rights, and any other forms of reproduction, please contact the Cognella Licensing Department at rights@cognella.com.

Trademark Notice: Product or corporate names may be trademarks or registered trademarks and are used only for identification and explanation without intent to infringe.

Cover image: Copyright © 2020 iStockphoto LP/paseven.
Copyright © 2021 iStockphoto LP/greyj.

Printed in the United States of America.

As I reflect on my career and the many people I have come across that have had an impact on my life, I can't help but think of my Uncle William, and the passion we shared for criminal justice over many decades. He has always taught me to be a critical thinker and never accept facts at face value. Go beyond what is obvious and ask, "Why?" And where there's a question mark, find the period. I learned from him to always be convinced and grounded in your arguments. His words of wisdom have collectively inspired me to be a writer and a theorist and for this reason I dedicate this book to him, my dear uncle William Yassa, you are the wind beneath the wings of many.

—Aida Hass-Wisecup

To my grandfathers, Edwin and Walter. The example you set for how to work hard, sacrifice for others, love and care for family, friends, and community, set a high bar; I love and miss you, always.

—Chris Moloney

Brief Contents

Module I: An Introduction to the Study of Crime Types and Criminals — 1

1. How Do We Study Crime Types and Criminals? — 2
2. Key Issues in the Study of Crime — 17
3. Developing a Criminal Typology — 35

Module II: Violent Crime Profiles — 55

4. Crimes of Interpersonal Violence: Homicide and Assault — 56
5. Crimes of Interpersonal Violence: Rape and Sexual Assault — 74
6. Crimes of Interpersonal Violence: Robbery — 88

Module III: Property and Drug Crime Profiles — 101

7. Property Crime — 102
8. Drug Crime — 113

Module IV: Cyber and Environmental Crime Profiles — 131

9. Cybercrime — 132
10. Green Crimes and Harms — 151

Module V: Crimes of Power: Organized and State Crime Profiles 169

11 Organized Crime 170

12 State Crime 185

Detailed Contents

Module I: An Introduction to the Study of Crime Types and Criminals — 1

1 How Do We Study Crime Types and Criminals? — 2
- Chapter Headings — 2
- Chapter Objectives — 2
- Key Terms — 2
- Opening Questions — 2
- True Crime — 3
- What Is Crime? — 3
- What Is Deviance? — 4
  - Social Definition and Social Norms — 5
  - The Role of Social Reaction in Defining Crime and Deviance — 6
- How Much Crime Is There? — 9
  - The Popular Image of Crime — 9
  - The Reality of Crime Data — 10
- Key Takeaways — 13
- Conclusion and Formal Summary Questions — 14
- E-Resources — 14
- References — 15

2 Key Issues in the Study of Crime — 17
- Chapter Headings — 17
- Chapter Objectives — 17
- Key Terms — 17
- Opening Questions — 17
- True Crime — 18
- Who Defines Crime? — 18
  - The Consensus Model of Law Creation — 19
  - The Conflict Model of Law Creation — 19
- What Is the Goal of Punishment? — 20
  - Punishment as Retribution — 21
  - Punishment as Deterrence — 22
  - Punishment as Rehabilitation — 23
- Crime Victimization in Context — 24
  - The Study of Crime Victims — 24
  - Trends in Victimization — 25

Social Correlates of Criminal Offending	27
Age and Crime	27
Race and Crime	28
Gender and Crime	29
Social Class and Crime	29
Location and Crime	30
Key Takeaways	31
Conclusion and Formal Summary Questions	31
E-Resources	32
References	32

3 Developing a Criminal Typology — 35

Chapter Headings	35
Chapter Objectives	35
Key Terms	35
Opening Questions	35
True Crime	36
What Are Typologies?	36
Legal Typologies	38
Felony Versus Misdemeanor	39
UCR Definition	39
Offender-Based Typologies	41
Physical Attributes	42
Personality of Offender	44
Motive/Method of Operation	46
Contextual Typologies	48
Victim-Based Typologies	50
Key Takeaways	51
Conclusion and Formal Summary Questions	51
E-Resources	52
References	52

Module II: Violent Crime Profiles — 55

4 Crimes of Interpersonal Violence: Homicide and Assault — 56

Chapter Headings	56
Chapter Objectives	56
Key Terms	56
Opening Questions	56
True Crime	57
What Are Crimes of Interpersonal Violence?	57
Various Categories of Homicide	58
Situational Homicide	59
Subculture of Violence	61

Serial Killing	62
Mass Murder	64
Various Categories of Assault	65
Intimate Partner Violence	65
Child Maltreatment	67
Elder Abuse	68
Homicide and Assault Offenders and Their Victims	69
Characteristics of Homicide and Assault Offenders	69
Characteristics of Homicide and Assault Victims	70
Key Takeaways	70
Conclusion and Formal Summary Questions	71
E-Resources	71
References	72

5 Crimes of Interpersonal Violence: Rape and Sexual Assault — 74

Chapter Headings	74
Chapter Objectives	74
Key Terms	74
Opening Questions	74
True Crime	75
What Is Rape and Sexual Assault?	76
Various Patterns of Rape	77
Date Rape	77
Spousal Rape	78
Same-Sex Rape	79
Gang Rape	80
Rape and Sexual Assault Offenders and Their Victims	81
Characteristics of Rape Offenders	81
Characteristics of Rape Victims	82
Key Takeaways	84
Conclusion and Formal Summary Questions	85
E-Resources	86
References	86

6 Crimes of Interpersonal Violence: Robbery — 88

Chapter Headings	88
Chapter Objectives	88
Key Terms	88
Opening Questions	88
True Crime	88
What Is Robbery?	89
Various Patterns of Robbery Offenses	90
Institutional Robbery	90
Personal Robbery	92
Home Invasion	93

Robbery and the Criminal Subculture	94
Robbery Offenders and Their Victims	95
Characteristics of Robbery Offenders	95
Characteristics of Robbery Victims	96
Key Takeaways	98
Conclusion and Formal Summary Questions	99
E-Resources	99
References	100

Module III: Property and Drug Crime Profiles   101

7 Property Crime   102

Chapter Headings	102
Chapter Objectives	102
Key Terms	102
Opening Questions	102
True Crime	102
What Is Property Crime?	103
The Scope and Scale of Property Crime	104
Property Crime Subtypes	105
Burglary	105
Larceny-Theft	106
Motor Vehicle Theft	107
Arson	108
Property Crime Characteristics	110
Key Takeaways	112
Conclusion and Formal Summary Questions	112
E-Resources	112
References	113

8 Drug Crime   113

Chapter Headings	113
Chapter Objectives	113
Key Terms	113
Opening Questions	113
True Crime	113
What Is Drug Crime?	114
The Scope and Scale of Drug Crime	116
Drug Crime Subtypes	118
The Cocaine Trade	118
The Heroin Trade	123
Drug Crime Characteristics	125
Key Takeaways	125

Conclusion and Formal Summary Questions	126
E-Resources	126
References	127

Module IV: Cyber and Environmental Crime Profiles   131

9 Cybercrime   132

Chapter Headings	132
Chapter Objectives	132
Key Terms	132
Opening Questions	132
True Crime	133
What Is Cybercrime?	133
The Scope and Scale of Cybercrime	135
How Much Cybercrime Is There?	135
The Evolution of Cybercrime	137
Cybercrime Subtypes	139
Computer Intrusions	139
Identity and Cyber Theft	140
Cyberbullying and Stalking	141
Virtual Black Markets	142
Cyberviolence	143
Cybercrime Characteristics	144
Cybercrime Offenders	146
Cybercrime Victims	147
Key Takeaways	148
Conclusion and Formal Summary Questions	148
E-Resources	149
References	149

10 Green Crimes and Harms   151

Chapter Headings	151
Chapter Objectives	151
Key Terms	151
Opening Questions	151
True Crime	152
What Is "Green" Criminology?	152
The Scope and Scale of Green Crimes and Harms	154
Subtypes of Green Crimes	156
Air Pollution and Water Pollution	156
Disposal of Hazardous and "E" Waste	160
Poaching and Illegal Wildlife Trafficking	162
Green Crime Characteristics	163

Green Crime Offenders	163
Green Crime Victims	164
Key Takeaways	165
Conclusion and Formal Summary Questions	165
E-Resources	165
References	166

Module V: Crimes of Power: Organized and State Crime Profiles 169

11 Organized Crime 170

Chapter Headings	170
Chapter Objectives	170
Key Terms	170
Opening Questions	170
True Crime	171
What Is Organized Crime?	171
The Organization of Organized Crime	171
The Scope and Scale of Organized Crime	174
The Catch-22—Law Enforcement Action May Create Organized Crime	174
The RICO Act and American Organized Crime	175
Organized Crime Subtypes	178
Narcotics Manufacturing, Trafficking, and Distribution	178
Weapons Trafficking and Distribution	178
Human and Organ Trafficking	179
Antiquities Theft, Fraud, and Trafficking	180
Organized Crime Characteristics	180
Key Takeaways	182
Conclusion and Formal Summary Questions	182
E-Resources	183
References	183

12 State Crime 185

Chapter Headings	185
Chapter Objectives	185
Key Terms	185
Opening Questions	185
True Crime	186
What Is State Crime?	186
The Difference Between State Crime and White-Collar Crime	187
Characteristics of White-Collar Crimes	188

The Scope and Scale of State Crime	189
State Crime Subtypes	191
State-Corporate Crime	191
Abuse of Power and Corruption	192
Crimes Against Humanity	193
Characteristics of State Crime	195
Key Takeaways	196
Conclusion and Formal Summary Questions	197
E-Resources	197
References	197

An Introduction to the Study of Crime Types and Criminals

MODULE 1

Chapter 1

How Do We Study Crime Types and Criminals?

Key Terms

Deviance
Social norms
Folkways
Mores
Taboos
Laws
Crime
Mala in se
Mala prohibita
Uniform Crime Report (UCR)
Summary Reporting System (SRS)
Hierarchy rule
National Incident-Based Reporting System (NIBRS)
National Crime Victimization Survey (NCVS)
Self-report surveys

Chapter Headings

1. Chapter opener
2. What is crime?
3. What is deviance?
   3.1. Social definition and social norms
   3.2. The role of social reaction in defining crime and deviance
4. How much crime is there?
   4.1. The popular image of crime
   4.2. The reality of crime data
5. Chapter summary

Opening Questions

Before you begin the chapter, take a few minutes to reflect on the following questions:

1. *Is it possible to agree on a single definition of crime? What about deviant behavior? Do you think people can agree on what's deviant and what isn't?*
2. *Are there certain social norms that guide our everyday interactions with people?*
3. *What is relativity? Do you think relativity can influence how people interpret behavior? Give an example to support your answer.*
4. *Is there a popular image of crime in our society; how does that measure up to the reality of crime data?*

Chapter Objectives

After reading Chapter 1, students will be able to do the following:

- *Distinguish between crime and deviance*
- *Become aware of social norms and how they influence the way we act*
- *Understand the role of social reaction in defining human behavior*
- *Recognize the reality of crime data and crime trends*

True Crime

Rush hour traffic can be very frustrating without a doubt! Many of us know the familiar bumper-to-bumper stream of reddish taillights adorning the streets and highways in cities everywhere in what seems like miles of lines of cars trying to get from work to home, child care, banks, and a variety of other destinations. Delay is inevitable, and the outcome of these dynamics can lead to impatience, frustration, tempers rising, and poor judgment ... but what about murder? What started off as a fender bender ended up with first-degree murder. How could this be? What would lead an average middle-aged woman to commit this unthinkable act?

The events unfolded on an ordinary evening in Springfield, MO on November 19, 2018, at around 5:15 p.m. Austyn Adams, a witness that day recalls confronting 46-year-old Elizabeth McKeown after what she did: "I looked in the driver's side and she was just sitting there staring, holding the steering wheel. And she looked over at me and just kind of looked back ... at me like no emotion, no anything, just staring. I told her it is like you just ran a person over, you're going to jail." Barbara Foster, the 57-year-old victim, got out of her car to check the damage after McKeown rear-ended her and that is when it happened. McKeown, apparently trying to get to her bank before it closed, backed up her car, sped up, and ran right over Foster, slamming into her and cutting her body in half. She told police she was mad that Foster stopped at the light, making her even later, so she "decided to hit it full out." Elizabeth McKeown was charged with first-degree murder and armed criminal action in the death of Barbara Foster (The Kansan City Star, 2018).

What Is Crime?

> *When a man is denied the right to live the life he believes in, he has no choice but to become an outlaw.*
>
> —Nelson Mandela (2011, p. 174). *Nelson Mandela by Himself: The Authorized Book of Quotations*, Pan Macmillan

What is crime? Is it an action or an event? Can it be a mere thought or words? Does it involve taking specific steps toward a behavior? When we think of the word *crime*, many images of actions that are evil, shameful, harmful, or immoral come to mind. These acts can be collectively regarded as violations that break the law and result in some type of formal sanction by a government entity. However, a closer examination of the concept of crime reveals a much wider scope of understanding that encompasses elements of actions that capture the meanings and intentions of individuals where the consequences are not always clear. Thus, when developing a comprehensive definition of crime, we must recognize that we are addressing a behavioral element whereby we strive to describe and explain the root cause of criminality and a definitional element that seeks to explain how certain acts come to be defined as crime while others do not (Taylor, 2019). Considering the variety of human behaviors that can be defined as crime, we begin to wonder where we get our images of a bank being robbed, a college student being mugged, a young woman being sexually assaulted, or a drug cartel ordering an execution.

Popular culture within the United States has become permeated with media attention to crime, criminal investigation, and criminal behavior. This attention is clearly manifested in television shows and documentaries, movies, news, reality programs, and social media that provide us with enough diversion to satisfy our appetites for information about detective work, crime scene analysis, police chases, and the handling of forensic evidence. While these outlets may have some entertainment value, they also serve to create a precarious foundation upon which we build our knowledge and understanding of crime and criminal behavior (Greer & McLaughlin, 2017). For this reason, it is imperative that we direct our attention to a more scholarly understanding and definition of crime that guides us in the direction of appropriate programs and interventions to prevent its causes.

Researchers have traditionally relied on an encompassing definition of crime that accounts for multiple perspectives, including legal, political, sociological, and psychological (Hass et al., 2016). From a *legal* perspective, crime is behavior that violates the laws of cities, states, and the federal government. This assumes that if the behavior is not so defined by law, then it is not a crime. The *political* perspective reminds us that acts are defined as crime by individuals with economic wealth and political advantage, and the acts that are defined as crime are defined as such to further their own positions of power. Thus, the process of law creation involves an attempt to control the actions of populations with little or no power from threatening the status of individuals with the power to define. The *psychological* perspective adds to our understanding of crime the notion that while politics and the law may intersect to create shared meanings of rules and regulations, we must also be aware of the human element of criminal action as a form of maladaptive behavior to environmental stimuli. Therefore, we should account for the definition of crime based on variations in human response. Finally, from the perspective of sociology, we begin to indulge in a broader insight and awareness of the contextual elements involved in the study and perception of crime. By recognizing that behavior does not occur in a vacuum absent of social interaction and structural circumstances, we see that there are forces shaping our definition of crime that must be accounted for. What are these forces, and how do they influence our definition of crime? We turn now to a discussion of these forces within a broader discussion of deviance and social norms.

What Is Deviance?

How are crime and deviance related? When we think of acts such as the abuse of a child, a gang-related shooting, and stealing money from an elderly person, the term *deviant behavior* seems to be quite appropriate. However, some acts that also violate the law do not elicit the same reaction—for instance, running a red light, pilfering from a fast-food restaurant, and drinking underage. Why is this the case? The term **deviance** refers to behaviors that violate the standards of conduct set forth by society (Downes et al., 2016). These standards, also called **social norms**, are the guiding informal and formal rules that create a set of criteria or boundaries within which we consider behaviors to be acceptable. Let's take a closer look at how social norms affect the definition of our conduct and ultimately shape our concept of criminal behavior.

Social Definition and Social Norms

Recent trends have revealed an unprecedented growth in the use of the electronic cigarette device known as "Juul" among young teenagers nationwide and reaching circles of younger children at epidemic proportions according to the Food and Drug Administration (Kaplan & Hoffman, 2018). "Vaping" is considered illegal when involving an underage minor. However, the image of a young child holding this device and smoking it goes beyond illegal to a level of dismay and anger that transmits the role of being illegal into one that is offensive and even far-reaching to parental or other adult authority figures whereby we want to assess blame for this action and place some responsibility on them for allowing this form of deviance to take place. These and other similar forms of behaviors and social conditions help us to recognize the role of social reaction in defining and interpreting human behavior (Lynch et al., 2016). First, however, we must develop a clear understanding of *why* variability in social reaction takes place by recognizing that social norms are not all equally binding, meaning, their violation does not elicit the same reaction.

From a very young age, we can recall someone, perhaps mom, dad, grandma, our neighbor, a school teacher, or another adult "telling us what to do": don't put your elbows on the table, cover your mouth when you cough, don't talk to strangers, look people in the eyes, share with others, etc. These are all examples of **folkways** or nonbinding social conventions (Manning, 2017). We go along with these and other norms that carry us through adulthood to guide our relationships with spouses, significant others, friends, strangers, bosses, and even landlords. It's why we wear boots in the snow, give up our seat on a bus for an older adult, tip the waitress who serves us well, and stay quiet during a long church service. Sometimes, we also recognize even stronger limits to our actions so as not to behave offensively and violate a **more** or strong conviction about right and wrong (Manning, 2017). We are told to silence our phones at the movies "or else," wear respectable clothes at a funeral, and clip our toenails in our own home and not at a public restaurant! Violating these mores would elicit a stronger social reaction that could lead to actions such as verbal reprimands or being removed from a premise. This goes beyond the typical stares of disapproval involving the violation of folkways. What about when actions are shocking, disturbing, and even disgusting to some, yet these actions do not violate the law? We refer to acts that are socially prohibited, socially offensive acts as **taboo** (Maryanski, 2018). Taboos are social norms that regulate acts pertaining to cultural customs, beliefs, and standards. In American Society, it is taboo to have sexual relations with a blood relative for example, while this might be quite acceptable in other cultures around the world that allow and even require first cousins to be married (Park & Burgess, 2019). Sometimes, acts that are socially forbidden require a reaction that goes beyond a collective disapproval to include formal mechanisms of control that intervene to ensure that the behavior does not threaten the social order. Here, we see that these behaviors become defined in **laws**, formal rules of conduct that proscribe and prohibit certain actions and have formal sanctions for their violation (Petrazycki & Trevino, 2017). So, while a parent or caretaker might not mind that their 10-year-old child uses a Juul, social disapproval and legal sanction have collectively made this act a crime. The same goes for underage drinking, failing to file income tax, paying someone to have sex, and committing first-degree murder.

Table 1.1 provides a summary of the social norms we have been discussing thus far. With a better understanding of these norms, we can gain a clearer picture of the dynamics involved in the definition of **crime** as conduct that is interpreted as a violation of society's norms and that must be controlled and sanctioned by legal decree. This interpretation, however, to be fully accounted for, must be assessed in light of the role of context in shaping meaning and influencing social reaction. This context is discussed by examining the role of time, place, and individual in evaluating and assessing human conduct.

TABLE 1.1 ARE ALL NORMS EQUALLY BINDING?

SOCIAL NORM	What Does It Mean?	A Violation of This Norm	Social Reaction to Violation	CONTINUUM OF BEHAVIOR
Law	Written down formal decrees with formal sanctions	Robbing a bank teller at gunpoint	Getting arrested and formally charged with robbery	Criminal
Taboo	Culturally and socially offensive informally formally behaviors	Having a sexual relationship with a blood relative	Shunned by family and friends; can lead to anger or physical violence	
More	Strong convictions about right and wrong that elicit a strong reaction	Talking loudly on your cell phone in the theater during a movie	Verbal or physical confrontation; can lead to being removed from theater	
Folkway	Nonbinding social conventions with little intervention to prevent	Wearing cut off shorts at a fancy wedding reception	Snide remarks, stares, laughter	Deviant

The Role of Social Reaction in Defining Crime and Deviance

Our discussion of social norms has brought us full circle toward a more comprehensive definition of crime and deviant behavior. This discussion would not be complete without an examination of the contextual variables of time, place, and individual in shaping our interpretation of human actions. Consider, for example, the following statements. Read each in isolation, and try to create an image of how the statement makes you "feel":

"I saw a man drinking."
"I saw a man drinking at 10:00 a.m."

"I saw a man drinking at 10:00 a.m., and it was vodka."
"I saw a man drinking vodka at 10:00 a.m. and slapping a child."
"I saw a man drinking vodka at 10:00 a.m. at church."
"I saw a man drinking vodka at 10:00 a.m. at church, and it was my pastor."

Each statement has elements of the same behavior; what changes is context. Here, with each variation, we see a change in how we interpret the situation depending on who the individual actor is, place this is happening, and the timing of the event. This illustration, as silly as it might seem, gives us a glimpse of how what we "see" might be a reflection of our attempt to make sense of the behavior based on the role of *time*, *place*, and *individual*. These three variables define for us the situation and shape our interpretation of human interactions, rendering them either right, wrong, or somewhere in between. For this reason, we say that the definition of what is deviant and ultimately what is considered crime is subject to relativity.

Box 1.1 provides us with a real-life case example of how these factors come into play and ultimately begin to define the concepts of **mala in se**, acts that are evil in and of themselves, and **mala prohibita**, acts that are wrong because they have been identified as wrong. When we refer to universally disapproved of acts, behaviors that are collectively agreed to be bad and inherently wrong, we are speaking of mala in se. Here, these acts are consensually detrimental, regardless of economic, social, and political context. With mala prohibita acts, there is less agreement, and we begin to assess the situational elements of time, place, and individuals to determine social reaction. These are rules and regulations that give some semblance of order and consensus but are regularly violated with little stigma attached to the offender. Consider the following examples to better illustrate these concepts Table 1.2):

TABLE 1.2 MALA IN SE OR MALA PROHIBITA

Behavior	Legal Example	Illegal Example (Mala in Se)	Illegal Example (Mala Prohibita)
Two people are fighting; one person gives the other a black eye	A sporting event such as boxing or wrestling	A man punches his wife in the eye because she didn't make his dinner on time	Two friends get into a heated argument, and one insults the other using a racial slur; the fighting gets physical
Two people are engaging in a sexual act	A married couple on their honeymoon in their hotel room	A young woman jogging in the park is forced to have sex against her will	An 18-year-old has sex with his 16-year-old girlfriend
A person is smoking	A 45-year-old man is smoking a pipe in the smoking section of a restaurant	A mother allows her 8-year-old daughter to smoke a cigarette	Two legally aged friends smoke marijuana at a party

(*Continued*)

TABLE 1.2 (Continued)

Behavior	Legal Example	Illegal Example (Mala in Se)	Illegal Example (Mala Prohibita)
Somebody takes something from someone else's possession	The repo man is following orders to take back a vehicle	Two people systematically steal social security checks from elderly citizens	A desperate father steals food from a grocery store to feed his family
Killing another person	A soldier takes a life while defending his country in the line of duty	A woman kills her coworker because she believes she deserved the promotion he got	A dad enraged takes the life of the person who raped and killed his daughter

WHO DID IT? DR. LARRY NASSER — BOX 1.1

"You used your position of trust … in the most vile way to abuse children. … I agree that now is a time of healing, but it may take them a lifetime of healing while you spend your lifetime behind bars thinking about what you did in taking away their childhood." These were the words of Judge Rosemarie Aquilina directed to Dr. Larry Nasser while in court for a plea hearing in Lansing, Michigan, in November of 2017. For years, Nasser served as a sports medicine physician working for USA Gymnastics and Michigan State University. While serving in this capacity and treating young girls for sports-related injuries, he committed multiple acts of sexual assault, penetrating the girls under the guise of "medical treatment." He later admitted that there was no medical reason behind his molestation and pled guilty to seven counts of criminal sexual conduct. This once world-renowned doctor who treated America's leading Olympic women gymnasts was now a public disgrace, a threat, danger, and menace to society. His criminal actions against more than 150 accusers spanning two decades were nothing short of wicked, evil acts, truly the epitome of the term *mala in se*. During his sentencing hearing, Randall Margraves, a father of three of Nasser's victims asked the judge if she would grant him "five minutes in a locked room with this demon." The judge said that she would not be able to allow that to happen. The father then lunged at the table where Nasser and his attorneys were seated, attempting to physically attack him before law enforcement officers in the courtroom tackled and restrained him. His actions were seen by millions of people around the world who viewed this exchange in recorded media and were applauded, justified, and seen as a heroic reaction by a distressed father who ached for the victimization of his girls. That father's behavior in contempt of court was completely dismissed by the judge, and no criminal charges were ever filed, a clear case of criminal behavior interpreted as *mala prohibita* under the circumstances.

Source: USA Gymnastics doctor admits to molesting and 'penetrating' 7 children under his care. Associated Press. 22 November 2017. Retrieved from https://www.crimeonline.com/2017/11/22/devil-doc-usa-gymnastics-doctor-admits-to-molesting-and-penetrating-7-children-under-his-care/

Source: Murphy, Dan. 2 February 2018. Father of three daughters not punished for trying to attack Larry Nassar in court. ESPN. Retrieved from http://www.espn.com/college-sports/story/_/id/22298251/father-three-daughters-tries-attack-larry-nassar-courtroom

How Much Crime Is There?

Crime and crime-related topics have become a vast industry in the entertainment media over the past several decades (Greer, 2019). Television programs like *Breaking Bad, Narcos, CSI,* and *Criminal Minds* dramatize for us the crimes of murder, drug trafficking, rape, and assault. We are left with a certain impression and understanding of why crime occurs, how to go about solving it, and the role of law enforcement, courts, and the criminal law in serving as aids in deconstructing crime-related facts. This shadow of understanding leaves us begging for more information when it comes to why ordinary individuals become involved in trafficking illegal drugs, doctors sexually assault their patients, politicians abuse their positions of power, priests engage in sexual acts with children, husbands kill their spouses, and businessmen and women cheat on their income taxes. A closer examination of the popular image of crime can help us better understand the reality of crime-related facts and separate it from distortions created by the entertainment value of television and other media sources (Garcia & Arkerson, 2017).

The Popular Image of Crime

Media portrayal of crime and crime-related data without a doubt paints a picture of criminals as raging lunatics who are out of control, impulsive, and a menace to society (Intravia et al., 2017). We can't help but associate this image with a fear and hysteria of violent crime rates growing exponentially, with strangers lurking around the corner ready to attack innocent victims in their homes, on the streets, at work, and throughout society. This fear, while justified in certain contexts, does not accurately portray the crime problem or crime trends in our society. We must instead recognize the many faces of crime and criminal offenders to become more informed citizens who approach the study of crime from a scholarly standpoint (Ditton & Farrall, 2017).

What's newsworthy and entertaining is rarely the mundane, ordinary day-to-day wrongful criminal actions committed by ordinary people. Rather, it is the unusual, dramatic, and shocking events that permeate our minds every time we turn on the news, watch a crime drama, or read the newspaper. The truth of the matter is that crimes such as murder, robbery, and rape portrayed by the "popular image" of crime in the media are often crimes that take place the least. As a matter of fact, studies show that violent crimes represent 60% to 90% of crime news stories while making up only 12% of all crimes (Surette, 2015). What is even more confounding is that while the crime rate in general and violent crime in particular have gone down over the past few decades (see Figure 1.1), media sources have become increasingly consumed with coverage and details of criminal events. With this coverage, one would hardly believe that violent crimes such as homicide and rape have gone down over 50% from 1993 to 2018. For this reason, it is important to approach the study of crime by acknowledging the distorted portrayal represented by the popular image of crime and relying on a more educated approach to understand the reality of crime data to develop appropriate safety and prevention measures and reduce fear (Maier & DePrince, 2020). We turn now to a closer look at crime data sources to shed some light on how much crime there really is.

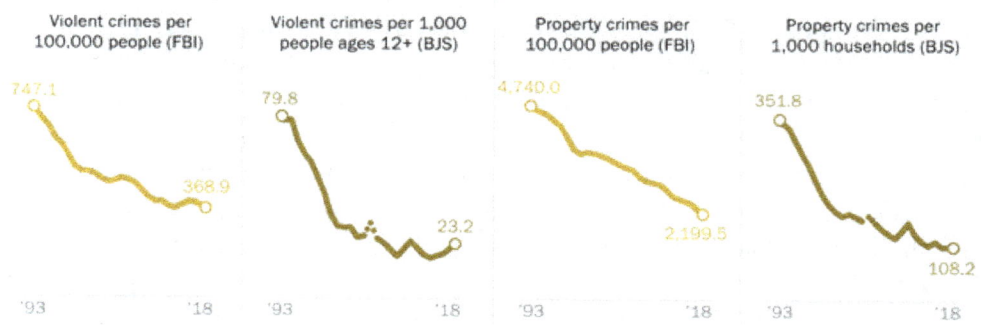

The Reality of Crime Data

FIGURE 1.1 Has Crime Really Gone Down in the United States?

In trying to capture the nature and extent of criminal behavior, we must rely on meaningful sources that provide us with reliable information as to variations, trends, and patterns of criminality. While the quality of the data may vary, we still can capture a more realistic understanding of "how much crime is there" beyond the sources of information we receive from media portrayals that are driven by the entertainment industry. Since there are significant variations in types of crime and criminality, we must approach the study of crime data with caution, recognizing that we are relying on the gathering of information in various contexts and settings that vary immensely depending on the source of information (Schwartz & Vega, 2017). With this in mind, we will take a look at different data sources on crime and identify each one's unique contribution to our comprehension of the characteristics of crime and criminals. Our first and most widely used official data source on crime is the **Uniform Crime Report (UCR)**. The UCR was created in 1929 as a recommendation from the International Association of Chiefs of Police to develop a more reliable, uniform method of data collection on crime (Federal Bureau of Investigation, 2020b). The information, gathered and compiled by the FBI, consists of data received from over 18,000 federal, state, city, county, and local law enforcement agencies that voluntarily participate in the program. The UCR can be broken down into four different collections of data: The National Incident-Based Reporting System (NIBRS), the Summary Reporting System (SRS), the Law Enforcement Officers Killed and Assaulted Program, and the Hate Crime Statistics Program. For our purposes, we will examine the NIBRS and the SRS.

At the inception of the UCR, data was provided relying on the **Summary Reporting System** or **SRS**. This method of data collection concentrates on crimes that are known to the police and focuses on what is considered by the FBI as the most serious offenses. It includes information on eight "index crimes": homicide, forcible rape, robbery, aggravated assault, burglary, larceny, arson, and motor vehicle theft. Arrest data for crimes considered by the FBI to be "less serious" such as public intoxication, drug offenses, simple assault, vagrancy, and gambling also are reported. Reporting is based on the compilation of crimes "known" to police, crimes where an arrest has been made, and cases that are *cleared*, where the suspect is known, but no arrest has been made. The SRS relies on what we call the **hierarchy rule** in recording crime, which means that in any given criminal incident, only the most severe crime is officially reported or counted. So, for example, if the police are called to a home where a robbery occurred and a murder, the hierarchy rule dictates that only the murder is reported by the agency to the UCR.

The most obvious problem with the SRS way of gathering data is its "mobilization of bias" toward certain categories of crime considered to be most important while ignoring other serious categories, such as embezzlement, fraud, terrorism, drug trafficking, and many others (Lantz et al., 2019). This distorts our image of crime to a certain extent by focusing on street crimes more traditionally committed by the lower classes. Moreover, critics also note that these reports are subject to inaccuracy and reflect police practices, reporting patterns, and estimates of total crime projections without taking into account crimes that are unreported, and the discretion involved at various stages throughout the criminal justice process that is not captured here (Wormeli, 2018).

Because of the limited amount of information that is collected by the SRS, and also the built-in biases discussed earlier, a more useful source of information on crime that we can rely on now is the **National Incident-Based Reporting System** or **NIBRS** (Federal Bureau of Investigation, 2020a). Implementation of the NIBRS began in 1982 in an effort to revise data collection on crime and provide a more comprehensive analysis of criminal events. Under this new system, law enforcement agencies provide the FBI with information on each crime occurring in a single incident. The NIBRS provides greater details on incidents of crime, allowing law enforcement agencies, researchers, and public officials to more effectively define the crime problem, develop resources and implement policies and practices that address crime efficiently. The following is a summary of the advantages of the NIBRS over the traditional, limited SRS, which was phased out in January of 2021 (Federal Bureau of Investigation, 2020a).

- *Provides greater specificity in reporting offenses.* Not only does NIBRS look at all of the offenses within an incident, but it also looks at many more offenses than the traditional SRS does. NIBRS collects data for 52 offenses, plus 10 additional offenses for which only arrests are reported. SRS counts limited data for 10 offenses and 20 additional crimes for which only arrests are reported.
- *Collects more detailed information.* This includes incident date and time, whether reported offenses were attempted or completed, expanded victim types, relationships of victims to offenders and offenses, demographic details, location data, property descriptions, drug

types and quantities, the offender's suspected use of drugs or alcohol, the involvement of gang activity, and whether a computer was used in the commission of the crime.
- *Helps give context to specific crime problems.* This includes drug/narcotics and sex offenses, as well as modern crime issues like animal cruelty, identity theft, and computer hacking.
- *Provides greater analytic flexibility.* Through NIBRS, data users can see many more facets of crime, as well as relationships and connections among these facets, than SRS provides.

One problem that we cannot overlook when discussing official crime data sources is the fact that they rely on crimes that are reported by and to law enforcement agencies. What about those crimes that go unreported or unnoticed by police? Another important crime data source that we rely on to capture this information often referred to as the "dark figure" of crime, is the **National Crime Victimization Survey (NCVS;** Bureau of Justice Statistics, Office of Justice Programs, 2018). The NCVS was first implemented in the early 1970s as a National Survey administered by the U.S. Bureau of Census to survey households across the United States about their experience as crime victims. Today, the NCVS surveys more than 240,000 individuals annually, gathering victimization data on approximately 160,000 individuals in about 95,000 households. Data is collected through interviews with household members above the age of 12, asking about each individual's experience with criminal victimization. Information is collected on the crimes of rape, sexual assault, robbery, aggravated assault, burglary, motor vehicle theft, and larceny. Personal information such as age, sex, race, marital status, education level, and income is captured, as well as characteristics of the offender such as age, race, sex, and their relationship to the victim. Survey respondents also provide information on the characteristics of the crime itself such as where it occurred, whether or not weapons were involved, any injuries sustained, the financial cost of the crime, whether the crime was reported to police, and their experience with the criminal justice system (United States Census Bureau, 2020).

NCVS data provides us with a clearer picture of the characteristics of crime and crime victimization by putting crime in context and gaining a perspective that is not simply a reflection of law enforcement policies and practices. Another source of data on crime that also provides us with additional perspective is the **Self-Report Survey** (Kim & Bushway, 2018). While there is no nationally administered form of this research technique, studies conducted by criminologists and other scholars using surveys asking samples of individuals whether they have committed certain crimes in a given time period or over the course of their lifetime have been conducted in research settings for the past several decades (Pollock et al., 2016). Findings from these studies consistently reveal that crime is not limited to a certain type or category of individual or the traditional forms of street crime captured in official data sources, but rather crime cuts across age, race, gender, education, and socioeconomic status and includes a greater variety of individuals and criminal activities (Marshall et al., 2019). Box 1.2 captures some of these findings from two pioneering self-reports that established these measures of crime data and laid the foundation for their use and administration for decades to follow.

BOX 1.2 — THE REAL DEAL: A CLOSER LOOK AT CRIME DATA

Official crime data have traditionally revealed a pattern of offending over the years, whereby there is a disproportionate number of arrests among lower class, uneducated, Hispanic, and African American males. Social scientists, recognizing the importance of having a more detailed depiction of the nature, volume, and scope of criminality, established the use of self-report surveys to highlight the volume of crime and delinquency among different categories of individuals based on their reported involvement. Using these studies, we have been able to get a better snapshot of the variations in race, social class, gender, and age in patterns of drug use, addiction, alcohol use, property crime, sexual assault, and a variety of other delinquent and criminal behaviors. Two major studies pioneered this survey methodology in the 1940s. One study conducted by Austin Porterfield compared juvenile delinquents to college students (Porterfield & Clifton, 1946) A questionnaire administered to Texas college students revealed over 90% of survey respondents admitted to committing at least one felony crime. Similar findings were reported in a study conducted by Wallterstein and Wyle where researchers surveyed a wide range of men and women working in professional occupations in New York City (Wallerstein & Wyle, 1947). Their study revealed that 90% of respondents admitted to committing one or more of 49 criminal offenses. Findings from these two studies have been replicated over the years with similar conclusions, noting that crime as a phenomenon is more evenly distributed throughout society and not an anomaly that is limited to a certain class of individuals with either common social-psychological characteristics of pathology or socio-demographic characteristics defining race, class, age, or gender.

A clearer picture of the definition of crime as well as its prevalence in our society will guide us throughout the rest of our journey toward understanding the various categories of criminal behavior and how we can evaluate these behaviors in a social context. First, however, we need to develop a concise perspective on some of the key issues involved in the study of crime, exploring first the question, "Who defines crime and creates law" in our next chapter.

Key Takeaways

Review the following list of bullet points for a quick overview of the key ideas and information in this chapter:

- Human behavior does not occur in a vacuum of isolated events but rather our behavior is guided by the norms and regulations of society, which are products of social definition and social reaction.
- Crime is behavior that is a product of social reaction, just like any other behavior created through social definition; because of this, the definition of crime is subject to the relative forces of time, place, and individual.

- There is a popular definition of crime that is created by the various common sources of information we receive about criminals and crime-related facts, largely influenced by the media and entertainment industry.
- The popular image of crime as an isolated occurrence limited to a certain group of individuals, social classes, and economic means does not measure up to the reality of crime data that social scientists have developed over the years.

Conclusion and Formal Summary Questions

This chapter opened the door to our future inquiry into the study of crime types and criminals. We learned the importance of looking at crime through a broader lens of social context that recognizes the role of social reaction and social definition in creating shared definitions of right and wrong, which ultimately shape our conceptualization of crime. While this often leads to a popular image of crime based on the mediating effect of media and its influence, we continue to explore a scientific measure of crime data that relies on the tools of criminology to better inform our understanding.

- *Can you describe how crime and deviance are different? In what ways are they similar?*
- *Can you define social norms and identify how they shape the way we act?*
- *Are you able to recognize the role of time, place, and individual in shaping social reaction to human behavior?*
- *Are you more aware of the popular image of crime and how that measures up to the reality of crime data?*

E-Resources

For more information on "juuling" trends among young teens in the United States, visit the *Truth Initiative* website at https://truthinitiative.org/research-resources/emerging-tobacco-products/data-suggest-teens-who-use-juul-are-not-just

For a vivid illustration of social interpretation and reaction to the violation of norms, take a look at https://www.bing.com/videos/search?q=social+norms+and+deviance+behavior&qpvt=social+norms+and+deviance+behavior&view=detail&mid=77DFB49193C9155A7F0777DFB49193C9155A7F07&&FORM=VRDGAR&ru=%2Fvideos%2Fsearch%3Fq%3Dsocial%2Bnorms%2Band%2Bdeviance%2Bbehavior%26qpvt%3Dsocial%2Bnorms%2Band%2Bdeviance%2Bbehavior%26FORM%3DVDRE

Read more on the use of self-report surveys about crime at https://study.com/academy/lesson/crime-surveys-self-report-surveys-implications-uses.html

References

Bureau of Justice Statistics, Office of Justice Programs. (2018). *Data collection: National crime victimization survey*. https://www.bjs.gov/index.cfm?ty=dcdetail&iid=245

Ditton, J., & Farrall, S. (Eds.). (2017). *The fear of crime*. Routledge.

Downes, D., Rock, P. E., & McLaughlin, E. (2016). *Understanding deviance: A guide to the sociology of crime and rule-breaking*. Oxford University Press.

Federal Bureau of Investigation. (2020a). *National Incident-Based Reporting System (NIBRS)*. https://www.fbi.gov/services/cjis/ucr/nibrs

Federal Bureau of Investigation. (2020b). *Uniform Crime Reporting (UCR) Program*. https://www.fbi.gov/services/cjis/ucr

Garcia, V., & Arkerson, S. G. (2017). *Crime, media, and reality: Examining mixed messages about crime and justice in popular media*. Rowman & Littlefield.

Greer, C. (Ed.). (2019). *Crime and media: A reader*. Routledge.

Greer, C., & McLaughlin, E. (2017). News power, crime and media justice. In A. Liebling, L. McAra, & S. Manura (Eds.), *Oxford Handbook of Criminology* (pp. 260–283). Oxford University Press.

Hass, A. Y., Moloney, C., & Chambliss, W. J. (2016). *Criminology: Connecting theory, research and practice*. Taylor & Francis.

Intravia, J., Wolff, K. T., Paez, R., & Gibbs, B. R. (2017). Investigating the relationship between social media consumption and fear of crime: A partial analysis of mostly young adults. *Computers in Human Behavior, 77*, 158–168.

Kaplan, S., & Hoffman, J. (2018, September 12). FDA targets vaping, alarmed by teenage use. *The New York Times*. https://www.nytimes.com/2018/09/12/health/juul-fda-vaping-ecigarettes.html

Kim, J., & Bushway, S. D. (2018). Using longitudinal self-report data to study the age–crime relationship. *Journal of Quantitative Criminology, 34*(2), 367–396.

Lantz, B., Gladfelter, A. S., & Ruback, R. B. (2019). Stereotypical hate crimes and criminal justice processing: A multi-dataset comparison of bias crime arrest patterns by offender and victim race. *Justice Quarterly, 36*(2), 193–224.

Lynch, M., Stretesky, P., & Long, M. (2016). *Defining crime: A critique of the concept and its implication*. Springer.

Maier, S. L., & DePrince, B. T. (2020). College students' fear of crime and perception of safety: The influence of personal and university prevention measures. *Journal of Criminal Justice Education, 31*(1), 63–81.

Manning, P. D. (Ed.). (2017). *On folkways and mores: William Graham Sumner then and now*. Routledge.

Marshall, I. H., Neissl, K., & Markina, A. (2019). A global view on youth crime and victimization: Results from the International Self-Report Delinquency Study (ISRD3). *Journal of Contemporary Criminal Justice, 35*(4), 380–385.

Maryanski, A. (2018). *Emile Durkheim and the birth of the gods: Clans, incest, totems, phratries, hordes, mana, taboos, corroborees, sodalities, menstrual blood, apes, churingas, cairns, and other mysterious things*. Taylor & Francis Group.

Park, R. E., & Burgess, E. W. (2019). *Introduction to the science of sociology*. Good Press.

Petrazycki L., & Trevino, A. J. (2017). *Law and morality*. Routledge.

Pollock, W., Hill, M. C., Menard, S., & Elliott, D. S. (2016). Predicting consistency between officially recorded and self-reported records of arrest. *American Journal of Criminal Justice, 41*(4), 623–644.

Porterfield, A. L., & Clifton, C. S. (1946). *Youth in trouble; studies in delinquency and despair, with plans for prevention*. Leo Potishman Foundation.

Schwartz, J., & Vega, A. (2017). Sources of crime data. In B. Teasdale & M. S. Bradley (Eds.), *Preventing crime and violence* (pp. 155–167). Springer, Cham.

Surette, R. (2015). Media, crime, and criminal justice. *Cengage Learning*.

Taylor, I. (2019). *Crime in context*. Routledge.

The Kansas City Star. (2018, November 28). Running late, a woman used her car to cut stopped driver "'in half,'" Missouri cops say. https://www.kansascity.com/news/state/missouri/article222296600.html

United States Census Bureau. (2020). *National crime victimization survey (NCVS)*. https://www.census.gov/programs-surveys/ncvs.html

Wallerstein, J. S., & Wyle, C. (1947). Our law-abiding law breakers. *Probation 25*, March/April, 107–112, 118.

Wormeli, P. (2018). Criminal justice statistics—An evolution. *Criminology & Public Policy, 17*(2), 483–496.

Figure Credits

Fig. 1.1: Source: https://www.pewresearch.org/fact-tank/2019/10/17/facts-about-crime-in-the-u-s/.

Chapter 2

Key Issues in the Study of Crime

Key Terms

Consensus model
Society
Conflict model
Punishment
Retribution
Code of Hammurabi
Enlightenment
Deterrence
Specific deterrence
General deterrence
Shaming
Incapacitation
Three-strikes laws
Rehabilitation
Positivism
Indeterminate sentencing
Victimology
Victim precipitation
Victim facilitation
Career criminals
Environmental criminologists

Chapter Headings

1. Chapter opener
2. Who defines crime?
   - 2.1. Consensus model of law creation
   - 2.2. Conflict model of law creation
3. What is the goal of punishment?
   - 3.1. Punishment as retribution
   - 3.2. Punishment as deterrence
   - 3.3. Punishment as rehabilitation
4. Crime victimization in context
   - 4.1. The study of crime victims
   - 4.2. Trends in victimization
5. Social correlates of criminal offending
   - 5.1. Age and crime
   - 5.2. Race and crime
   - 5.3. Gender and crime
   - 5.4. Social class and crime
   - 5.5. Location and crime
6. Chapter summary

Opening Questions

Before you begin the chapter, take a few minutes to reflect on the following questions:

1. *How is a law created? Do you think we agree on the definitions of right and wrong?*
2. *Why do we punish people who break the law? Are there certain types of punishment that work better than others to stop crime?*
3. *In what ways does crime impact victims? Does crime affect some groups more than others?*
4. *Are there particular characteristics of individuals who commit crimes? Does offending vary by such things as age, race, gender, and social class? What about differences in crime by location or region?*

Chapter Objectives

After reading Chapter 2, students will be able to do the following:

- *Distinguish between the consensus and conflict models of law creation*
- *Understand the goals of punishment in stopping crime*
- *Identify various dimensions in the study of victimization*
- *Recognize different trends in criminal offending*

True Crime

Two heads are better than one is an expression we often hear, indicating that the judgment of two people or their problem-solving skills together, make for a better resolution of a difficult task, complex decision, or moral dilemma. However, this was far from the truth when six teenagers got together on an August Tuesday in the early hours of the morning just after midnight and decided to burglarize a home in Old Mill Creek, Illinois, a town about 50 miles north of Chicago. What started off as teens behaving badly, carelessly, and recklessly ended up in the death of the youngest one of the group, a 14-year-old boy who was shot and killed by the homeowner. The 75-year-old was rightfully defending his and his wife's safety when he noticed the six boys on his property, and after yelling at them to leave multiple times, two boys began to approach him, with one appearing, to be "holding something in his hand."

This tragedy, the death of a young kid, was not the only thing shocking about the events that unfolded that day. This story made national news media when the five surviving teenagers involved in the burglary attempt, ranging from ages 16 to 18, were all charged as adults with the first degree, premeditated murder of their friend, under a state statute that allows for this charge to be made when a death occurs during the commission of a forcible felony. How can this be? As heartbreaking as this story is for the family of the teenager who was shot and killed, is this the true meaning of criminal homicide? Does the law in the State of Illinois really intend to define the actions of the teenagers that day as a premeditated attempt at murder (Jacob, 2019)?

Who Defines Crime?

> *For the powerful, crimes are those that others commit.*
> —Noam Chomsky, *Imperial Ambitions: Conversations on the Post-9/11 World*

Let's stop and think for a moment about the law: Where does it come from? How do we arrive at a shared understanding of right and wrong? When you were growing up, as a young child, there were rules and regulations made in your household governing certain behaviors, tasks, obligations, and expectations. For example, most people have a curfew, a time that is set to determine when it is acceptable to come home in the evening or at night. What was that magic number for you? Was it 10, 11, or midnight? Did it vary from person to person in your household? Why does it matter? Did that number change from weekday to weekend or as the years went by? Did you agree with that number or was it forced on you? This complexity of deliberation is an illustration of the dynamics involved in the debate over law creation. We eventually come to an agreement over terms and rules, but the real question is, how do we reach agreement? There are two opposing viewpoints on how right and wrong become embedded into our formal social norms of law: the consensus view and the conflict view. Let's examine these two perspectives in greater detail. This will give us a better picture of the relationship between deviant behavior, crime, social reaction, and the law.

The Consensus Model of Law Creation

A quick scan of the world around us leads us to wonder how we ever come to agreement on the definitions of right and wrong, as social, economic, and political debates permeate media and news outlets over subjects such as gun control, immigration, health care, and taxes (Garimella et al., 2017). This is particularly challenging in light of what we discovered in Chapter 1 about the role of social reaction in defining crime and deviance, and the relativity of social interpretation with regard to time, place, and individual. However, amidst the polarization of government and society, we are still able to establish certain ground rules and expectations that we generally view as advancing the public good, enhancing self-preservation, and ensuring social conformity.

Renowned sociologist Emile Durkheim developed our perspective on law and order by arguing that "social conformity is achieved through sanctions that society imposes on those who choose to deviate" (Cotterrell, 1999). The implication here is that society achieves agreement over right and wrong by identifying behaviors that we collectively disapprove of and coerce individuals to adhere to these set standards or social norms. This is the **consensus model** of law creation, whereby the criminal law is a measure of all those actions we as a society deem morally reprehensible, harmful, and subject to formal social control. Here, **society** is defined as the collectivity of individuals who live in a particular country, region, or area, and adhere to a common set of values, morals, and beliefs (Park & Burgess, 2019). Therefore, such acts as murder, rape, stealing, child abuse, and kidnapping are clearly detrimental to the safety of citizens, and the collective group has deemed them necessary to control for the preservation of individuals and the well-being of society. What about other actions, however, such as the legal drinking age, prostitution, recreational drug use, and gambling, that are not as clearly defined by social standards of right and wrong (Gottdiener, 2019)? Such acts present us with various moral dilemmas, and the conflict model of law creation gives us greater insight into the resolution of these dilemmas in the evolution of criminal law.

The Conflict Model of Law Creation

The distribution of power in any given society is inevitably tipped in favor of some individuals more than others (McDonald, 2019). Even in a model of interaction such as that of a household or family, rules and regulations are made and enforced by those individual members who have the most influence. So, in all likelihood, when you were a teenager and fought for your "rights" to stay up late, drive the family car, and get paid an allowance, the ultimate decision pertaining to those matters was made by your parents, largely because they exercised the most control over what goes on in your life. Think, for a moment, what gave them that control and power of decision to make the rules?

The **conflict model** of law creation recognizes power differentials in society and argues that the competition of interest between various groups in society leads to disagreement over right and wrong. This competition arises from variations in norms and values that exist in a complex society consisting of diverse groups of individuals from various backgrounds, races, social classes, religions, and cultures who all strive to advance their own definitions of law. This is clear in the struggle over laws governing issues pertaining to gay rights, the use of military power, abortion, capital punishment, and the availability of health care. According to the conflict model of law creation, those groups with the greatest access to financial resources and political power have the most amount of influence and control over legislation. Therefore, the law is a reflection of definitions of behavior that go against or threaten their own interests. Proponents of this perspective would argue that criminal law is a "tool of the rich and powerful to control the behavior of the less powerful, in an effort to advance their own interests and maintain their privileged position in society … and even laws forbidding crimes such as robbery and murder, which on the surface appear to be in the interests of protecting society as a whole, nevertheless are designed to maintain the overall social order by ensuring that the anger and hostility of the poor and powerless does not become directed at the wealthy and privileged" (Hass & Chambliss, 2016). Figure 2.1 presents us with a summary of the conflict v. consensus perspective of law creation. With these opposing viewpoints on the evolution of law, the next question becomes one of enforcement and outcome, to which we now turn to a discussion of punishment and its various goals as a mechanism of social control in society to prevent criminal behavior.

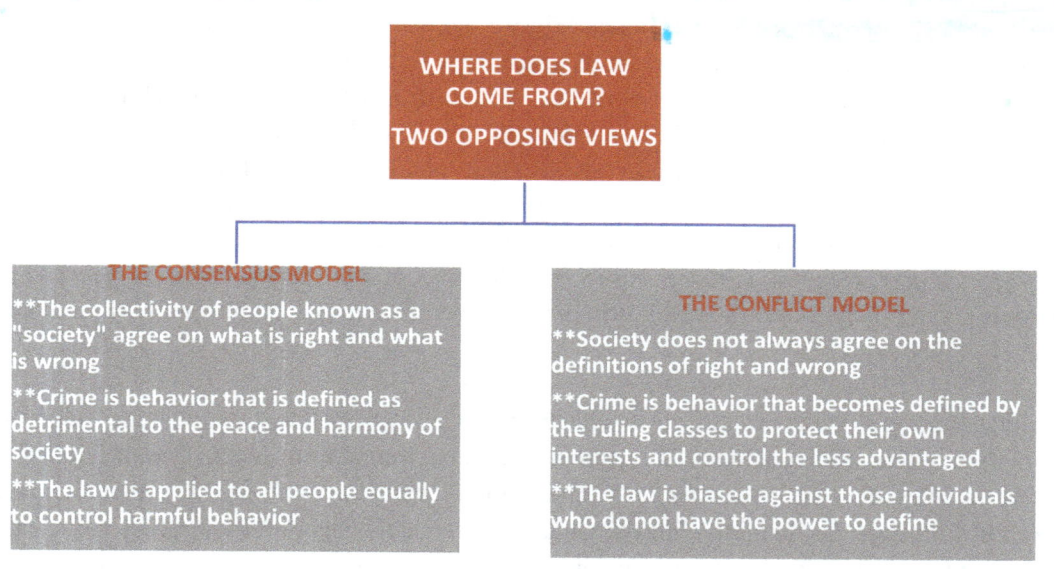

FIGURE 2.1   Consensus or Conflict: What Do You Think?

What Is the Goal of Punishment?

To recognize the goal of punishment, we must first deconstruct the concept of punishment, its meaning, institutionalization, and philosophical foundation. The term *punishment* conjures up images of some sort of discomfort, unpleasantry, and even the imposition of harm. We are confounded with equating such a concept with legitimate authority and, therefore, must come to understand the term and its connection to outcome or consequences. We must also consider matters of fairness in the distribution of punishment, as well as principles of proportionality and reciprocal outcomes (Mungan, 2019). **Punishment**, as we move forward in its study, can be defined as something undesirable or unpleasant that is imposed on an individual or group of people by some type of authority figure or legitimate entity (Lerman, 2019). Here, we see that punishment as an action can be recognized in various contexts, including the discipline of children by parents, actions taken by school authorities, and formal sanctions by law enforcement officers, court officials, and correctional personnel.

For punishment to be perceived as fair and legitimate, the justification for its imposition must be connected to a stated goal or outcome that is not necessarily the harm caused by the action itself (Meško, 2020). So, for example, when a child is "sent to the principal's office" after disrespecting the teacher, and that child's parents are called about the incident, the outcome of these dynamics must be connected with a particular goal or meaning, and the punishment is a form of action intended to stop a behavior from occurring again in the future. However, if the action taken by the child went beyond disrespect to include assaulting another student, then that child might be expelled from school. In this case, the welfare of other children and their need for protection become the intended outcome of the punishment. These various contexts of punishment become clearer when we discuss the specific goals of punishment as retribution, deterrence, and rehabilitation.

Punishment as Retribution

Since the beginning of time, the concept of good versus evil has led us in the direction of understanding the goal of punishment as one that exacts some type of harm upon an individual to make right a wrong committed (Waller, 2020). This form of **retribution** acts as a mechanism of vengeance stemming from public outrage, moral disgrace, or personal harm caused by the actions of another. Historically, the evolution of punishment reflected this ideology, and early sources of law such as the **Code of Hammurabi** (1700 B.C.) emphasized the application of punishment in a very precise and harsh manner, an "eye for an eye," to destroy evil and get revenge on the actions of the wicked (Greco, 2019). Thus, it was very common from that time forward throughout the progression of civilizations, to use the death penalty for hundreds of acts ranging from adultery and theft to sexual assault and murder.

As our concepts of good and evil changed over time, however, so did our perception of criminal behavior and its root cause. The **Enlightenment,** a social movement spanning the 17th and 18th centuries, ushered in an era of innovative thinking directing our attention to scientific teachings, and the ideas of rationality and free will (Outram, 2019). Also known as the "age of reason," this time period questioned, among many other things, the use of punishment as an end in and of itself to drive out evil and retaliate against the offender. Criminology as a discipline began to search for a more scientific explanation of crime causation that ultimately restructured our concepts of crime and punishment.

Punishment as Deterrence

The conceptualization of punishment has a long-standing history with the evolution of criminological theory. Early Classical theorist **Cesare Beccaria** (1764) argued that human beings are rational actors who seek to maximize their own pleasures and benefits and minimize pain and discomfort. Thus, from this perspective, the goal of punishment in stopping criminal behavior should be to deter individuals from making bad choices just because it is for their own personal gain (Schram & Tibbetts, 2019). The criminal law is therefore established as a mechanism of **deterrence**, setting rules and regulations to preserve the social order by curbing the harmful choices individuals might make while seeking their own selfish desires and personal pleasures. Beccaria also noted that punishment is a means to an end, criminal desistance, and this was possible because human beings are rational actors and, therefore, their behavior is predictable and ultimately preventable (Bun et al., 2019). Thus, punishment can be used as a form of **specific deterrence**, to stop the individual charged with a crime from committing future offenses, as well as **general deterrence**, to discourage society at large from committing similar offenses, knowing the consequences that might befall them. Some forms of punishment such as **shaming**, depicted earlier, are designed to influence the future decision of the individual offender, and also let the public know the outcome of criminal choices. The question, however, is, what punishment is right and how much punishment is enough for it to "work"?

For centuries, the debate over what punishment works to stop crime has perplexed criminologists, philosophers, psychologists, researchers, and policymakers all over the world. Amidst these discussions, social scientists have come to recognize the strong connection between punishment outcome, crime, and theoretical criminology. In essence, the answer to the question of "what works" is strongly connected to our understanding of "why crime" or what causes an individual to make criminal choices. For this reason, the goal of deterrence has taken on several forms over the decades, with laws shifting to accommodate changes in our understanding of crime causation, our perception of criminal offenders, and our need for public safety. Box 2.1 illustrates this process of change in the evolution of three-strikes laws, designed to deter persistent, habitual criminal offenders through **incapacitation**, sentencing them to life in prison after committing three felony crimes.

THE REAL DEAL: A CLOSER LOOK AT THREE-STRIKES LAWS | BOX 2.1

Get-tough-on crime measures began in the early 1990s in response to public disdain and fear over escalating crime rates, as well as political rhetoric affirming the rational nature of human beings and their responsibility for making criminal choices. This ideology culminated in the enactment of three-strikes laws implemented first in Washington State in 1993, spreading to the federal government and over half of all states by the end of the decade. While each state has its own unique version of these laws, the spirit of their practice requires that offenders who are convicted of a serious violent felony and who have two prior felony convictions of any kind serve a life sentence in prison (Sloan, 2017). These laws are geared toward the general goal of incapacitating habitual, chronic felony offenders, and the long-term goal of criminal deterrence through fear of harsh punishment. Has this been the case, however, in the trend of declining criminal activity in states that have enacted such laws?

The state of California leads the nation in its use and implementation of three-strikes laws, accounting for an estimated 90% of cases across the country. Advocates of such measures support the use of three-strikes laws, pointing to significant declines in crime rates since their passage, with California attorney general Dan Lungren's office reporting a 26.9% drop in violent crime rates just 4 years after enacting this law. Critics of three-strikes law note, however, that such statistics are misleading, and the empirical data does not stand up to closer scrutiny. Research studies have found that any deterrent effect is marginal at best and comes at a very high cost (Datta, 2017). Notably, regarding statistics on California, the stated decline in crime rates reflected a general trend of decline in violent crime rates in California and nationwide that had started prior to the implementation of three-strikes laws and would have likely continued without them. Furthermore, California counties that enforced the three-strikes laws more aggressively than counties that used them more sparingly did not experience a greater decline in violent crime rates, with some more lenient jurisdictions actually experiencing greater declines.

With such conflicting findings, we must rely on our scientific understanding of crime trends and their relationship to law and the theoretical support for reducing criminal behavior. When such reasoning is implemented, we look for measures that are grounded in research, and to this extent, criminologists rely on science, not emotion, public frenzy, and political manipulation in the search for a solution to the crime problem.

Source: Males, M., & Macallair, D. (1999). Striking out: The failure of California's "three-strikes you're out" law. Stanford Law and Policy Review, 11(1), 65. Retrieved April 3, 2020, from https://heinonline.org/HOL/LandingPage?handle=hein.journals/stanlp11&div=13&id=&page=

Punishment as Rehabilitation

One of the most recently formulated models of punishment in American correctional history hinges on the goal of **rehabilitation** and the idea that punishment should serve the purpose of treatment to the offender for them to return to society as a fully functioning, law-abiding member of the community (McNeil, 2018). This concept began during the 1930s as an offshoot of **positivism**, a philosophical approach that relies on the scientific method to study diverse phenomena and explain changes in behavior. This perspective ushered in decades of interventions that called for the implementation of policies and programs to treat the specific causal variables of crime that were found in the individual and their immediate social environment. Under this approach, a treatment specialist would assess and diagnose the cause of the individual's criminal behavior, then recommend a plan for treatment to change the individual's ways, and determine when that individual has become rehabilitated. This often led to the practice of **indeterminate sentencing**, or a sentence that accounts for a maximum and minimum range of time to account for an evaluation of interventions.

The rehabilitative goal of punishment proved to be a more humane and scientific approach in responding to criminal behavior and providing solutions geared toward criminal desistance. Over the years, however, the practical application of rehabilitative measures experienced periods of attack and criticism for their inability to stop criminal behavior and reduce rates of reoffending. As the field of criminology continued to grow in its scope of understanding crime, punishment, and criminal behavior, another branch of the discipline emerged to shed light on crime types and criminals through the study of criminal victimization and its various dimensions. We turn now to an examination of victimology.

Crime Victimization in Context

The study of crime victims and victimization has not always been at the forefront of criminological discourse. Historically, awareness of the effect of crime on victims and the need for justice was a personal matter that left it up to the victim or the victim's family to recover from the loss or harm (Daigle & Muftic, 2019). This often led to the enactment of retaliation to the offender where the punishment or method of revenge was equal to the harm committed. The study of crime victimization emerged as a discipline during the 1940s and 1950s, validating the need to shift attention in the response to crime to be more centered around the harm caused to the victim and how to respond to that harm. This prompted a victims' rights movement, spanning decades of research and reform to address the impact of crime on victims, advance the needs of victims of crime, and protect them from further victimization by criminal justice proceedings.

The Study of Crime Victims

One of the earliest pioneering criminologists to direct our attention to the study of crime victimization was Hans Von Henting, who investigated factors contributing to the victimization of certain individuals more than others (Lasky, 2019). His research helped develop our current conceptualization of the various traits and characteristics that are linked to both criminal offending and crime victimization. In his 1948 seminal book *The Criminal and His Victim*, he elaborated on the overlap in victimization and offending by recognizing the fallacy of studying criminal offenders and crime victims as two distinct categories (Hentig, 1948). Rather, he argued, causal variables of criminal offending can also be a contributive factor in determining and predicting crime victimization. His work advanced the further analysis of crime victimization and significantly contributed to the expansion of research into the field of victim studies.

Victimology, as a discipline, came of age in the late 1940s when Benjamin Mendelson, considered the "father of victimology," coined the term known as the scientific study of crime victims (Mendelsohn, 1976). Today, we define **victimology** as the study of the causes of victimization, its consequences, and how the criminal justice system addresses the needs of victims, as well as the role of society in responding to victims of crime (Daigle & Muftic, 2019). Mendelson became interested in studying victims of crime and their relationship to offenders through his work and observations during interviews as a criminal defense attorney. Recognizing that victims and offenders were more often than not entangled with one another in some type of relationship or interaction, he developed a classification of crime victims based on their degree of culpability, recognizing the importance of differentiating victimization based on the behavior or reactions of the victim. We will consider this dynamic next in greater detail. First, however, we must assess the value of these historical contributions to the more modern-day *victim rights movement.*

The social climate of the mid-1900s redirected our attention to various problems and conditions within society, leading to conflict, discrimination, and chaos in a search for resolution (Pemberton et al., 2019). During this time, and largely as an outgrowth of other social movements such as the *women's movement* and the *civil rights movement,* a sympathetic interest in victims of crime and their hardships culminated in a victim rights movement that moved the study of victimization to the frontage of research and data collection. This movement spanned decades of victim advocacy, ushering in programs, policies, and practices aimed at raising social and cultural awareness of the effect of victimization on individuals, creating special organizations to address victim needs, and prompting national campaigns and federal task forces to address victim rights and protections, as well as the compensation of victims of crime. The victim rights movement contributed to the growth and expansion of the field of victimology and its study as a discipline. Let's turn now to some of the highlights of this study to better understand the consequences of criminal behavior on crime victims, as well as the role of victimization in the study of criminal typologies.

Trends in Victimization

To properly study crime victimization and its relationship to crime types and criminals, we must first assess the crime victim by determining who the typical victim is or who is most at risk of becoming a victim and why. Victimization surveys such as the National Crime Victimization Survey (NCVS; discussed in Chapter 1) have helped criminologists identify categories of individuals we consider to be members of vulnerable populations that are targeted by criminals. The most current 2019 NCVS data report reveals that trends in violent crime victimization increased for individuals aged 12 and older from 2.7 million in 2015 to 3.3 million in 2018, while property victimizations fell from 118.6 per 1,000 households in 2016 to 108.2 per 1,000 in 2018. The increase in violent crimes was largely due to increases in the number of victims of rape or sexual assault, aggravated assault, and simple assault (Morgan & Oudekerk, 2019). A closer look at NCVS demographic data collected per criminal incident reveals some interesting findings that indicate crime does not occur uniformly but rather a definite pattern emerges surrounding such variables as age, race, social class, and gender. Table 2.1 provides a summary of some of these trends and findings:

TABLE 2.1   PATTERNS AND TRENDS IN CRIME VICTIMIZATION

	NCVS Data Reveal ...
What about age?	People between 18 and 24 years old are more likely to be the victim of a violent crime than any other age group; the risk of being a victim declines steadily after age 24, with people over the age of 65 accounting for the fewest incidents of violent crime victimization.
What about race?	The offender was of the same race or ethnicity as the victim in 70% of violent incidents involving Black victims, 62% of those involving White victims, 45% of those involving Hispanic victims, and 24% of those involving Asian victims.
What about gender?	Except for the crimes of rape and sexual assault, men are more likely to be the victims of all crimes and twice as likely to be the victims of violent crimes.
What about income?	The lower the social class, the greater the likelihood that one will be the victim of a crime, especially violent street crime that occurs in many neighborhoods where drug abuse, poverty, and social deprivation are prevalent.

Research studies on crime victimization have also been able to guide us in better evaluating the role of victims in a criminal event. In fact, the very beginnings of the study of crime victimization centered on the investigation of victim characteristics and behavior patterns contributing to their own victimization. The term **victim precipitation** was developed to assess the extent to which a victim is "responsible" for their own victimization (Lasky, 2019). This concept recognizes that while some victims do not bear any responsibility at all in their victimization, others share some burden of action through provocation, incitement, or reaction before, during, or after the incident. **Victim facilitation** occurs when a victim makes it "easier" for a criminal act to occur through their own actions or omissions (De Heer, 2019). This can happen, for example, when someone leaves their car door unlocked when running into a grocery store, or another individual leaves their purse on a table to go refill a drink at a fast-food restaurant. While these individuals certainly don't deserve to be victimized, their actions, while not blameworthy, definitely made them an easier target for theft, explaining why some individuals are more likely to be victimized than others.

While historical attempts at various forms of victim blaming have been abandoned over the years through the evolving victim rights movement, these concepts continue to play a role in helping us create targeted strategies that increase victim awareness of the dynamics involved in becoming targeted for crime and how to avoid those structural and contextual components that increase the odds of victimization.

The context of crime victimization has provided us with a unique perspective that provides a more far-reaching, complete approach to the study of criminal typologies that goes beyond the exclusive focus on criminal offenders, their motives, and the causal variables contributing to their offending. Crime is a harm, a form of unwanted behavior, and not simply a violation of the law (Hass-Wisecup & Saxon, 2018). The field of victimology has emerged to help us better understand the social, emotional, and physical impact of this harm to victims. To properly assess this harm and address it comprehensively, however, we must first evaluate crime from the standpoint of various social correlates that criminologists have found to be associated with criminal offenders, to which we now turn to a discussion of what these are.

Social Correlates of Criminal Offending

Another piece of the crime picture that we must look at when studying criminal typologies is the social correlates of criminal offending. Criminologists studying personal and demographic variables associated with crime have found consistencies in the amount, type, and frequency of certain categories of crime and age, race, gender, social class, and geographic location. Let's take a look at some of their findings.

Age and Crime

Theoretical criminology has a long-standing support of the strong correlation between age and crime, notably, that criminal behavior declines significantly with age (Hirschi & Gottfredson, 1983). Generally speaking, the incidence of crime increases dramatically between ages 12 and 16, and peaks in the adolescent years from about age 17 or 18 to about age 24 consistently across various other demographic variables such as race, income, and education. This holds true for violent crimes, as well as for most other categories of crime (see Figure 2.2). One way criminologists explain this trend is by attributing the criminality of youth as largely a function of adolescent traits such as impulsivity, neurological underdevelopment, and lack of maturity, as well as factors such as peer pressure, seeking independence, and rebellion against adult supervision (Seidl et al., 2020). Other studies note the variables of strain, increasing economic demand on young adults, and exposure to violence as social correlates of this age group that increase their propensity to respond to stress and conflict through criminal means (Nsubuga, 2019).

Further studies on the age-crime curve, however, have proved this connection to be a far more complex matter, and researchers caution us against overlooking other trends showing clusters of individuals who become involved in offenses during their later years in life, such as occupational crimes involving stock market fraud for example or insider trading, types of "white-collar crimes" that we will discuss in later chapters. We also don't want to neglect the study of **career criminals**, that group of offenders who are habitual repeat offenders who commit crimes throughout the course of their lives and age out at a much later stage of life because of their developmental and environmental exposure to criminogenic forces (Sampson & Laub, 2005).

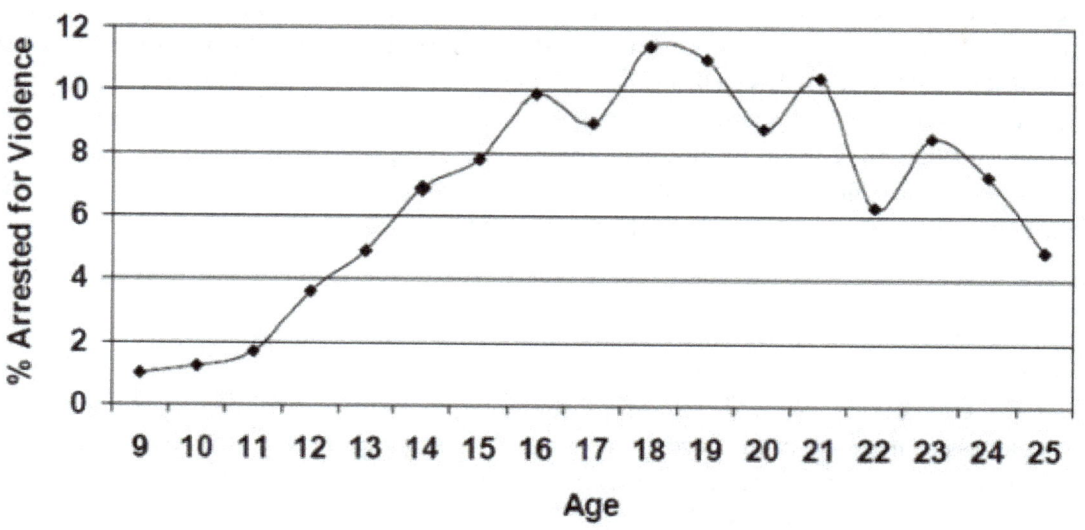

FIGURE 2.2   The Age-Crime Curve

Source: https://nij.ojp.gov/sites/g/files/xyckuh171/files/images/2019-06/age-crime-curve.jpg

Race and Crime

Racial disparities in arrests have been a prevalent finding in official crime data reports for quite some time. A consistent pattern has been the disproportionate arrest rate of African Americans, who comprise roughly 13% of the population but represent about 25%–30% of all arrests (Federal Bureau of Investigation, 2020). Moreover, according to the most current full publication of *Crime in the United States* (2018), the African American arrest rate for homicide was 53.3% and 54.2% for robbery. These statistics, however, must be viewed with caution. We must recall that official crime reports rely on arrest data provided by law enforcement agencies, and therefore, we are only provided with information on such crimes as, burglary, assault, robbery, murder, and a few other index crimes (see Chapter 1).

So, while these findings on racial disparity seem to lead us to believe that African Americans are responsible for the majority of criminality, that is simply not true, as we are neglecting data on crimes such as government corruption, corporate fraud, human trafficking, and domestic violence. Moreover, findings from official data reports on crime, especially violent crime, affect police departments and their practices, as they lead to patterns of patrolling in certain neighborhoods that are predominantly African American (Brantingham et al., 2018). This further compounds the problem by leading to an increase in arrests for young, minority African American males because of police bias and visibility caused by an increase in surveillance in areas where nonwhites live. It is also important to note that the overwhelming majority of victims and offenders are of the same race, and therefore, the relationship between crime and race also applies to victimization, most notably for violent crime (Bureau of Justice Statistics, Office of Justice Programs, 2018).

Gender and Crime

The variable of gender has also proved to have a significant role in the prediction of criminal offending. According to Uniform Crime Report data, men are 4 times as likely to be arrested for a violent crime as women, with the ratio of male to female arrests for homicide being 7 to 1 (Federal Bureau of Investigation, 2020). Moreover, men are more than 4 times as likely to commit the crime of burglary than women, and almost 3 and a half times as likely to steal a car. When it comes to larcenies such as shoplifting, however, the picture is quite different, with men only slightly (0.4%) higher than women. Information from other data sources such as the NCVS (discussed in Chapter 1) also shows similar findings, indicating that men are responsible for the majority of serious crimes such as murder, rape, and robbery.

While the majority of criminologists do not dispute this very obvious trend, research studies explaining the reason for this gender disparity are in less agreement. A body of literature centering upon studying innate, biological differences in the constitution of men and women attribute the difference in criminality, especially with regard to violent crimes, to genetic traits of males as more aggressive, stronger, and antagonistic (Conover-Williams & Schwartz, 2019). Other studies of gender differences in crime rates between men and women examine the effects of socialization as mediating the gap, arguing that males grow up learning to be assertive, aggressive, and powerful, while women are socialized into gender roles that are more nurturing, adaptive, and submissive (Isom & Mikell, 2019). While both of these perspectives merit further exploration, it is important to note that with regard to gender and crime, although gaps continue to exist between men and women, that gap has declined over the course of time, with converging rates of criminality, especially with regard to property crime, becoming a trend with the increasing role of women as breadwinners, primary family providers, and leaders in the workforce (Durrant, 2019; Gould & Hulon, 2019).

Social Class and Crime

The relationship between social class and criminality has been a complex phenomenon for criminologists to study. There are several theoretical perspectives that attribute high rates of crime to low-income, socially disadvantaged neighborhoods characterized by poverty, unemployment, alcoholism, and violence (Snowden, 2019). These explanations focus on concentrated pockets of street crimes such as robbery, drug use, gang activity, and homicide as products of the disorganized structure of the environment. Other theories of crime maintain that social class mediates the type and amount of crime owing to criminal justice system practices that discriminate against certain types of individuals and certain neighborhoods (Kurlychek & Johnson, 2019). Here, we see that poor, minority, uneducated individuals with lower socioeconomic status show up disproportionately in crime statistics because of biased police practices that focus on controlling these individuals, which ultimately creates a sense of personal stigma from being labeled as a "criminal type," causing a self-fulfilling prophecy and increasing the likelihood of future criminality. Box 2.2 illustrates this dynamic interaction between social class, crime, and the criminal justice system.

WHO DID IT? "THE SAINTS VERSUS THE ROUGHNECKS" — BOX 2.2

"The Saints and the Roughnecks" is a research study conducted through observations and interviews with two delinquent gangs. The Saints were a group of eight promising young men from "good" White upper-middle-class families. They were active in school affairs, received good grades, and played on athletic teams. At the same time, they were some of the most delinquent boys at Hannibal High. However, their technique for covering truancy was so successful that teachers did not even realize that the boys were absent from school much of the time. The local police also saw the Saints as good boys who were among the leaders of the youth in the community. On rare occasions when they were stopped in town for speeding or running a stop sign, the Saints were always polite, contrite, and pled for mercy. Although constantly occupied with truancy, drinking, wild driving, petty theft, and vandalism, none of them was officially arrested for any misdeed during the 2 years they were observed.

Although their rate of delinquency was about equal to that of the Saints, the Roughnecks were constantly in trouble with police, who suspected that they were engaged in criminal activities. They knew this partly from catching them, mostly from circumstantial evidence, and because they shared the view of the community in general that this was a bad bunch of boys. Because they were constantly involved with the police, teachers also saw the boys as heading for trouble. What was the cause of this disparity in treatment between the Saints and the Roughnecks, and what was the result? Why did the Roughnecks and the Saints in fact have quite different careers after high school, which, by and large, lived up to the expectations of the community?

The community responded to the Roughnecks as boys in trouble, and the boys agreed with that perception. Once their pattern of deviance was reinforced, the boys acquired an image of themselves as deviants, selecting friends who affirmed that self-image. As that self-conception became more firmly entrenched, they also became willing to try new and more extreme deviances. With their growing alienation came a freer expression of disrespect and hostility for representatives of the legitimate society. This disrespect increased the community's negativism, perpetuating the entire process of commitment to deviance.

Source: Aida Y. Hass, Chris Moloney, and William J. Chambliss, Selections from Criminology: Connecting Theory, Research and Practice, pp. 438-439. Copyright © 2017 by Taylor & Francis Group. Reprinted with permission.

Location and Crime

During the mid-1980s, a branch of criminology emerged to examine the effect of location on criminal activity. **Environmental criminologists** study the characteristics of communities that contribute to high rates of crime in those areas, drawing a link between criminal behavior patterns and the geographic location and physical features of certain neighborhoods (Andresen, 2019). This field has contributed significantly to our development of criminal typologies based on the immediate context within, which criminal behavior occurs. This theoretical approach is supported by crime data sources which show that criminal behavior is not randomly distributed but rather a product of variables such as time, place, and situation that facilitate and mediate criminal opportunities (Brantingham et al., 2020).

Location is a very important social correlate of crime, as it guides us in developing criminal typologies based on an understanding of what contributes to criminal events, how to intervene to prevent them from occurring, and what tools to use to predict and prevent future patterns of offending. Chapter 3 will examine these dynamics in greater detail as we begin to explore the blueprints of criminal behavior by building various categories of crime types and criminals.

Key Takeaways

Review the following list of bullet points for a quick overview of the key ideas and information in this chapter:

- Criminal law develops in different ways. While we sometimes agree on right and wrong, modern, complex societies are composed of a diversity of individuals with differing values and, therefore, conflict over law leads to debates about what is right and wrong. The outcomes are rules and regulations that favor those with more power.
- Part of law and order in our society revolves around the issue of punishment. Historically, the goal of punishment has been to exact revenge on the offender, with no regard to human rights. As civilization evolved, and the field of criminology developed, the goals of punishment shifted to a more logical imposition of sanctions designed to deter crime and rehabilitate offenders.
- The study of crime victimization helps us better understand the physical, social, and psychological harms experienced by victims, how to address those harms, and how to create interventions that target those populations at risk for victimization.
- Criminologists have been able to identify personal and demographic variables associated with crime; traits such as age, race, gender, social class, and geographic location are integral to the study of criminal typologies.

Conclusion and Formal Summary Questions

This chapter began our journey toward a more comprehensive look at the connections we need to make between crime, victimization, and the role of criminal law in shaping the outcome of punishment and intervention. We learned that the matter of defining right and wrong is not always an easy task, and therefore, while some regulations are the product of consensus over moral values, other rules are ultimately shaped by deliberations that sort out the disagreements, with those in power usually having the upper hand in legal definitions. Criminal law has evolved over time, with changing social norms redefining society's principles and standards of conduct. These changes also influenced the goal of punishment and its implementation. Society no longer settled on traditional notions of vengeance and harm, and the goal of punishment moved from a focus on retribution to one of a more meaningful application of deterrence and rehabilitation. This focus expanded our study of criminal offenders, their relationship to victims of crime, as well as the various social correlates that can be identified as parallels of criminal behavior.

- *Can you identify the main differences between the consensus and conflict models of law creation?*
- *Are you able to list the various goals of punishment we have in our effort to stop criminal offending?*
- *Can you describe the field of victimology and how it helps us study crime victimization?*
- *Do you know what we mean by social correlates of criminal offending and what they are?*

E-Resources

For more information on "what works" in crime prevention, visit the Justice Research Center website at http://thejrc.com/wwi-principles.asp

Learn more about victim assistance programs by visiting the National Organization for Victim Advocacy at https://study.com/academy/lesson/crime-surveys-self-report-surveys-implications-uses.html

Check out this short prison documentary about a career criminal (Shotgun Joe Scanlon): https://www.youtube.com/watch?v=OLAD4h98xj8

References

Andresen, M. A. (2019). *Environmental criminology: Evolution, theory, and practice*. Routledge.

Brantingham, P. J., Brantingham, P. L., Song, J., & Spicer, V. (2020). Crime hot spots, crime corridors and the journey to crime: An expanded theoretical model of the generation of crime concentrations. In K. M. Lersch & J. Chakraborty (Eds.), *Geographies of Behavioural Health, Crime, and Disorder* (pp. 61–86). Springer, Cham.

Brantingham, P. J., Valasik, M., & Mohler, G. O. (2018). Does predictive policing lead to biased arrests? Results from a randomized controlled trial. *Statistics and Public Policy*, 5(1), 1–6.

Bun, M. J., Kelaher, R., Sarafidis, V., & Weatherburn, D. (2019). Crime, deterrence and punishment revisited. *Empirical Economics*, 1–31.

Bureau of Justice Statistics, Office of Justice Programs. (2018). *Data collection: National crime victimization survey*. https://www.bjs.gov/index.cfm?ty=dcdetail&iid=245.

Conover-Williams, M., & Schwartz, J. (2019). Masculinity theory and female offending. In F. P. Bernat, K. Frailing, L. Gelsthorpe, S. Kethineni, & L. Pasko (Eds.), *The encyclopedia of women and crime* (pp. 1–3). Wiley-Blackwell.

Cotterrell, Roger. (1999). *Emile Durkheim: Law in a moral domain*. Edinbergh University Press.

Daigle, L. E., & Muftic, L. R. (2019). *Victimology: A comprehensive approach*. SAGE Publications.

Datta, A. (2017). California's three strikes law revisited: Assessing the long-term effects of the law. *Atlantic Economic Journal*, 45(2), 225–249.

De Heer, B. (2019). Victim blaming. In F. P. Bernat, K. Frailing, L. Gelsthorpe, S. Kethineni, & L. Pasko (Eds.), *The encyclopedia of women and crime* (pp. 1–5). Wiley-Blackwell.

Durrant, R. (2019). Evolutionary approaches to understanding crime: Explaining the gender gap in offending. *Psychology, Crime & Law, 25*(6), 589–608.

Federal Bureau of Investigation. (2020). *Uniform crime reporting (UCR) program.* https://www.fbi.gov/services/cjis/ucr

Garimella, K., De Francisci Morales, G., Gionis, A., & Mathioudakis, M. (2017, June). *The effect of collective attention on controversial debates on social media.* Proceedings of the 2017 ACM on Web Science Conference.

Gottdiener, M. (2019). New urban sociology. In A. M. Orum (Ed.)., *The Wiley Blackwell Encyclopedia of Urban and Regional Studies* (pp. 1–5). Wiley.

Gould, L. A., & Hulon, K. (2019). Gender disparity and arrests. In F. P. Bernat, K. Frailing, L. Gelsthorpe, S. Kethineni, & L. Pasko (Eds.), *The encyclopedia of women and crime* (pp. 1–4). Wiley-Blackwell.

Greco, A. (2019). The code of Hammurabi in later school tradition. *The Code of Hammurabi in Later School Tradition* (pp. 69–79).

Hass, A. Y., Moloney, C., & Chambliss, W. J. (2016). *Criminology: Connecting theory, research and practice.* Taylor & Francis.

Hass-Wisecup, A., & Saxon, C. (2018). *Restorative justice: Integrating theory, research, and practice.* Carolina Academic Press.

Hentig, H. V. (1948). *The criminal & his victim; studies in the sociobiology of crime.* Yale Univ. Press.

Hirschi, T., & Gottfredson, M. (1983). Age and the explanation of crime. *American Journal of Sociology, 89*, 552–584.

Isom Scott, D. A., & Mikell, T. (2019). 'Gender' and general strain theory: Investigating the impact of gender socialization on young women's criminal outcomes. *Journal of Crime and Justice, 42*(4), 393–413.

Jacobo, J. (2019). 5 teens charged with murder after Illinois homeowner shoots 14-year-old during burglary attempt. *ABC News.* https://abcnews.go.com/US/teens-charged-murder-illinois-homeowner-shoots-14-year/story?id=64967872.

Kurlychek, M. C., & Johnson, B. D. (2019). Cumulative disadvantage in the American criminal justice system. *Annual Review of Criminology, 2*, 291–319.

Lasky, N. V. (2019). Victim precipitation theory. In F. P. Bernat, K. Frailing, L. Gelsthorpe, S. Kethineni, & L. Pasko (Eds.), *The encyclopedia of women and crime* (pp. 1–2). Wiley-Blackwell.

Lerman, D. C. (2019). Punishment. In S. Hupp & J. D. Jewell (Eds.), *The encyclopedia of child and adolescent development* (pp. 1–9). Wiley.

McDonald, L. (2019). *Sociology of law & order.* Routledge.

McNeill, F. (2018). Rehabilitation, corrections and society: The 2017 ICPA distinguished scholar lecture. *Advancing Corrections Journal, 5*, 10–20.

Mendelsohn, B. (1976). Victimology and contemporary society's trends. *Victimology, 1*(1), 8–28.

Meško, G. (2020). Punishment and legitimacy. In R. Hacin & G. Meško (Eds.), *The dual nature of legitimacy in the prison environment* (pp. 9–15). Springer, Cham.

Morgan, R. E., & Oudekerk, B. (2019). *Criminal victimization: 2018.* U.S. Department of Justice, Office of Justice Programs. https://www.bjs.gov/content/pub/pdf/cv18.pdf.

Mungan, M. C. (2019). Salience and the severity versus the certainty of punishment. *International Review of Law and Economics, 57*, 95–100.

Nsubuga, F. (2019). *Stress, peer pressure and delinquency among adolescents* [Doctoral dissertation, Makerere University].

Outram, D. (2019). *The enlightenment* (vol. 58). Cambridge University Press.

Park, R. E., & Burgess, E. W. (2019). *Introduction to the science of sociology.* Good Press.

Pemberton, A., Mulder, E., & Aarten, P. G. (2019). Stories of injustice: Towards a narrative victimology. *European Journal of criminology*, *16*(4), 391–412.

Sampson, R. J., & Laub, J. H. (2005). A life-course view of the development of crime. *The Annals of the American Academy of Political and Social Science*, *602*(1), 12–45.

Schram, P. J., & Tibbetts, S. G. (2019). *Introduction to criminology: Why do they do it?* SAGE Publications.

Seidl, H., Nilsson, T., Hofvander, B., Billstedt, E., & Wallinius, M. (2020). Personality and cognitive functions in violent offenders—implications of character maturity? *Frontiers in Psychology*, *11*, 58.

Sloan III, J. J. (2017). Three strikes laws. In K. R. Kerley (Ed.), *The encyclopedia of corrections* (pp. 1–7). Wiley-Blackwell.

Snowden, A. J. (2019). Exploring violence: The role of neighborhood characteristics, alcohol outlets, and other micro-places. *Social Science Research*, *82*, 181–194.

Waller, B. N. (2020). Rethinking punishment, written by Leo Zaibert. *Journal of Moral Philosophy*, *17*(1), 122–124.

Chapter 3

Developing a Criminal Typology

Key Terms

Typology
Legally based typology
Felony
Misdemeanor
Offender-based typology
Biological theories
Atavistic features
Ectomorph
Mesomorph
Endomorph
Homology
Psychological theories
Instrumental crimes
Expressive crimes
Environmental criminology
Collective efficacy
Situational context typology
Victim-based typology

Opening Questions

Before you begin the chapter, take a few minutes to reflect on the following questions:

1. How many crime categories can you think of? Are crime categories shaped by their legal definition?
2. What characteristics do some crime categories share with one another? What about criminal offenders?
3. Can we understand a crime scene better by identifying the motive of the offender?
4. Does the relationship between the victim and the offender matter in the study of criminal typologies?

Chapter Headings

1. Chapter opener
2. What are typologies?
3. Legal typologies
   3.1. Felony versus misdemeanor
   3.2. UCR definition
4. Offender-based typologies
   4.1. Physical attributes
   4.2. Personality of offender
   4.3. Motive/method of operation
5. Contextual typologies
6. Victim-based typologies
   6.1. Structural position of victim
   6.2. Behavior pattern of victim
7. Chapter summary

Chapter Objectives

After reading Chapter 3, students will be able to do the following:

- Understand what we mean by the term typologies
- Determine the role of typologies in the study of criminal behavior
- Identify various criminal typologies and how they are created
- Recognize the value of criminal typologies in a criminal investigation

True Crime

History is riddled with examples of bizarre, inexplicable, shocking acts of criminal actions perpetrated by a variety of individuals, from ordinary housewives, members of the clergy, and medical doctors, to schoolteachers, presidents of countries, and professional athletes. None was more scandalous than the 1994 attack on Olympic hopeful skater Nancy Kerrigan. While practicing at a Detroit, Michigan, ice skating rink just 2 days before the Olympic trials in January, a man walked in and hit Kerrigan with a club on the back of the knee. Her shrieks of pain, confusion, and panic became an image of horror captured in the minds of Americans watching this attack, for many years to come. What became an even greater shock to the integrity of sportsmanship and the spirit of competition was the story that emerged surrounding this crime when we learned that Kerrigan's chief rival for placement on the 1994 U.S. Olympic Figure Skating Team, Tonya Harding, was caught up in the conspiracy to perpetrate this attack to eliminate Kerrigan from the competition.

Sometime during the middle of December 1993, Harding's ex-husband, Jeff Gillooly, approached a man by the name of Shawn Eckardt about devising a scheme to remove Kerrigan from the competition, as she was a major rival to Harding. Eckardt set up a meeting between Gillooly and two other men, Derrick Smith and Shane Stant, who agreed to be paid in exchange for injuring Kerrigan. Stant carried out the attack and fled the scene in Smith's getaway car, leaving Kerrigan unable to skate, and leading to Harding winning the championship and placing on the 1994 Olympics Figure Skating Team. Shortly after the attack, Smith and Stant were arrested and confessed to their role in the crime, implicating Gillooly, who was charged with conspiracy to assault Kerrigan. While initially denying any knowledge of this attack, Harding later admitted she knew about the plan but didn't inform authorities. The unfolding events of a crime like this raise many questions in our minds, even after we have allegedly "solved" the mystery. What would motivate a young, successful, talented athlete to become entangled with such heinous behavior? What could have been done to protect Kerrigan from this victimization? How are the different "players" in this drama going to pay for their crimes? What should we charge them with according to our perception of their actions and according to the criminal law? The development of criminal typologies helps us answer some of these as well as other lingering questions.

What Are Typologies?

> *The kind of violence, looting, destruction that we saw from a handful of individuals in Baltimore, there's no excuse for that. That's not a statement. That's not politics. That's not activism. That's just criminal behavior.*
>
> —Barack Obama, *At This Hour with Kate Bolduan and John Berman,* www.cnn.com, April 29, 2015

Crime by any other name is crime; it's obvious, straightforward, and not subject to debate. Right? Absolutely not! While former President Obama's statement may have defined the actions of protesters in Baltimore as brazen examples of crime and violence similar to how we would describe the actions of the perpetrators in our true crime story, there are more pieces to the puzzle that we must put together to get an accurate depiction of crime types and criminals. Why is there a handful of individuals? Who is this handful? Can their actions ever be construed as "making a statement"? What does politics have to do with it? Let's explore some of these questions as we begin to study criminal typologies.

So far in our exploration of the study of crime types and criminals, we have examined the conceptualization of crime, its definition, and relationship to social reaction, as well as its evolution according to developments in standards of conduct as set forth by the social climate. In Chapter 2, we set out to establish an understanding of criminal behavior that is guided by the evolution of laws that define for us right and wrong and provide sanctions for those who violate criminal codes. Now as we move forward in our study, we will attempt to capture the varieties of these behaviors collectively referred to as *crime* to gain a comprehensive road map of criminal behavior in its various forms, causes, and manifestations throughout society. We will do this by developing typologies of criminal behavior. This road map is imperative in order to analyze such a complex phenomenon as crime and its various dimensions.

Typologies, therefore, help us gain a more concise understanding of facts, events, and behaviors. The more complex the behavior, fact, or event, the more we need to create a typology that categorizes it according to certain common features or characteristics. Crime **typologies** serve to simplify the social reality of crime by identifying homogeneous groups of criminal behaviors that are different from other clusters of crime (Miethe et al., 2005). Consider, for example, the following news headlines describing various forms of criminal events:

- *College professor stabbed in front of students*
- *Priest charged with possessing child pornography*
- *Several arrested in gang-related shooting*
- *Unmasking a massive abuse of power by the president*
- *Police videotaped attacking girl*
- *Man charged with hate crime*
- *Ex-Dolphins running back aggravated battery charge dropped*

As we try to make sense of the events surrounding these headlines, we begin to see the need to outline the various contexts, actions, traits, and characteristics of the individuals involved in these crimes. This exercise clearly dictates that criminal behaviors must be dissected according to certain variables. The variables criminologists have identified to be most useful in understanding crime and criminal behavior surround the following dimensions outlined in Table 3.1:

TABLE 3.1 THE MAKING OF A CRIMINAL TYPOLOGY

What We Ask ...	What We Are Looking For ...
Who is the offender?	<ul><li>Gender</li><li>Age</li><li>Race</li><li>Relationship to victim</li><li>Former convictions</li><li>Background, history of violence</li><li>Mental health status</li></ul>
Who is the victim?	<ul><li>Gender</li><li>Age</li><li>Race</li><li>Relationship to offender</li><li>Former victimizations</li><li>Mental health status</li></ul>
What is the situational context of the crime?	<ul><li>The physical setting of the crime, including location, time, weapons used, etc.</li></ul>
What were the exact actions taken?	<ul><li>Beaten</li><li>Stabbed</li><li>Multiple stabs</li><li>Attacked</li><li>Slaughtered</li><li>Molested</li><li>Broke in</li><li>Etc.</li></ul>
What legal definitions apply to the actions?	<ul><li>First-degree murder</li><li>Second-degree murder</li><li>Manslaughter</li><li>Rape</li><li>Assaults</li><li>Larceny</li><li>Embezzlement</li><li>Etc.</li></ul>

Criminologists expand these elements to create the classification of crimes into categories of events that we can better identify, analyze, and determine cause. Let's take a closer look at the major criminal typologies that have been developed to help us sort out the varieties of crime types and criminals.

Legal Typologies

In the social sciences, we come to draw conclusions through the basic lens of observation of the world around us. Thus, the first step of observation in developing typologies of criminal behavior is to categorize crimes according to their legal connection to the law. Put simply, laws have been developed for centuries to create various divisions, levels, and stratifications of actions that have been deemed harmful to society and, therefore, necessary to formally regulate and sanction. From this, our understanding of crime has been shaped by a **legally based typology** of classification within the criminal law, which in its most basic form distinguishes between crimes according to the severity of the offense and the legal consequences of the behavior (Bergman, 2020).

Felony Versus Misdemeanor

One of the most useful aspects of legal typologies is their ability to give us a better picture of the crime problem by allowing us to come up with meaningful categories of acts that can be defined and measured. These categories enable us to assess the amount of crime, where it occurs, and how to take proactive measures to prevent it from becoming an even bigger problem. The broadest legal classification of crime is determined by the action's severity and the subsequent legal consequence. From this perspective, we can categorize a crime as either a *felony* or *misdemeanor*. A **misdemeanor** crime is one that is less serious, and in most states and under federal law is considered a criminal offense that is punished by a potential jail term of less than 1 year. Moreover, some states further break down the classification of misdemeanor crimes into specific "classes" of offenses delineating the punishment range (Bergman, 2020). When it comes to more serious crimes, the law recognizes acts as **felony** crimes, acts that are serious in terms of their severity of punishment and the depth of harm caused to a victim or to society. That harm can be physical harm, the threat of harm, or significant financial damage or loss. Felonies almost uniformly throughout the United States refer to crimes that can be punishable by more than 1 year in prison (Simester et al., 2019).

While this is a useful step in the right direction of categorizing criminal acts, it leaves us with less than a complete understanding of various important dynamics that shape a comprehensive criminal typology. The classification of crimes according to felony or misdemeanor does not tell us much beyond seriousness and punishment outcome. We need to further break down crimes according to a more standard scheme of legal definition. For that endeavor, we turn to a discussion of some of the major categories of crime as described by the Uniform Crime Report (UCR).

UCR Definition

Renowned author and criminologist William J. Chambliss once noted that "trying to capture the varieties of crime is like trying to draw a map of the world. If the map has all the details in it, it is as large as the world and worthless as a map. If it leaves out all the rivers and mountains, roads and alleys, it is compact but does not tell us enough to give us a sense of where we are or where we are going" (Chambliss, 1988). This profound statement recognizes the difficult task of demarcating all acts under the umbrella of crime and sorting them into specific types or groups. For this reason, we rely on the widely used definitions established by the UCR to develop a better grasp of the varieties of criminal behavior by relying on their legal definitions contained within this widely used data source. Table 3.2 presents us with some of the major crime categories and their description according to their description in the UCR, as well as other federal and state codes and statutes. For the sake of organization, we divided these crimes into groups according to the nature and meaning of the crimes, their targeted victims, and their source of offense. While this doesn't capture all crimes that are defined by legal statute in all jurisdictions throughout the United States, it nevertheless gives us enough detail to build upon and develop more adequate criminal profiles.

TABLE 3.2 A CLOSER LOOK AT THE LEGAL CLASSIFICATION OF CRIME

Violent Crimes	Property Crimes	Crimes Against the Public Order	Crimes Committed by People in Positions of Power or Authority	Crimes of National or Global Nature
Murder—The willful (non-negligent) killing of one human being by another human being. **Rape**—Penetration of the vagina or anus with any body part or object, or oral penetration by a sex organ of another person, without the consent of the victim. **Assault**—The attempted commission of bodily injury to another human being. Assault can also mean putting an individual in fear of imminent bodily harm, injury, danger, or threat. An assault can therefore include threats, taunting, intimidation, and harassment; it requires no physical contact.	**Larceny**—The unlawful taking away of someone's property without using force, violence, or by fraud. **Burglary**—The unlawful entry into a building or structure to commit a theft or felony. **Arson**—The willful and malicious burning of a home, vehicle, building, or other structure or property. **Motor Vehicle Theft**—The theft or attempted theft of a motor vehicle.	**Prostitution**—The unlawful engaging in sexual activities for profit. **Pornography**—The portrayal or depiction of sexually explicit material. **Drug Abuse**—The violation of laws pertaining to the possession, use, manufacture, or sale of controlled substances.	**White-Collar Crime**—Nonviolent acts involving deception, concealment, and guile committed by individuals, businesses, and corporations, for the purposes of obtaining money, avoiding loss, or gaining personal advantage. **State Crime**—Illegal activities by government officials to advance their political agendas or promote their own interests. **Organized Crime**—The illegal activities of groups of individuals in the course of some type of illegal business or enterprise set up for monetary gain.	**International Crime**—Systematic practices involving the infringement of human rights, peace agreements, or other violations of international laws. **Political Crime**—Crimes committed to threaten, oppose, or challenge the government in power. **Technology Crimes**—Criminal offenses that are perpetrated using some type of network communication device such as the Internet.

Violent Crimes	Property Crimes	Crimes Against the Public Order	Crimes Committed by People in Positions of Power or Authority	Crimes of National or Global Nature
Robbery—The taking or attempting to take anything of value from the care, custody, or control of a person or persons by force or threat of force or violence and/or by putting the victim in fear.				
Hate Crime—Crimes directed at certain individuals because of their race, sexual orientation, religion, national origin, political orientation, or physical condition.				

Source: Aida Y. Hass, Chris Moloney, and William J. Chambliss, *Selections from Criminology: Connecting Theory, Research and Practice*, pp. 21. Copyright © 2017 by Taylor & Francis Group. Reprinted with permission.

The UCR is an important classification system that we rely on to be able to describe criminal actions from a legal standpoint. It helps us as a society to reference crime in a way that holds individuals accountable under the law. However, this type of sorting out of crime falls short of giving criminologists and researchers the necessary tools to study crime types and criminals. We still do not know much about the offender, their motive, their relationship to the victim, the circumstances of the crime, and other aspects of the offense and the social context of the criminal act. Moreover, legal definitions of crime may vary by state, as well as, as we previously discussed in Chapter 1, by time, place, and location (Ručman, 2019). In addition, there is an underlying assumption that offenders with the same type of legal label (murderer, rapist, arsonist, etc.) are all similar or products of the same environment or circumstances. This is far from the truth, and for this reason, criminologists have studied crime and researched criminal behavior to provide us with more detailed typologies that help us distinguish the enormous varieties of criminals and criminal acts. One of these typologies that we will now turn to focuses on the study of offenders.

Offender-Based Typologies

For years, criminologists have studied criminal behavior in order to grasp a sense of how and why a crime was committed and connect these causal variables to the physical and demographic attributes of an offender and their social environment. Various theoretical paradigms have emerged to facilitate the research into offender characteristics, traits, and motivations in order to be able to use scientific measures to intervene and prevent crime from happening or mediate scenarios that can lead to violent behavior. While a plethora of theories exists to explain criminal behavior, our focus on developing **offender-based typologies** of crime will entail the study of the physical attributes and personality traits of criminals and their motives for committing crimes (Abreu et al., 2019).

Physical Attributes

Is it possible that criminal offenders are somehow physically distinct from nonoffenders? Can biological makeup play a role in triggering outbursts of violence and aggression? **Biological theories** explain violence and crime by studying the physiological basis of human behavior and drawing a link between traits such as aggression, impulsivity, and intelligence and the onset of criminal behavior. Through these studies, criminologists have been able to develop physical typologies of criminal offenders based on manifest body features, common brain dysfunctions, and innate biological drives.

Italian criminologist Cesare Lombroso was one of the first researchers to study the relationships between crime and the physical features of convicted criminals in the early 1900s (Lombroso, 2019). Influenced by evolutionary theories of the time, he hypothesized that some human beings were not as biologically advanced as others and were more characteristic of earlier forms of human civilizations characterized by traits of aggression, impulsivity, and lack of sensitivity to pain (Lombroso, 2019). These less evolved "throwbacks" were incapable of functioning in a more advanced society, which led them to commit criminal acts of violence and aggression. Moreover, they could be readily identified by their very distinct physical features according to his study of the postmortem bodies of Italian prisoners. Lombroso identified what he referred to as **atavistic features**, physical anomalies that included low cranial capacity, a receding chin, long arms, large teeth and fleshy lips, a crooked nose, attached earlobes, and excessive body hair, among other physical variances (Laws, 2020). Unfortunately, Lombroso's study was flawed in its design, as he failed to compare his subjects and their bodies to those of noncriminals to see if they had similar atavistic features. Future studies also did not support his findings, and researchers began looking into other ways at linking human physical features to criminality.

Another famous study that focused on developing a physical typology of offenders was developed by William Sheldon, a psychologist, and physician. In 1949, Sheldon published *Varieties of Delinquent Youth* in which he described three basic body types and their corresponding temperaments, **ectomorph**, **mesomorph**, and **endomorph** summarized in Figure 3.1 (Little, 2018). Sheldon based his study on the classification of physical body features of 200 boys in a rehabilitation facility, comparing them to 200 college students that were nondelinquent. He

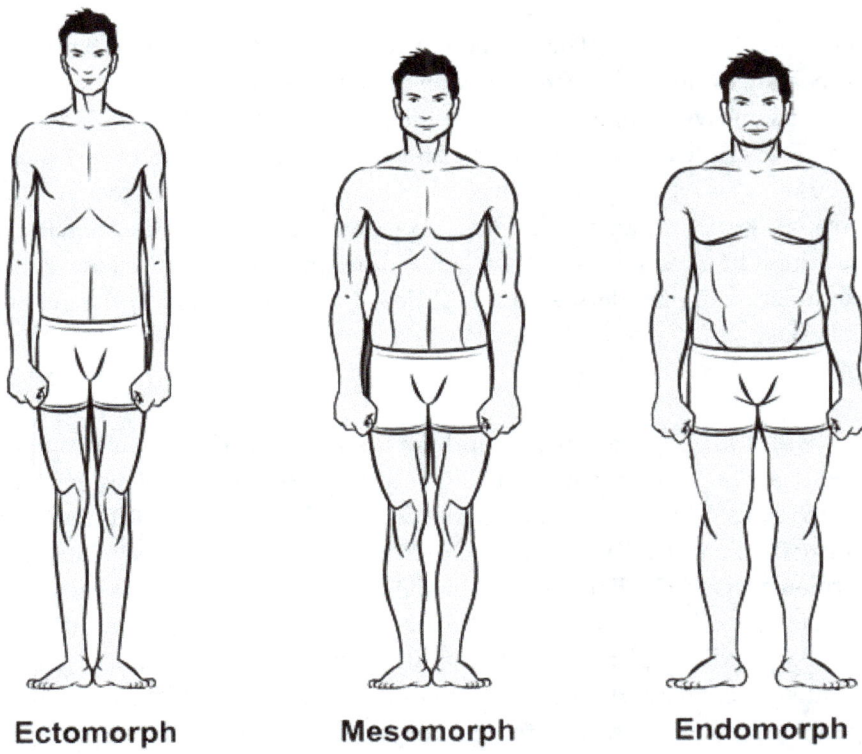

Ectomorph   **Mesomorph**   **Endomorph**

FIGURE 3.1 Body Type and Crime: Is There a Link?

found a higher rate of the physical body type of the mesomorph among the delinquents versus the nondelinquents, concluding that there is a strong correlation between body type and personality since mesomorphs are physically more muscular and tolerant to pain, they were also more likely to become aggressive and callous (Ikeda, 2018).

Sheldon's body type classification of delinquent youth as physically distinct from nondelinquents is quite compelling; however, his findings must be approached with caution. Offender-based typologies of crime relying on the physical attributes of offenders don't take into account the significant influence of sociological dynamics involved in labeling certain individuals as deviant-based variables unrelated to personal appearance (Ivanich & Warner, 2019). We saw this process unfold in Chapter 2 in our discussion of "The Saints and The Roughnecks" and how social labels can create a trajectory of crime and delinquency based on personal appearance and bias.

Offender-based physical typologies have been widely criticized for their reliance on physical traits to identify crime-prone types of individuals in the perception and surveillance of criminal behavior (Fagan & Geller, 2020). This has been especially true in recent times where images of police bias and brutality in the treatment of African Americans have proliferated social media outlets and led to a public movement calling for racial justice and the fair treatment of all individuals regardless of physical appearance. The movement away from offender-based typologies relying on physical appearances alone has been a growing trend for decades that has shaped the study of crime and criminal behavior in the direction of the concept of **homology**, the idea that certain similar categories of crimes are committed by offenders with similar traits and characteristics (Abreu et al., 2019). This type of profiling has led us to rely more heavily on behavioral manifestations of personality rather than physical features that are identifiable, lest we falter and begin to discriminate based on categories of race, cultural origin, and sexual orientation. Let's turn now to an examination of offender-based typologies of crime informed by the personality and mind of the offender.

Personality of Offender

As we interact with the people around us and try to "make sense" of their actions, we begin to see the need to assign them into categories that distinguish their traits or behavior patterns from other individuals. This is a common social process that becomes part of our nature and understanding of interactions as we adapt to the social rules, norms, and regulations governing society (Liberman et al., 2017). For example, in high school, we label groups of individuals into categories such as "jocks," "Goths," "nerds," "overachievers," "class clown," and "stoner" based on a shared understanding of how these individuals dress, wear their hair, carry themselves, interact with others, achieve certain grades, or possess certain talents and abilities. Such categorizing of people and their actions represents our attempt to simplify the complexity of social interactions by linking various components of human behavior to aspects of personality and interpersonal traits.

Criminologists also have a long-standing history of analyzing the behavior of offenders based on specific traits and components of personality driving their actions (Dargis & Koenigs, 2018). Studies based on **psychological theories** of crime that analyze the behaviors and personalities of pedophiles, rapists, arsonists, serial killers, and other types of offenders show a significant link between the offender's personality and their motive for the crime (Gadd & Corr, 2017). Most notably, researchers have found evidence between components of personality such as self-confidence, impulsivity, conscientiousness, and thrill seeking, and motivations behind crimes such as corporate fraud, embezzlement, sexual assault, rape, and murder (Edwards et al., 2017; see Box 3.1, "Who Did It?"). Figure 3.2 gives us a summary of some of the major personality typologies established through criminological research with corresponding behavioral traits that have been found to be correlated with types of criminal offending:

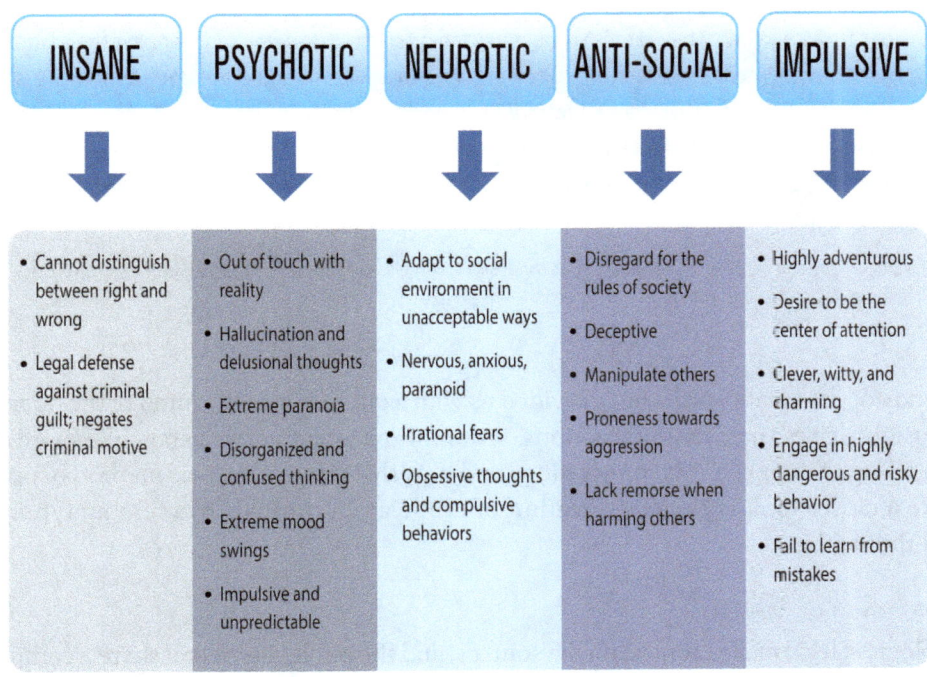

FIGURE 3.2 Personality Profiles and Their Corresponding Traits

| WHO DID IT? DENNIS RADER: HUSBAND, FATHER, BOY SCOUT LEADER … SERIAL KILLER | BOX 3.1 |

On August 18, 2005, Dennis Rader was sentenced to 10 consecutive life terms in prison after pleading guilty to 10 murders from 1974 to 1991. At the time of his arrest and trial, the 60-year-old Rader had clearly been leading a double life for decades. On the one hand, he was a devoted family man and company worker, as well as a Boy Scout leader and an active member of his church. On the other hand, he was a monstrous killer who referred to himself as BTK for "bind, torture, and kill," his method of operation in his murderous pursuits. Interviews of Rader revealed graphic details involving a desire to inflict pain on his victims and thrill in exercising control over them and torturing them. He eluded police for years, playing cat and mouse games and leaving behind clues taunting law enforcement, the public, and potential victims. Silent for years, his alter ego resurfaced in 2004 when he sent letters to local authorities and media outlets detailing some of his crimes.

Are there certain personality traits that are found to be the motive behind the behavior of some serial killers? According to criminologist Dr. Scott Bonn, the answer is yes. Thrill-seeking, hedonistic killers have narcissistic personalities with an intense desire for stimulation and excitement that is fulfilled by the capture

(Continued)

and torture of their victims. They target strangers often after stalking them and planning their kidnapping. They appear to derive intense satisfaction from murdering their victims and experience a thrill or rush from the killing, very much akin to that derived from a drug, sport, or roller-coaster ride. Their pathological personalities make them incapable of feeling regret or remorse or having compassion or a sense of empathy for their victims. These were clearly traits possessed by Dennis Rader and manifested in his years of torturing and killing his victims.

Source: Bonn, S. A. (2015). "The Zodiac and other thrill killers." Psychology Today. https://www.psychologytoday.com/us/blog/wicked-deeds/201509/the-zodiac-and-other-thrill-killers.

The study of personality traits has provided us with a glimpse into the mind of the offender and what possibly drives their criminal actions. From this perspective, we can gain a more detailed understanding of their criminal motivations and how this influences their method of operation. Let's take a closer look at the classification of crime and criminals by creating typologies of criminal motivation.

Motive/Method of Operation

Criminologists, legal professionals, media sources, and the public in general share a common goal when it comes to understanding criminal behavior, namely, the attempt to answer the question "why"? Why did a husband kill his wife, why did a politician abuse their power, why did a wealthy actress steal from a clothing store, why did a priest sexually assault a teenage boy, why, why, why? The question of "why" leads us to develop a profile of offending based on various categories of motive behind criminal behavior. Here, we will begin to connect the concept of motive, the particular driving force behind committing the crime to the actual pattern of criminal offending, as well as the implications for crime control and prevention.

An important distinction when it comes to discerning between types of criminal intents and motivation is the difference between instrumental and expressive crimes. **Instrumental crimes** are those that reflect some type of desired outcome or goal (Adjorlolo & Chen, 2017). The crime is therefore used as a means to an end. This end could be money, inheritance, revenge, status, control, etc. **Expressive crimes** are those committed out of emotions, with very little thought about the outcome of the crime itself (Walters, 2018). Thus, the crime is an end in and of itself, and most often the outcome of some type of interpersonal conflict or dispute that leads to anger, frustration, rage, jealousy, etc. These distinctions are important, as they not only delineate the way law enforcement approaches the investigation of the crime but also the degree of criminal responsibility. Thus, for example, the charge of first-degree murder is based on a premediated instrumental goal to kill, whereas the less serious charge of second-degree murder is considered a crime of passion not based on previous calculations.

As we further develop our understanding of criminal typologies based on offender behavior and motivation, another important element of classification that is important to consider is the offender's method of operation based on the selection of victim and the level of planning involved in committing the crime. A prevalent image we sometimes have of criminal offenders is that they are very calculated in their selection of victims at one end of the spectrum or on the other hand execute random nonsensical acts of crime and violence with no target consideration at all. The truth is, this might be the case, but it is more important to assess target selection by evaluating the criteria involved in rational criminal thinking. These criteria have more to do with situational considerations such as convenience or familiarity with the target, the absence of "guardianship," and the expected outcome or yield (Wikström, 2019). This evaluation of the target also influences the level of planning involved, which is discerned by the offender's execution of the crime. For example, was it a spontaneous act based on some type of opportunity that they stumbled upon, or was the criminal action sought out, strategized, and deliberate? These are important distinctions when developing crime types, as they are theoretical elements of consideration when determining legal responsibility and intervention to deter criminals, rehabilitate them, or incapacitate them from future offending (Baron, 2019). Based on these dynamics of offender behavior and motivation, the following criminal profiles can be used to distinguish between categories of offenders; this typology provides criminologists, researchers, and law enforcement a useful tool in developing theories of crime causation, means of intervention that are specifically designed to address criminal behavior, and informed investigation of crime scenes based on an understanding of the offender's pattern of offending and method of operation:

- *Occasional Criminals.* These criminals commit a crime when an opportunity presents itself. Can be expressive or instrumental in motive, and target selection is often linked to both prospect and the degree of ease. Patterns of offending are irregular, with little to no attention to planning. Some examples of this type of criminal can be the shoplifter, the vandal, and some types of car thieves (Manning et al., 2016).
- *Habitual Criminals.* Crime is a way of life, and these types of offenders have had many convictions for the same type of crime or for various kinds of criminal behaviors. They are sometimes referred to as chronic or repeat offenders and are in and out of the criminal justice system and correctional institutions almost their entire lives. Their method of operation and target selection are specific to the type of crime committed. These can include sex offenders, drug users, and gang members (Walters, 2019).
- *Professional Criminals.* These offenders are also habitual, but their criminal behavior includes a degree of offense specialization and organization in terms of planning, execution, and target selection. Their crimes are built upon the notion of a "profession" and are therefore a way of life and means of financial resource. Some examples are professional thieves, the professional fence, and an organized crime syndicate (Holmes, 2017).
- *Passionate Criminals.* With this type of offender, crime tends to be situational, often provoked by unusually stressful circumstances or life events. The crime is motivated by intense emotions of anger, rage, frustration, or resentment toward a very specific person or group of people. This offender is manifested in crimes of passion, such as

second-degree murder and spontaneous acts of assault or the destruction of property. We also see some forms of passionate criminals in crimes involving sexual assault and arson (Guan et al., 2017).

- *Hedonistic Criminals.* These offenders commit crimes for the sheer pleasure they derive from their actions. They are driven by a heightened state of thrill associated with the criminal act. Their crimes often involve a degree of planning that is sometimes associated with the rush of excitement of the experience. This category explains the crimes of many serial killers, rapists, vandals, and arsonists (Smith, 2018).

Typologies of crime based on offender classification have been the foundation of criminological studies for years. They have served as the foundation for research into the minds and behaviors of criminal offenders in an effort to understand their criminal actions and make sense of their behavior in order to better inform law enforcement, the apprehension of suspects, and the prevention of future crimes (Blasko, 2016). The picture would not be complete, however, without analyzing personality and its relationship to environmental variables. We turn now to an examination of various elements of context involved in the commission of crime that can more clearly account for the variations in human behavior and how differences in personality and the mind interact with other conditions and social situations.

Contextual Typologies

During the mid-1980s, a branch of criminology emerged to study the different ways that diverse attributes of individuals are influenced to commit crime by various elements within their immediate social and physical environment. This branch of study known as **environmental criminology** highlights the importance of analyzing the immediate context within which crime occurs to better understand how potential offenders, their victims, and the environment interact to shape the type and amount of criminal activity (Moir et al., 2019). Studies from this theoretical approach have helped us develop policies and interventions that target specific crime-prone situations and help law enforcement in controlling and preventing crime. The assumption here is that criminal behavior is significantly influenced by the structure of the environment in which it occurs and, therefore, patterns of criminal activity are not distributed randomly but rather vary according to contextual elements of time, place, and situations that facilitate criminal opportunities (Wortley & Townsley, 2016). What are these crime-prone situations and interactions, and how do they help us create more comprehensive criminal typologies? Box 3.2 provides an "anatomy" of dangerous, crime-prone places and situations:

THE REAL DEAL: ELEMENTS OF CRIME-PRONE CIRCUMSTANCES — BOX 3.2

- The Variable of *Space*. This dimension analyzes the physical environment to determine whether certain spatial aspects are correlated with certain types of criminal activity. Variables within the environment found to be correlated with higher rates of criminal activity include the presence of rundown and abandoned apartments, buildings with broken or boarded up windows or that are abandoned, blind spots from untamed shrubs and bushes, public spaces that are unkempt and full of trash, excessive amounts of graffiti on building and other street areas, and streets and neighborhoods that are poorly lit.
- The Variable of *Time*. This dimension analyzes temporal issues to note variations in criminal activity because of changes in time. With regard to crime-prone times of the day, the evening/night hours have higher rates of crime, with businesses open all night being at the greatest risk for criminal activity. In some instances, especially those involving juvenile delinquency, the hours of unsupervised time between 3 and 6 p.m. present the greatest risk.
- The Variable of *Guardianship*. This refers to the presence of protective factors that are likely to inhibit criminal activity within a given social environment. Here, it is noted that the absence of security systems, guard dogs, informal neighborhood surveillance and watches, as well as weak ties between families and neighborhoods can all increase the likelihood of crime occurring. Moreover, guardianship disintegrates in a climate of fear and suspicion, which reduces the **collective efficacy** of communities, their banding together to fight crime through measures such as informally patrolling streets, advocating for their safety in city council meetings, and keeping an eye on strangers.
- The Variable of *Target Selection*. Victims of crime constitute a major component of study when analyzing the contextual events and circumstances involved in the criminal event. In the section to come, we will study typologies of crime based on the victim. For now, we recognize target selection as an environmental variable characterized by certain traits, such as regular or predictable patterns of movement, vulnerability owing to being alone, the presence of drugs and alcohol, living in a highly disorganized neighborhood or community, high rate of residential instability, and fearful of crime and victimization.
- The Variable of *Offender*. The context of crime is very often shaped by certain elements of interaction that take place between the offender and their immediate social environment. These become defining points of criminal actions that are specific to circumstances, such as sudden financial loss, the weakening of social ties because of divorce or other loss, unemployment or idleness, network ties to other offenders or criminal opportunities, and triggers of provocation leading to anger or frustration, lack of social or community services to address personal needs.

Source: Andresen, M. A. (2019). Environmental criminology: Evolution, theory, and practice. Routledge.

The study of **situational context typologies** has provided us with a more informed understanding of crime-prone situations, circumstances, and environments that constitute "hot spots" of criminal activity. We are also able to characterize categories of crime based on their settings or "domains"(Haart, 2020). We can now immediately relate elements of different criminal acts, whether they are acts of violence, harassment, or abuse, in terms of victim-offender dynamics of interaction, as well as their location or contextual framework. This has helped us create such categories as school shootings, workplace violence, domestic violence, public order crime, gang-related murder, international crime, and various other categories. These typologies have been an integral part of criminal investigation and the study of crime types and criminals. However, our study would not be complete without an examination of the role victims play in a criminal event.

Victim-Based Typologies

Contextual typologies guided our study of crime from a very important perspective, emphasizing the relevance of time and space in dictating the outcome of encounters between criminal offenders and crime victims. Another important dimension to consider when classifying criminal behavior into different categories is the unique characteristics of victims, their actions, and their relationship to the offender. What is the relationship between victims and offenders, before, during, and after crimes, and how does that dynamic help us better understand criminal typologies? Let's explore this question in some detail.

Victim-based typologies examine the unique role or position of the victim in relation to the criminal event (Walklate, 2017). Criminologists have developed victim typologies that are based on the personal characteristics of victims and their actions during their encounters with criminal offenders. While there are many complex factors to consider, the most salient elements that have been researched over the years pertain to a victim's level of *shared responsibility* and their *structural position*, which determines their degree of vulnerability. Through the hallmark contributions of classifications developed by criminologists such as Mendelsohn (Mendelsohn, 1956, 1976), we have been able to apply the concepts of victim facilitation and victim precipitation that we discussed in Chapter 2 to the classification of crimes based on the actions of the victim, which was either provocative in nature or led to their selection as a target. Again, we must always emphasize that this level of interpretation does not negate criminal responsibility or place the blame on the victim to where we are implying, they deserved what happened. Rather, we are recognizing the behavioral patterns of victims where through their actions or omissions, knowingly, carelessly, or negligently, they create the context for criminals to go through with their crimes (Pratt & Turanovic, 2016). Moreover, we also recognize that the classification of crime is also subject to the actions of victims where they play a more active role in provoking the offender, such as, for example, throwing the first punch or hurling an insult or racial slur at someone. These distinctions have served as the foundation for classifying the seriousness of different categories of violent crimes according to the degree of shared responsibility of the victim in their encounter with the offender.

Another important aspect we consider when developing victim-based typologies is derived from the personal characteristics of the victim that define their socio-structural position within society. Criminal psychologist Hans von Hentig expanded upon victim typologies based on situational factors to include aspects of the victim's physical, sociological, and psychological vulnerabilities (Von Hentig, 1948). Included in this analysis are variables such as age, gender, race, sexuality, disability, and mental impairment. These identified traits impact the potential for victimization by situating individuals in a place of vulnerability through physical weakness, powerlessness, the target of prejudice, or the object of bullying and predatory behavior (Adeyemi, 2020). From this typology, we are able to develop an understanding of targeted violence that has come to be defined in categories such as crimes against the elderly, child pornography, and hate crime, identifying groups of victims who share common traits, as well as common experiences in victimization.

Key Takeaways

Review the following list of bullet points for a quick overview of the key ideas and information in this chapter:

- Criminal behavior is complex and comes in many different forms, perpetrated by a variety of offenders with diverse motives. Typologies of crime help us make sense of this complexity by mapping out crime into categories of facts, events, and behaviors that share common features and characteristics.
- Criminal typologies have been developed to help us recognize the differences between criminal offenders and their actions. By understanding what makes them distinct from one another, we can also begin to recognize their common traits. This allows criminologists to develop a more theoretical approach to studying crime causation that can guide prevention measures in the control of criminal offending.
- Organizing criminal behavior into categories has relied on the development of typologies that analyze various dimensions of crime. Over the years, criminologists have created typologies of crime based on legal classification, criminal offenders and their personal traits and characteristics, situational context of the crime, and victim-offender interaction.
- Without criminal typologies, crime scene investigations would lack significant understanding. Knowing the relationship between offenders and their victims, and how that influences environmental variables discovered through crime scene analysis can help in apprehending suspects, solving crimes, and identifying potential criminal actions before they occur.

Conclusion and Formal Summary Questions

We have seen in this chapter the importance of developing criminal typologies in organizing the immense diversity of criminal behaviors. We learned that this is not a straightforward task but rather relies on a comprehensive analysis of the various dimensions and elements involved in the study of criminal behavior. Through a combination of theoretical developments, we are able to classify crime according to multiple facets, including legal definition, the offender's traits and motives, the situational context of the crime, and behavioral and personal aspects of the victim. Through this scope of understanding, we can better inform criminal justice operations, the investigation of crime, and the intervention to prevent criminal behavior and control its occurrence.

- *Do you have a better understanding of what we mean by criminal typology?*
- *Can you identify the role of typologies in the study of criminal behavior?*
- *Are you able to describe the various criminal typologies and how they are created?*
- *Can you recognize the value of criminal typologies in criminal investigation?*

E-Resources

Learn how the FBI's Behavioral Analysis Unit was created to study serial killers by visiting https://www.fbi.gov/news/stories/serial-killers-part-2-the-birth-of-behavioral-analysis-in-the-fbi

Visit the Environment Criminology Research Institute website at http://www.geographicprofiling.com/index.html for additional facts on this field of study.

Check out this article for a detailed overview of Mendelsohn's typology of crime victims: https://files.eric.ed.gov/fulltext/ED140138.pdf

References

Abreu, V., Barker, E., Dickson, H., Husson, F., Flynn, S., & Shaw, J. (2019). Investigating homicide offender typologies based on their clinical histories and crime scene behaviour patterns. *Journal of Criminological Research, Policy and Practice*, 5(3), 168–188. https://doi.org/10.1108/JCRPP-03-2019-0022.

Abreu, V., Barker, E., Dickson, H., Husson, F., Flynn, S., & Shaw, J. (2019). Investigating homicide offender typologies based on their clinical histories and crime scene behaviour patterns. *Journal of Criminological Research, Policy and Practice*, 5(3), 168–188.

Adeyemi, O. E. (2020). Gender and victimization: A global analysis of vulnerability. In J. O. Ayodele (Ed.), *Global perspectives on victimization analysis and prevention* (pp. 114–133). IGI Global.

Adjorlolo, S., & Chan, H. C. (2017). The nature of instrumentality and expressiveness of homicide crime scene behaviors: A review. *Trauma, Violence, & Abuse, 18*(2), 119–133.

Baron, E. T. (2019). The borders of criminal responsibility: Difficult cases for the law's default understanding of people. *Psychology, Crime & Law, 25*(6), 693–708.

Bergman, Paul. (2020). *Felonies, misdemeanors, and infractions: Classifying crimes.* Nolo. https://www.nolo.com/legal-encyclopedia/crimes-felonies-misdemeanors-infractions-classification-33814.html

Bergman, Paul. (2020). *Felonies, misdemeanors, and infractions: Classifying crimes.* Nolo. https://www.nolo.com/legal-encyclopedia/crimes-felonies-misdemeanors-infractions-classification-33814.html

Blasko, B. L. (2016). Overview of sexual offender typologies, recidivism, and treatment. In E. L. Jeglic & C. Calkins (Eds.), *Sexual violence* (pp. 11–29). Springer, Cham.

Chambliss, William J. (1988). *Exploring criminology*. Macmillan Publishing.

Dargis, M., & Koenigs, M. (2018). Personality traits differentiate subgroups of criminal offenders with distinct cognitive, affective, and behavioral profiles. *Criminal Justice And Behavior, 45*(7), 984–1007.

Edwards, B. G., Albertson, E., & Verona, E. (2017). Dark and vulnerable personality trait correlates of dimensions of criminal behavior among adult offenders. *Journal of Abnormal Psychology, 126*(7), 921.

Fagan, J., & Geller, A. (2020). Profiling and consent: Stops, searches, and seizures after Soto. *Virginia Journal of Social Policy and the Law, 27*(1), 16; Gabbidon, S. L., & Higgins, G. E. (2020). Correlates of the decision to report incidents of "consumer racial profiling": A preliminary study. *Victims & Offenders, 15*(4), 418–429.

Gadd, D., & Corr, M. L. (2017). Beyond typologies: Foregrounding meaning and motive in domestic violence perpetration. *Deviant Behavior, 38*(7), 781–791.

Guan, M., Li, X., Xiao, W., Miao, D., & Liu, X. (2017). Categorization and prediction of crimes of passion based on attitudes toward violence. *International Journal of Offender Therapy and Comparative Criminology, 61*(15), 1775–1790.

Hart, T. C. (2020). Hot spots of crime: Methods and predictive analytics. In K. M. Lersch & J. Chakraborty (Eds.), *Geographies of behavioural health, crime, and disorder* (pp. 87–103). Springer, Cham.

Holmes, T. (2017). Professional criminals and white-collar crime in popular culture. In H. N. Pontell (Ed.), *Oxford research encyclopedia of criminology and criminal justice*. Oxford.

Ikeda, M., Tanaka, S., Saito, T., Ozaki, N., Kamatani, Y., & Iwata, N. (2018). Re-evaluating classical body type theories: Genetic correlation between psychiatric disorders and body mass index. *Psychological Medicine, 48*(10), 1745–1748.

Ivanich, J. D., & Warner, T. D. (2019). Seen or unseen? The role of race in police contact among homeless youth. *Justice Quarterly, 36*(5), 816–840.

Laws, D. R. (2020). Criminal anthropology: Lombroso's search for criminal man. In D. R. Laws (Ed.), *A History of the Assessment of Sex Offenders: 1830–2020* (pp. 63–88). Emerald Publishing Limited.

Liberman, Z., Woodward, A. L., & Kinzler, K. D. (2017). The origins of social categorization. *Trends in Cognitive Sciences, 21*(7), 556–568.

Little, M. A. (2018). Sheldon, William H. In W. Trevathan (Ed.), *The international encyclopedia of biological anthropology* (pp. 1–2). Wiley-Blackwell.

Lombroso, G. (2019). *Criminal man, according to the classification of Cesare Lombroso*. Good Press.

Manning, L., Smith, R., & Soon, J. M. (2016). Developing an organizational typology of criminals in the meat supply chain. *Food Policy, 59*, 44–54.

Mendelsohn, B. (1956). The victimology. *Etudes internationales de psycho-sociologie criminelle, 3*, 25–26; Mendelsohn, B. (1976). Victimology and contemporary society's trends. *Victimology, 1*(1), 8–28.

Miethe, T. D., McCorkle, R. C., & Listwan, S. J. (2005). *Crime profiles: The anatomy of dangerous persons, places, and situations*. Roxbury Publishing Company.

Moir, E., Hart, T. C., Reynald, D. M., & Stewart, A. (2019). Typologies of suburban guardians: Understanding the role of responsibility, opportunities, and routine activities in facilitating surveillance. *Crime Prevention and Community Safety, 21*(1), 1–21.

Pratt, T. C., & Turanovic, J. J. (2016). Lifestyle and routine activity theories revisited: The importance of "risk" to the study of victimization. *Victims & Offenders, 11*(3), 335–354.

Ručman, A. B. (2019). What is crime? A search for an answer encompassing civilisational legitimacy and social harm. *Crime, Law and Social Change, 72*(2), 211–226.

Simester, A. P., Spencer, J. R., Stark, F., Sullivan, G. R., & Virgo, G. J. (2019). *Simester and Sullivan's criminal law: Theory and doctrine*. Bloomsbury Publishing.

Smith, J. (2018). *Application of investigative psychology to psychodynamic and human development theories: Examining traits and typologies of serial killers* [Doctoral dissertation, Drexel University]. ProQuest One Academic.

Von Hentig, H. (1948). *The criminal and his victim: Studies in the sociobiology of crime*. Yale University Press.

Walklate, S. (2017). Other visions of victimisation and victimology. In S. Walklate (Ed.), *Handbook of victims and victimology* (2nd ed., p. 143). Routledge.

Walters, G. D. (2018). Black–white and male–female differences in criminal thinking: Examining instrumental and expressive motives for crime in federal supervisees. *The Prison Journal, 98*(3), 277–293.

Walters, G. D. (2019). The crimes of first-time offenders: Same or different from the crimes of habitual criminals? *Journal of Criminal Psychology, 10*(1), 1–15.

Wikström, P. O. H. (2019). Situational action theory: Toward a dynamic theory of crime and its causes. In H. N. Pontell (Ed.), *Oxford research encyclopedia of criminology and criminal justice*. Oxford.

Wortley, R., & Townsley, M. (Eds.). (2016). *Environmental criminology and crime analysis*. Taylor & Francis.

Figure Credits

Fig. 3.1: Copyright © by Granito diaz (CC BY-SA 4.0) at https://commons.wikimedia.org/wiki/File:Bodytypes.jpg.

Violent Crime Profiles

MODULE 2

Chapter 4

Crimes of Interpersonal Violence
Homicide and Assault

Key Terms

Interpersonal violence
Criminal homicide
Malice aforethought
Premeditation
Situational homicide
Expressive homicide
Instrumental homicide
Subculture
Subculture of violence
Code of the streets
Serial killing
Mass murder
Assault
Battery
Simple assault
Aggravated assault
Intimate partner violence
Child maltreatment
Elder abuse

Chapter Headings

1. Chapter opener
2. What are crimes of interpersonal violence?
3. Various categories of homicide
   3.1. Situational homicide
   3.2. Subculture of violence
   3.3. Serial killer
   3.4. Mass murder
4. Various categories of assault
   4.1. Intimate partner violence
   4.2. Child maltreatment
   4.3. Elder abuse
5. Homicide and assault offenders and their victims
   5.1. Characteristics of homicide and assault offenders
   5.2. Characteristics of homicide and assault victims
6. Chapter summary

Opening Questions

Before you begin the chapter, take a few minutes to reflect on the following questions:

1. What crimes come to mind when you think of the term "interpersonal violence"?
2. How are different types of homicide and assault similar? What makes them different?
3. Who are the perpetrators of homicide and assault, and what motivates their crimes?
4. Do victims of homicide and assault share common characteristics?

Chapter Objectives

After reading Chapter 4, students will be able to do the following:

- Define the term interpersonal violence and what behavior it applies to
- Distinguish between various typologies of criminal homicide and assault
- Identify various characteristics of homicide and assault perpetrators
- Recognize common traits of victims of homicide and assault

True Crime

When we think of the term "homicide," we often conjure up images of a random act of violence where we hear of victims' lives being taken by a stranger who is in a heightened state of rage and opens fire in a public place. We also think of homicide in the context of dangerous neighborhoods where people are at the wrong place at the wrong time and succumb to shots fired in gang-related retaliations or drug deals gone wrong. We rarely, however, think of violence and homicide as a common phenomenon between a married couple in a loving relationship and expecting a baby on the way. This reality of homicide became a national tragedy when we learned that a pregnant Laci Peterson disappeared from her home on Christmas Eve in 2002 and her body, along with the remains of her unborn child, washed up along the shores of Berkeley Marina in the San Francisco Bay area of California, nearly 4 months later after a spring storm. What happened to this young woman, a daughter, wife, and expecting mother is not only shocking but unthinkable.

Scott and Laci Peterson were married on August 9, 1997. A little over 5 years later, Laci Peterson, who was 8 months pregnant, was found dead. Because her body was severely decomposed, it was difficult to tell much about how she died from the forensic evidence, but her cause of death was determined to be smothering or strangulation. Speculations about her murder turned to her husband Scott Peterson. Initially, Peterson told police that his wife disappeared after leaving their home to walk their dog. His image of a distraught, devoted, and loving husband began to fall apart when weeks later, a 28-year-old massage therapist came forward to tell police that she was having an affair with Peterson. In April of 2003, Scott Peterson was arrested and charged with two counts of murder. He was found carrying a large amount of cash, his brother's passport, and seemingly in "disguise" with a new haircut and color. During his trial, prosecutors presented evidence to further implicate him as a monster who didn't care about his wife or anybody else, with 174 witnesses and hundreds of pieces of evidence showing Peterson as a cold, calculated, and heartless man who was a manipulative liar who cheated on his wife. On November 12, 2004, after a week of deliberation, a jury found Scott Peterson guilty of the first-degree murder of his wife and the second-degree murder of his unborn son. Peterson was originally sentenced to death for his crimes, however, in December of 2021, a California judge resentenced him to life in prison without the possibility of parole.

What Are Crimes of Interpersonal Violence?

> *Returning violence for violence multiplies violence, adding deeper darkness to a night already devoid of stars.*
>
> —Dr. Martin Luther King Jr.

Acts of harm and violence have proliferated societies across the globe since the beginning of time. These acts have particularly become manifest in recent times with the expansion of social media and the use of camera and cell phone technology to record the actions of law enforcement officers' interactions with the public. The embedding of violence as a mechanism of protest and a reflection of social discord was so clearly portrayed in the events following the murder of George Floyd on May 25, 2020, when a police officer knelt on his neck while he was handcuffed and lying face down on the street, killing the 46-year-old man (Fitz-Gibbon, 2020). Videos of this horrible act flooded media outlets for several days, leading to a chain of protests that included citizens uniting in peaceful demonstrations against such acts of injustice. However, there were several eruptions of violence, including looting, assault, and murder against innocent citizens that terrorized and brutalized communities across the United States. **Interpersonal violence** has many faces and most broadly refers to actions taken by any individual that include physical, emotional, or emotional acts or threats of acts that create in another feelings of fear, terror, threat, or intimidation (Hass et al., 2016).

Acts perpetrated by individuals who commit interpersonal violence share some common characteristics, the most notable being the harm created to individuals and the shared feelings of fear and helplessness of victims. However, there are many contextual and situational differences that separate the various categories of interpersonal violence and make each a unique type of crime that is characterized by similarities in offender motivation, planning, and interaction with the victim (Hass et al., 2016). In this chapter, we will examine two typologies of interpersonal violence, criminal homicide, and assault.

Various Categories of Homicide

When we think of the crime of homicide, we recognize immediately that the act is malicious, willful, and deliberate. However, we also acknowledge that taking the life of another individual is not always illegal. Additionally, there are some circumstances that place a greater legal burden on the offender when their actions are calculated, planned, and without any emotions. How then do we define the crime of homicide? Are there elements common to murder? What makes some killings legal and justified? Let's take a closer look at some of these questions to get a more comprehensive definition of this crime category.

Criminal homicide is most broadly defined as the unlawful killing of one human being by another without legal justification or excuse (Reed & Bohlander, 2018). When we examine this definition, we see that the terms "legal justification or excuse" imply that sometimes the killing of one human being by another is not considered criminal. This would be the case, for example, in self-defense or military line of duty. Criminal homicide can be divided into several categories based on the offender's state of mind and their actions prior to and during the offense. Take a look at Table 4.1 for a detailed description of the different forms of criminal homicide according to their legal classification:

TABLE 4.1   THE FACES OF CRIMINAL HOMICIDE

Type of Homicide	Legal Elements of Classification
First-Degree Murder	• Requires **malice aforethought**, a wicked and evil intent to kill • Requires **premeditation**, the killing is thought out, plotted, planned; deliberation to commit the act is proven by the mere passage of time, demonstrating the individual has a chance to think about the intent to kill and to retreat from those thoughts
Second-Degree Murder	• Requires only malice aforethought, a wicked and evil intent to kill • The law recognizes the offender's state of mind as noncalculating and nondeliberating but rather in the heat of the moment, acting because of intense emotions of rage, anger, jealousy, or frustration
Voluntary Manslaughter	• Does not require malice aforethought or premeditation • An unlawful killing that arises out of mitigating circumstances, such as a barroom brawl or fight • Circumstances of provocation or poor judgment also can be included • Actions leading to the homicide are criminal in nature
Involuntary Manslaughter	• Also does not require malice aforethought or premeditation • The killing is a result of noncriminal acts of negligence, carelessness, or reckless behavior

While legal classification is important to understand and to ensure the proper criminal charge is filed and the offender is held accountable for their particular actions, the development of different profiles of homicide based on our understanding of criminal typologies gives us a more accurate and meaningful description of this crime category that captures various elements of context, as well as the interactions that take place between victims and offenders that shape the evolution of criminal homicide. Typologies of homicide based on contextual elements have yielded four unique categories: *situational homicide, subculture of violence, serial killing,* and *mass murder.*

Situational Homicide

One of the most distinct characteristics of criminal homicide is that it is riddled with human interactions that have gone wrong. Ordinary persons in a unique state of mind, circumstances, poor judgment, provocation, or lack of self-control given the right environmental triggers take the life of other individuals for many different reasons. Central to these dynamics is the concept of **situational homicide**, a homicide that occurs out of certain interactions between the victim and the offender. The assumption here is that if it weren't for the circumstances that led up to the conflict, the homicide would not have occurred (Parker & McKinley, 2018). To better understand this concept, we must further distinguish between two categories of situational homicide: situational homicide that is expressive and situational homicide that is instrumental.

Expressive homicide is the most common type of homicide and occurs between family members, neighbors, coworkers, friends, and acquaintances (Adjorlolo & Chan, 2017). In this type of homicide, the killing is primary, meaning there is no other motive aside from an expression of intense emotion because of some type of interpersonal conflict that has spurred feelings of anger, resentment, hatred, jealousy, rage, or frustration. Interpersonal conflicts leading to expressive situational homicide often revolve around disputes over money, ownership, relationships, domestic disagreements, and love triangles. **Instrumental homicide** is "nothing personal" against the victim, and very often, the killing is secondary to an ulterior motive or the victim is in the wrong place at the wrong time (Adjorlolo & Chan, 2017). Here, a fine line separates emotions and heightened states of mental turmoil from calculated, intentional actions to take another human being's life. In some contexts of instrumental homicide, an event or incident brings two individuals together who have no relationship at all, as the victim might be in the way of a shooting or high-speed car chase, trying to prevent a crime from happening, or resisting an offender during a robbery. In other contexts of instrumental homicide, the victim and offender can have a direct relationship. In such instances, the offender, under different sets of circumstances, becomes motivated to eliminate the victim to obtain some type of goal, such as monetary inheritance, getting out of a relationship, or avoiding prosecution for a drug trafficking case. Box 4.1 gives us a glimpse into expressive and instrumental homicide and how emotions and situational context intersect to create two very distinct typologies of murder.

WHO DID IT? TWO VERY DIFFERENT MURDERERS — BOX 4.1

On August 18, 2017, a jury convicted 25-year-old Nicholas Johnson of second-degree murder in the killing of his lover Virgil Jack. The two were having an affair when the 31-year-old woman lied and told Johnson she was pregnant by him. After telling Jack that he was not going to leave his girlfriend to be with her, she began to send him as well as his girlfriend angry and nasty messages. Desperate and pressured, and in the words of the prosecutor, in "one frenzied episode," Johnson viciously stabbed Jack 126 times at a northwest Toronto park, killing her. This type of emotional killing that involves emotions of desperation and heightened states of rage and anxiety are associated with expressive homicide and crimes of passion. The crime scene is indicative of a pre-existing relationship between the victim and the offender, whereby evidence is consistent with the role of emotions in the killing as apparent in a crime scene where there is an excessive use of violence.

On April 5, 2018, Stacie Mendoza and her husband Jose Mendoza tortured and killed 70-year-old Vietnam Veteran Kenneth Coyle by blunt force trauma and suffocation in an attempt to get information from him to access his bank account and steal all of his money. In the months prior to this vicious act, Stacie Mendoza struck up a relationship with the victim while working as a waitress at a restaurant in Hanford, California. Coyle was a regular at the restaurant who was just looking for friendship and conversation. Mendoza had no intention of becoming a friend but rather became greedy and tried to use his trust to defraud him out of money. When things didn't work out the way she wanted, she and her husband killed Coyle and then drove his dead body to rural Madera County where they burned his remains in front of their three children. They face charges of torture, elder abuse, and first-degree murder, among several other charges relating to the abuse of their children. Cold and calculated acts of violence perpetrated on innocent victims, unprovoked and without any prior indication of a relationship that led to betrayal and anger are the hallmark attributes of instrumental homicide, motivated by greed and a callous disregard for the life of human beings.

Source: Powell, B. (2019, December 12). Man convicted of murder in love-triangle stabbing. The Hamilton Spectator. https://www.thespec.com/news/ontario/2019/12/12/man-convicted-of-murder-in-love-triangle-stabbing.html

Source: Magness, J. (2018, April 19). Couple tortured veteran to get money—and burned his body while kids watched, California cops say. The Fresno Bee. https://www.fresnobee.com/news/nation-world/national/article209326149.html

In this section, we were introduced to two situational homicides that arise out of circumstances and contexts that have a direct impact on the interactions that take place and lead to murder. In the section to come, we will explore a completely different context of homicide that does not at all rely on situation to understand but rather on the nature of interactions that take place on a daily basis within a subculture of violence.

Subculture of Violence

Society is composed of a variety of individuals, each with a unique set of values, beliefs, customs, and traditions. This is a basic sociological observation made about the world around us (Foner et al., 2019). Some individuals value technology and are consumed by the material acquisition of any new gadgets, cell phones, electronics, smartwatches, and exercise trackers that add value to their lives and personal experiences. Other groups of people living in the United States, such as the Amish, forbid the use of most forms of technology at all, including basic things such as electricity and automobiles. We see groups of individuals riding on motorcycles, wearing similar jackets with common emblems, sporting bandannas, sunglasses, and long hair, characterizing the common traits of a biker. We recognize their commonality and the traits that make them unique to each other but different from the majority of others in society. What makes some people different in these ways defines for us the concept of **subculture, individuals or groups of people who adhere to values, norms, and beliefs that are similar to one another** but vary significantly from the dominant culture in which they live (Johansson & Herz, 2019).

Subcultures allow individuals to unite around common interests when experiencing problems and situations not common to mainstream society or when unable to identify with and acclimate with the dominant culture. Not all subcultures are necessarily at odds with the dominant values and norms of society (Johansson & Herz, 2019). However, the study of criminal typologies and theoretical criminology has identified a type of criminal subculture sustained by a **subculture of violence**, embedded in many lower class, urban communities where the dominant street culture is permeated by gangs, trouble, lawlessness, criminal activity, and animosity toward authority.

Sociologists Marvin Wolfgang and Franco Ferracuti identify the subculture of violence as a response to unique problems faced by lower class urban youth who join gangs and resort to delinquency and violence in order to respond to social conflicts, settle disputes, and maintain reputations (Ferracuti & Wolfgang, 2013). Research suggests these behavior patterns emerge as a result of common, shared problems faced by these youth, including poverty, discrimination, lack of opportunity, and inability to integrate into the dominant culture of a law-abiding society (Walach, 2019). In a classic study of the subculture of violence, Elijah Anderson describes the **code of the streets** whereby urban youth "often show a lack of consideration for other people and have a rather superficial sense of family and community … the seeming intractability of their situation, caused in large part by the lack of well-paying jobs and the persistence of racial discrimination, has engendered deep-seated resentment and anger in many of the poorest blacks, especially young people" (Anderson, 2000).

The subculture of violence becomes a symbol of alienation from society, especially social institutions representing law, order, and norms and standards of the dominant culture. A sense of belonging, order, and respect become redefined according to the standards of conduct that rely on toughness, autonomy, and violence to establish a reputation. This helps us understand why homicide becomes a normative response to conflict and disagreement in certain neighborhoods, as violence is embedded in the very culture of interaction between individuals; is expected and sustained by a standard set of rules, norms, and values; and is essentially a way of life (Anderson, 2000). Murder can therefore be a means by which an individual achieves their goals, conferring power upon a threat to their reputation, or a means of settling a dispute that escalates into a violent confrontation (Anderson, 2019). These dynamics of interaction are "understandable" to the extent that the violent response is motivated by a culture of violence through generations of exposure to behaviors and interactions that emerge through the shared experiences of individuals who adhere to a set of conduct norms reinforcing such acts. Let us turn now to a typology of homicide that is more difficult to comprehend, analyze, and discern its distinct characteristics.

Serial Killing

The popularized image of murder in U.S. entertainment media, literature, and documentaries portrays notorious, ambiguous, and murderous killers who spread fear, shock our minds, and leave us bewildered with their acts of violence and torture. These are usually individuals who strike multiple times, taking the lives of many innocent victims. **Serial killing is best defined as unlawfully taking the life of at least three individuals in separate events** (Hass et al., 2016). Because this crime is sensationalized in the media, there are many associated myths and stereotypes associated with serial killers, most notably that they are low-life loser types who are sociopaths and shady characters that have a certain "look" or "appearance." However, studies have shown that serial killers are usually mainstream individuals who hide their actions, lead ordinary lives, and manifest a variety of psychosocial traits as well as diverse backgrounds (Marono et al., 2020). Moreover, there is a misperception that serial killing occurs at epidemic proportions in comparison to other forms of homicide and that it is a crime motivated by anger toward a relative, a traumatic childhood experience, or some type of sexual sadism. The following statements dispel some of these myths by providing a more realistic typology of serial killing (Kaplan, 2020):

- Serial killers do not have a physical appearance that is distinct and clearly identifiable
- Most serial killers are legally sane and therefore recognize the wrongfulness of their behavior
- The crime of serial murder is not common at all and is probably the least common of all forms of criminal homicide
- Serial killers are not sociopaths who are constantly at odds with the norms of society
- Pornography is not the primary motive or drive behind the actions of serial killers
- The majority of serial killers have not experienced traumatic childhoods
- Serial killers generally do not select victims who remind them of family members they are angry with
- Most serial killers are not sexual sadists but are rather motivated for a variety of different reasons
- Serial killers might leave clues behind but not because they are "crying for help" or "want to be found" but rather as part of their game with law enforcement

Researchers have studied the patterns of offending, personalities, and driving forces behind the crime of serial murder for many years. This has provided us with a typology of offending based on victim selection, motivation for the killing, and method of carrying out the murder. Table 4.2 provides us a summary of four types of serial killers:

TABLE 4.2 **SERIAL KILLERS: WHO ARE THEY?**

SERIAL KILLER TYPOLOGY	DESCRIPTION
Visionary/Missionary Serial Killer	I hear voices and have visions to kill people. I am often on some type of mission to save the world of evildoers or get rid of people because I think I can or should because I feel that sometimes I am God, or God tells me to.
Comfort Serial Killer	I am greedy and devise schemes to select wealthy people and kill them for material profit or financial and personal gain. I prey on the elderly or lonely, vulnerable rich men. I am sometimes referred to as a "black widow."
Thrill-Motivated Hedonistic Serial Killer	I kill for the pleasure and excitement I feel when I inflict pain on my victims. I choose victims carefully to ensure I can fulfill my desires and carry out my violent fantasies, which are sometimes also sexual.
Thrill Seeking Power-Dominance Serial Killer	I enjoy the feeling of power associated with controlling my victims and their fate of life and death. I like eluding authority and watching the chaos, fear, and confusion my killing causes.

Source: Cummins, I., Foley, M., & King, M. (2019). Serial killing: A modern phenomenon. In I. Cummins, M. Foley, & M. King (Eds.), Serial killers and the media (pp. 67–87). Palgrave Macmillan, Cham.

Serial killing has indeed received a great deal of attention in media despite its low incidence in homicide statistics (less than 1%). We turn now to another pattern of homicide that is also fairly uncommon and yet receives a great deal of attention.

Mass Murder

The U.S. Department of Justice defines **mass murder** as the killing of four or more individuals in a single event or during a short time period. It is understandable why mass murder takes on such a public nature, as the crime is often nationally and even globally shocking and newsworthy, very often involving many victims from a variety of backgrounds and demographic characteristics. Mass murders involve unexpected eruptions of violence in places considered to be safe or personal, such as schools, malls, airplanes, restaurants, churches, or office buildings. Unlike serial killers, mass murders rarely elude law enforcement, as they either turn themselves over after their murderous rampage or turn the weapon on themselves. Mass murderers vary in their typologies and researchers have a difficult time understanding their criminal actions, as many of them commit suicide after carrying out their plans (King & Jacobson, 2017). What we do know, however, is that the majority of mass murderers are not insane and display a variety of motives, various levels of planning, and different target selections. Based on these manifested traits, criminologists have been able to identify four main types of mass murderers (Clemmow et al., 2020):

- **Mass Murder for Terror.** Commit mass murder to create fear and panic in society, send out a warning or message, or advance political rhetoric
- **Mass Murder for Profit or Personal Gain.** Commit mass murder in the pursuit of financial or material benefit
- **Revenge.** Commit mass murder to get even with individuals or categories of people from specific ethnic or racial groups, walks of life, or religious beliefs
- **Love.** Commit mass murder to "protect" or "save" individuals they love from some type of danger or threat, or from a fear of losing them

Studies of mass murderers have revealed that events leading up to their actions are the product of various "triggers" (Peter et al., 2019). These can by years of accumulated anger and frustration over personal failure, rejection or social ridicule and isolation, or sparking events such as losing a job, political imprisonment of a terrorist group leader, or facing a divorce. Triggers such as these lead to the devastating acts of mass violence by shooters who want to be seen and heard. When their stories make headlines, immediately as a society, we experience fear, sadness, and vulnerability as a collective group; seek protection; and want answers to the senseless killing of innocent people (Silver et al., 2019). Later in this chapter, we will explore some of these questions about homicide by examining the various characteristics of homicide offenders and their victims. First, however, let's take a look at another typology of interpersonal violence, by investigating the crime of assault.

Various Categories of Assault

Developing typologies of criminal behavior is particularly challenging when there is a diversity of traits and characteristics that distinguish between the various elements of situational context, offender and victim interaction, and the motive behind the crime. This diversity is a distinct feature of the crime of **assault**, most broadly defined as the inflicting of unwanted physical contact, injury, or harm upon a person, including threatening or putting a person in fear of imminent bodily injury, harm, or danger. Under this definition, we see that the crime of assault can include acts involving no physical contact and therefore encompasses verbal threats, taunting, bullying, and intimidation. Some states specifically distinguish this element of physical versus nonphysical acts of assault by differentiating between assault and assault with **battery**, a nonconsensual physical contact. According to various data sources on crime, assault with battery is the most common violent crime in the United States (Kaplan, 2020). In the sections to come, we will therefore focus our attention on categories of assault with battery, recognizing an important distinction between **aggravated assault**, which results in serious bodily injury or harm to an individual and involves the use of a weapon, and **simple assault**, which results in minor bodily injury or harm to an individual and usually involves no weapon. With this distinction in mind, we turn now to a discussion of three broad categories of assault: *intimate partner violence, child maltreatment,* and *elder abuse*.

Intimate Partner Violence

Interpersonal violence involves a significant breach of trust when it is perpetrated between people in a position of friendship, collegiality, or acquaintance. It is even a more significant violation of sanctity when it involves individuals in an intimate relationship. According to the U.S. Office on Violence Against Women, **intimate partner violence** involves a pattern of abusive behavior used by one partner over another partner in an intimate relationship to gain power or maintain control (Miller & McCaw, 2019). The term *intimate partner* refers to current or former spouses, lovers, and individuals who are dating. This type of interpersonal form of violence ranges from a single episode of eruptive behavior to chronic and severe episodes of violence and abuse that can last over many years. The tools of this pattern of abuse involve various forms of violence and aggression, including the following:

- *Physical violence/aggression*—using physical force such as hitting, slapping, kicking, or other forms of physical violence to hurt your partner, also includes forcing your partner to use alcohol or drugs and denying medical care or treatment
- *Psychological/emotional aggression*—using either verbal or nonverbal communication to control your partner by harming them mentally or emotionally through attacking their sense of self-worth or self-esteem, including excessive and constant criticism, name-calling, economic or financial control, damaging relationships with family and friends, or causing fear by intimidation or threat of physical harm

- *Sexual violence/aggression*—using force to coerce your partner to take part in sexual acts without consent or treating your partner in a sexually demeaning manner
- *Stalking*—using repeated patterns of unwanted harassment or obsessive attention that causes your partner to fear for their own safety or the safety of someone close to them

According to the Centers for Disease Control and Prevention, about 1 in 4 women and 1 in 10 men have experience one of these four forms of intimate partner violence over the course of the life span (Centers for Disease Control and Prevention, 2019). This staggering number is difficult to understand in light of the nature of intimate relationships and the forms of aggression and violence that take place in otherwise loving forms of human interaction. In a classic study, researcher Lenore Walker interviewed 1,500 battered women, finding that the overwhelming majority of them identify the violence in their relationships to fall along a similar cycle or pattern of interaction with their intimate partners (Wilson, 2019). Figure 4.1 provides us with an overview of this cycle of violence to help guide our understanding of this typology of criminal behavior.

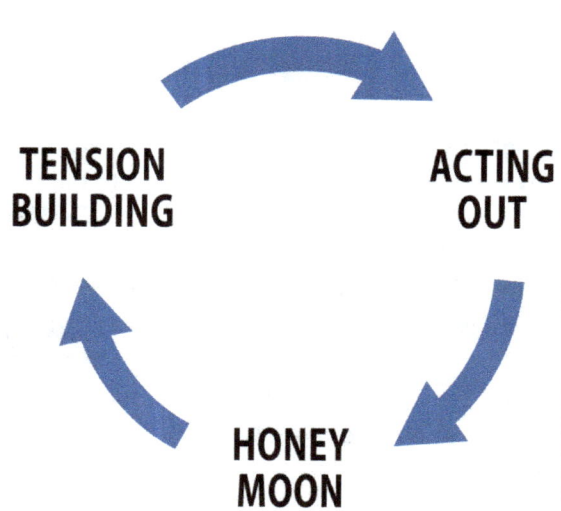

TENSION BUILDING: A breakdown in communication disrupts routine interactions between intimate partners and leads to a building of anxiety and fear in resolving ordinary disagreements and managing life stresses. Tension escalates when the abusive partner exercises power and control in dealing with the situation.

ACTING OUT: The abusive partner begins to take control of the victim through an explosive incident involving the abuser verbally or physically assaulting their partner, to control the environment and create fear. Victims are left isolated, confused, hurt and betrayed. The victim is left hurt, betrayed, confused, and afraid.

HONEY MOON: The abuser expresses remorse, apologizing to the victim and promising an end to the violence, often showering them with gifts, love and affection. Once the abuser gains the forgiveness and trust of the victim and after a period of withdrawal from the abuse, the same cycle begins over again, with this stage getting shorter or disappearing over time.

FIGURE 4.1 The Cycle of Violence

The escalation of interpersonal violence in intimate relationships is a global issue that has been the subject of much research and policy changes over the years (Wood et al., 2019). Another crime of interpersonal violence that is even more difficult to comprehend when developing a typology is the crime of child maltreatment. Let's turn now to a closer look at the second form of violence that occurs within an intimate family setting, child maltreatment, to see whether there are patterns of similarity between it and intimate partner violence.

Child Maltreatment

While corporal punishment and correction have historically been elements of parental or other authority figure control over the behavior of children, there is a clear line of separation between acceptable forms of discipline and what constitutes child abuse and neglect. The term **child maltreatment** is used to refer to all forms of abuse and neglect to children who are under the age of 18 years, including physical, emotional, sexual, and commercial exploitation. The law is designed to protect minor children from actions taken by parents, caretakers, or any other adult in a position of trust or power over the child (Saini et al., 2020). While there is not always uniformity in the nature and meaning of child maltreatment, the following terms are used to apply to very specific forms of child abuse and neglect (U.S. Department of Health and Human Services, 2019):

- *Physical abuse*—nonaccidental and purposeful infliction of physical harm to a child, including burning a child or hitting, punching, kicking, or beating with hands, belt, stick, or another object
- *Neglect*—actions that put a child at risk of harm or detriment to health and well-being, including deprivation of adequate food, clothing, shelter, medical care, or safety
- *Sexual abuse*—the use of a child through persuasion, inducement, enticement, or coercion to engage in any sexually explicit conduct or simulation of such conduct; the rape or statutory rape, molestation, prostitution, or other forms of sexual exploitation of children or incest with children
- *Emotional abuse*—verbal or physical acts of parents or caretakers that cause or can cause serious mental injury including depression, anxiety, withdrawal, and aggression in a child. This can include traumatic punishments such as locking a child in the closet or using verbally abusive or derogatory language

Much like intimate partner violence, child maltreatment is a global problem that has long-term and often lifelong consequences on the physical and emotional health, development, and well-being of victims. Statistics, however, are often difficult to use in assessing the problem, as definitions of what exactly constitutes abuse and neglect often vary, many cases go unreported, and long-term data on physical trauma leading to death are often not well documented (Kim & Drake, 2019). Box 4.2 highlights some significant trends and findings based on studies and data compiled by the World Health Organization:

> **THE REAL DEAL: SOME FACTS ABOUT CRIMES AGAINST CHILDREN** — BOX 4.2
>
> *The following facts are presented by the World Health Organization:*
> - Nearly 3 in 4 children—or 300 million children—aged 2-4 years regularly suffer physical punishment and/or psychological violence at the hands of parents and caregivers.
> - One in 5 women and 1 in 13 men report having been sexually abused as a child aged 0-17 years.
> - One hundred twenty million girls and young women under 20 years of age have suffered some form of forced sexual contact.
> - Every year, there are an estimated 40,150 homicide deaths in children under 18 years of age, some of which are likely due to child maltreatment. This number almost certainly underestimates the true extent of the problem since a significant proportion of deaths because of child maltreatment are incorrectly attributed to falls, burns, drowning, and other causes.
> - International studies reveal that nearly 3 in 4 children aged 2-4 years regularly suffer physical punishment and/or psychological violence at the hands of parents and caregivers, and 1 in 5 women and 1 in 13 men report having been sexually abused as a child.
> - Consequences of child maltreatment include impaired lifelong physical and mental health, and the social and occupational outcomes can ultimately slow a country's economic and social development.
> - A child who is abused is more likely to abuse others as an adult so that violence is passed down from one generation to the next. It is therefore critical to break this cycle of violence and in so doing create positive multigenerational impacts.
>
> Source: World Health Organization. (2020, June 8). Child maltreatment, key facts. https://www.who.int/news-room/fact-sheets/detail/child-maltreatment

Elder Abuse

Over the past several decades, life expectancy has increased significantly, with a growing number of individuals falling into the age category of the elderly and, consequently, problems associated with abuse have become more prevalent in modern societies (Ross et al., 2019). **Elder abuse** is defined as the intentional neglect, mistreatment, or abuse of an adult 60 years and older by a caregiver or other individual involved in their care or in a position of trust or expectation of care (Van Den Bruele et al., 2016). While many cases of elder abuse go unrecognized and therefore unreported, research indicates that the overwhelming majority of victims are women, with the most vulnerable population being individuals who have no family or friends to check on the care they are receiving, elderly with dementia, memory problems, or physical disabilities and individuals who rely on others for their everyday care and life functions (Storey, 2020).

Elder abuse can happen to any older adult, especially if they are frail and appear to be an easy target (Storey, 2020). It can take place in their home or some type of nursing care facility. According to the National Institute on Aging, the following types of abuse have been identified as forms of elder abuse (U.S. Department of Health and Human Services, National Institute on Aging, 2016):

- *Physical abuse*—hitting, pushing, punching, or slapping causing bodily injury or harm
- *Emotional abuse*—yelling, threatening, cursing at or saying derogatory words, or purposely ignoring
- *Neglect*—failing to respond to expected needs entrusted to the caregiver
- *Abandonment*—leaving an elderly adult senior alone without planning for their care
- *Sexual abuse*—forcing an older adult to watch or be part of sexual acts
- *Financial abuse*—stealing money or belongings, forging checks, taking retirement funds, altering bank accounts, life insurance policies, and wills
- *Health-care fraud*—overcharging, overbilling, or falsifying medical records, care, and claims by hospital staff and health-care providers

Acts of violence and abuse take on many forms, as we have seen so far. In the final sections of this chapter, we will explore the characteristics of both offenders and their victims involved in the interpersonal crimes of violence discussed in this chapter.

Homicide and Assault Offenders and Their Victims
Characteristics of Homicide and Assault Offenders

Developing a typology of individuals who commit the violent crimes of assault and homicide is considerably stifled by one limitation—notably, that studies of offenders are generally based on those who have been arrested, prosecuted, and convicted criminals. Despite this limitation, some basic characteristics of homicide and assault offenders have emerged to provide us with some general trends portraying those who commit these crimes, with one persistent finding showing that a majority of violent offenders also have prior arrest records for both violent and nonviolent crimes (Hester, 2019). Moreover, homicide and assault offenders disproportionately experience violent victimization at some point in their lives, and their acts of violence are often triggered by some type of argument or altercation with the victim (Berger & Felson, 2020).

Various crime data sources show that the overwhelming majority of homicide and assault offenders are men, a global trend that has varied over the years in terms of proportion but remains a constant trait, with males being responsible for over 90% of homicides and nearly 80% of aggravated assaults (U.S. Department of Justice, Federal Bureau of Investigation, 2019). Moreover, homicide and assault offenders tend to be more youthful, with a significant majority being under the age of 25 and rates of violence declining steadily after the age of 30 (U.S. Department of Justice, Federal Bureau of Investigation, 2019). Perpetrators of violence can come from many walks of life, especially when we are talking about the various forms of domestic violence we discussed. However, since we rely heavily on statistics to develop typologies of offenders, studies have shown that arrests are highest for individuals who come from neighborhoods that are socioeconomically deprived and deteriorated and who have achieved lower levels of educational and occupational success (Stansfield & Doherty, 2019). With regard to race and typologies of homicide and assault offenders, the subject has stirred up considerable controversy. Critics note that data on arrest and imprisonment reflect discriminatory practices of law enforcement and courts, therefore, skewing the numbers disproportionally toward a higher rate of criminality among certain racial and ethnic groups, with some minorities reflected more than others relative to their numbers in the general population (Holliday et al., 2020).

Characteristics of Homicide and Assault Victims

As we have determined, developing a typology of offenders depends largely upon data sources reflecting crimes that have been committed and recorded or "become known" to authorities. This often skews our total understanding of criminal offenders and, likewise, also skews the typology of their victims. For this reason, we also gather information on crime victimization from self-report survey research, as well as sources such as the NCVS discussed in Chapter 1. One consistent finding from various data sources on crime is that a significant majority of homicide and assault victims are young males from lower socioeconomic classes who are also members of ethnic or racial minority groups (Bureau of Justice Statistics, 2018). In addition, those individuals who are at the greatest risk of victimization are also among the same groups that are most likely to commit violent crimes, and therefore, victims of homicide and assault tend to share similar demographic characteristics as their offenders (Berg & Mulford, 2020).

With regard to female victims of violence, the greatest threat of assault and homicide for women is from men with whom they are intimately involved, with studies finding rates as high as 35% of female murder victims to be killed by a boyfriend or husband, and African American females experiencing higher rates of intimate partner violence than Caucasian females (Hanlon et al., 2016). Compared to men, research findings show that females are 4 times as likely to be killed by an intimate partner (Femicide Watch, 2019). These findings have created international concern for the safety of women and have sparked various organizations to examine gender-related issues addressing women's equality in education, the workforce, political representation, and health and safety concerns (Peace Corps, 2020).

Key Takeaways

Review the following list of bullet points for a quick overview of the key ideas and information in this chapter:

- There are various categories of interpersonal violence involving victims and offenders engaged in some type of violent encounter. These categories include homicide, assault, rape, and robbery.
- Interpersonal acts of violence such as homicide and assault share the common trait of creating harm to individuals and feelings of fear and helplessness in their victims, families, and communities. However, each situation and context of violence is different and

therefore creates various categories of offenses based on offender motivation, planning, and interaction with the victim.
- With the exception of domestic violence, homicide and assault victims and offenders tend to share common characteristics such as age, race, and gender, with the majority of both being young males from ethnic and racial minorities.

Conclusion and Formal Summary Questions

This chapter has provided us with a detailed overview of the most common category of interpersonal violence, assault, and the least common category, homicide. The overlap in the two offense typologies or common theme is the escalation of violent encounters between offenders and victims, which leads to the various forms of assault and homicide we discussed. With the exception of serial and mass murder, this violence occurs within the context of victims and offenders who know each other, live together, or somehow interact with one another in a situation that leads to criminal action. Heightened emotions can play a significant role in the onset of homicide and assault, as well as structural and contextual elements of situations that mediate the violent interaction. A typology of these criminal offenses reveals a diversity of motive, context, and victim-offender relationships, with the common element of violence, fear, and helplessness to the victim permeating our understanding of the effect of these forms of interpersonal violence.

- *Do you have a better understanding of the term interpersonal violence?*
- *Can you define the crimes of homicide and assault?*
- *Are you able to describe the various typologies of homicide and assault?*
- *Do you know what homicide and assault offenders have in common?*
- *Can you identify the characteristics of homicide and assault victims?*

E-Resources

For more information on the global study of violence against women, visit the *World Health Organization* website at https://www.who.int/news-room/fact-sheets/detail/violence-against-women.

Get to know the resources available for victims of child abuse and neglect by visiting the *Centers for Disease Control* website at https://www.cdc.gov/violenceprevention/childabuseandneglect/resources.html.

Check out this video to learn more about the evolving relationship between media and violence: https://www.youtube.com/watch?v=2PHxTr-59hE.

Learn more about some of the most notorious unsolved mass murders in U.S. history at https://listverse.com/2019/05/08/10-worst-unsolved-mass-murders-in-us-history/.

References

Adjorlolo, S., & Chan, H. C. (2017). The nature of instrumentality and expressiveness of homicide crime scene behaviors: A review. *Trauma, Violence, & Abuse, 18*(2), 119–133.

Anderson, E. (2000). *Code of the street: Decency, violence, and the moral life of the inner city*. W. W. Norton & Company.

Anderson, E. (2019). Code of the street. In A. M. Orum (Ed.), *The Wiley Blackwell encyclopedia of urban and regional studies* (pp. 1–3). John Wiley & Sons.

Berg, M. T., & Felson, R. (2020). A social interactionist approach to the victim-offender overlap. *Journal of Quantitative Criminology, 36*(1). 153–181.

Berg, M. T., & Mulford, C. F. (2020). Reappraising and redirecting research on the victim–offender overlap. *Trauma, Violence, & Abuse, 21*(1), 16–30.

Bureau of Justice Statistics. (2018). *Data collection: National crime victimization survey (NCVS)*. https://www.bjs.gov/index.cfm?ty=dcdetail&iid=245

Centers for Disease Control and Prevention. (2019, February 26). *Preventing intimate partner violence.* https://www.cdc.gov/violenceprevention/intimatepartnerviolence/fastfact.html

Clemmow, C., Gill, P., Bouhana, N., Silver, J., & Horgan, J. (2020). Disaggregating lone-actor grievance-fuelled violence: Comparing lone-actor terrorists and mass murderers. *Terrorism and Political Violence*, 1–26. https://doi.org/10.1080/09546553.2020.1718661

Femicide Watch. (2019, July 8). *2019 study on global homicide: Gender-related killings of women and girls | UNODC.* http://femicide-watch.org/products/2019-study-global-homicide-gender-related-killings-women-and-girls-unodc

Ferracuti, F., & Wolfgang, M. E. (Eds.). (2013). *The subculture of violence: Towards an integrated theory in criminology.* Routledge.

Fitz-Gibbon, Jorge. (2020, May 28). Here's everything we know about the death of George Floyd. *The New York Times.* https://nypost.com/2020/05/28/everything-we-know-about-the-death-of-george-floyd/.

Foner, N., Duyvendak, J. W., & Kasinitz, P. (2019). Introduction: Super-diversity in everyday life. *Ethnic and Racial Studies, 42*(1), 1–16.

Hanlon, R. E., Brook, M., Demery, J. A., & Cunningham, M. D. (2016). Domestic homicide: Neuropsychological profiles of murderers who kill family members and intimate partners. *Journal of forensic sciences, 61*, S163–S170.

Hass, A. Y., Moloney, C., & Chambliss, W. J. (2016). *Criminology: Connecting theory, research and practice.* Taylor & Francis.

Hester, R. (2019). Prior record and recidivism risk. *American Journal of Criminal Justice, 44*(3), 353–375.

Holliday, C. N., Kahn, G., Thorpe, R. J., Shah, R., Hameeduddin, Z., & Decker, M. R. (2020). Racial/ethnic disparities in police reporting for partner violence in the national crime victimization survey and survivor-led interpretation. *Journal of Racial and Ethnic Health Disparities, 7*(3), 468–480.

Johansson, T., & Herz, M. (2019). Subcultures and transitional spaces. In T. Johansson & M. Hertz (Eds.), *Youth studies in transition: Culture, generation and new learning processes* (pp. 41–53). Springer, Cham.

Kaplan, J. (2020). Jacob Kaplan's concatenated files: Uniform crime reporting program data: Offenses known and clearances by arrest, 1960-2018.

Kim, H., & Drake, B. (2019). Cumulative prevalence of onset and recurrence of child maltreatment reports. *Journal of the American Academy of Child & Adolescent Psychiatry, 58*(12), 1175–1183.

King, D. M., & Jacobson, S. H. (2017). Random acts of violence? Examining probabilistic independence of the temporal distribution of mass killing events in the United States. *Violence and Victims, 32*(6), 1014–1023.

Leary, T., Southard, L., & Aamodt, M. (2019). Serial killers and intelligence levels: Variability, patterns, and motivations to kill. *North American Journal of Psychology, 21*(4), 787.

Marono, A. J., Reid, S., Yaksic, E., & Keatley, D. A. (2020). A behaviour sequence analysis of serial killer' lives: From childhood abuse to methods of murder. *Psychiatry, Psychology and Law, 27*(1), 126–137.

Miller, E., & McCaw, B. (2019). Intimate partner violence. *New England Journal of Medicine, 380*(9), 854–857.

Parker, B. L., & McKinley, A. C. (2018). Homicide event motive: A situational perspective. *Salus Journal, 6*(2), 78.

Peace Corps. (2020). *Global issues: Gender equality and women's empowerment.* https://www.peacecorps.gov/educators/resources/global-issues-gender-equality-and-womens-empowerment/

Peter, E., Seidenbecher, S., Bogerts, B., Dobrowolny, H., & Schöne, M. (2019). Mass murders in Germany—classification of surviving offenders based on the examination of court files. *The Journal of Forensic Psychiatry & Psychology, 30*(3), 381–400.

Reed, A., & Bohlander, M. (Eds.). (2018). *Homicide in criminal law: A research companion.* Routledge.

Ross, M. E. T., Thomas, K. L., Pickens, S., Bryan, J., & Asghar-Ali, A. A. (2019). Elder Abuse. In M. Balasubramaniam, A. Gupta, & R. R. Tampi (Eds.), *Psychiatric ethics in late-life patients* (pp. 165–181). Springer, Cham.

Saini, M., Laajasalo, T., & Platt, S. (2020). Gatekeeping by allegations: An examination of verified, unfounded, and fabricated allegations of child maltreatment within the context of resist and refusal dynamics. *Family Court Review, 58*(2), 417–431.

Silver, J., Horgan, J., & Gill, P. (2019). Shared struggles? Cumulative strain theory and public mass murderers from 1990 to 2014. *Homicide Studies, 23*(1), 64–84.

Stansfield, R., & Doherty, E. (2019). Neighborhood health, social structure and family violence. *Social Science Research, 81*, 12–22.

Storey, J. E. (2020). Risk factors for elder abuse and neglect: A review of the literature. *Aggression and Violent Behavior, 50*, 101339.

U.S. Department of Health and Human Services, National Institute on Aging. (2016, December 29). *Elder abuse.* https://www.nia.nih.gov/health/elder-abuse

U.S. Department of Health and Human Services. (2019, February 6). *The child abuse prevention and treatment act (CAPTA).* https://www.acf.hhs.gov/cb/resource/capta

U.S. Department of Justice, Federal Bureau of Investigation. (2019). *Crime in the United States.* https://ucr.fbi.gov/crime-in-the-u.s/2019/preliminary-report/home

Van Den Bruele, A. B., Dimachk, M., & Crandall, M. (2019). Elder abuse. *Clinics in Geriatric Medicine, 35*(1), 103–113.

Walach, V. (2019). On narrative violence: How stories inflict harm in a street context. *Deviant Behavior, 42*(1), 1–14.

Wilson, J. K. (2019). Cycle of violence. In F. P. Bernat, K. Frailing, L. Gelsthorpe, S. Kethineni, & L. Easko (Eds.), *The encyclopedia of women and crime* (pp. 1–5). Wiley-Blackwell.

Wood, S. N., Glass, N., & Decker, M. R. (2019). An integrative review of safety strategies for women experiencing intimate partner violence in low-and middle-income countries. *Trauma, Violence, & Abuse, 22*(1), 68–82.

Chapter 5

Crimes of Interpersonal Violence

Rape and Sexual Assault

Key Terms

Rape, Abuse & Incest National Network (RAINN)
Sexual assault
Sexual harassment
Rape
Forcible rape
Statutory rape
Attempted rape
Acquaintance rape
Stranger rape
Date rape
Spousal rape
Same-sex rape
Gang rape
Anger-retaliatory rapist
Power-dominance rapist
Sadistic-excitement rapist
Masculine identity conflict rapist
Pathological personality rapist
National Intimate Partner and Sexual Violence Study

Chapter Headings

1. Chapter opener
2. What is rape and sexual assault?
3. Various patterns of rape
   3.1. Date
   3.2. Spousal
   3.3. Same-sex
   3.4. Gang
4. Rape and sexual assault offenders and their victims
   4.1. Characteristics of attackers
   4.2. Characteristics of rape victims
5. Chapter summary

Opening Questions

Before you begin the chapter, take a few minutes to reflect on the following questions:

1. What are the various types of rape and sexual assault offenses?
2. Do the crimes of rape and sexual assault occur more often between strangers or acquaintances?
3. Are certain types of individuals more likely than others to be rapists?
4. How can rape and sexual assault victims be identified, and what traits do they share?

Chapter Objectives

After reading Chapter 5, students will be able to do the following:

- *Define and distinguish between the crimes of rape and sexual assault*
- *Recognize various patterns of rape and sexual assault offenses*
- *Present a profile of rape and sexual assault offenders and what motivates them*
- *Identify characteristics of rape and sexual assault victims*

True Crime

One fact that is universally true about crime, especially crimes involving interpersonal violence, is the trauma of the event does not end just because the victim survives the attack. Rather, the crime itself leaves a mark of pain that transcends time and often leaves the individual with permanent scars that go beyond any physical or material well-being to permeate their development of self-worth, personal safety, and emotional healing. This is particularly true when experiencing the type of crime that is perpetrated within a context of trust, that violates not only an individual's sense of security but also robs them of something physical, psychological, and social, a crime that often breaches all imaginable elements of self-control and humanity. This crime is often riddled with conflicting stories, accusations, and disbelief, with all elements adding to the victim's trauma and their inability to experience full justice, hiding the truth in their own minds, and always wondering if their cries will be heard, and even if heard, truly believed. The following excerpt describes this type of crime in the words of a survivor:

> I was doing the cash register, it was a Sunday, so liquor sales didn't start until noon. Lawrence and Ziyad sat in the office until noon when the liquor sales started; then Lawrence and I traded places. For the longest time, Ziyad and I sat in the office talking and getting to know each other. We talked about people, sports, cars, just small talk. Then he began making perverted comments to me. Feeling very uncomfortable, I went up to the cash register with Lawrence. I didn't tell him about his cousin. Now I know I should have.
>
> At about 2:30, Lawrence sent me and Ziyad into that back room to do some work. I was back there, minding my own business and doing my thing. Ziyad grabbed me by my arms and drug me into the bathroom. I screamed. He put this hand over my mouth and started to undo his pants. Knowing what was about to happen, I froze. My whole body went numb. I couldn't move. After he was done, he got dressed and walked out of the bathroom like nothing happened. He left me there with my tears. When he walked out the door, he took with him my pride, my security, and my virginity. I had so many thoughts going through my mind. What if I tell someone and they don't believe me? Was it my fault? I thought Lawrence was my friend, if he was, how could his cousin do this to me? Not to mention the multiple feelings I had. Shame. Guilt. Anger. Fear. But most of all disbelief. How could this happen to me?
>
> About 10 minutes later, I walked out of the bathroom, past the office, and up to the cash register, where Lawrence, not knowing anything yet, was standing. As I walked past the office, I noticed that Ziyad's cousin Firas was there to pick him up. As I walked by, he said, "You know what Lindsie, you're a slut." So, that means that Ziyad went in there and bragged that he "got some."
>
> After Ziyad left, I began to cry. Lawrence continually asked me, "What's wrong Lindsie; what's wrong"? Finally, I blurted out, "Your cousin raped me." He hugged me and gently kissed my head. At first, he told me not to tell anyone; later on, he told me to do what I felt was right. He also said he'd always be here for me. The funny thing is, I believed him. …

Later that night, my sister came to pick me up. As soon as I got in her car, I started crying. I told her what happened. She told me I had to tell my parents. I didn't want to. She did. My whole family was crying ... my parents ... my two brothers ... and my sister. My mom called the police. After they got there, and we made a police report, they took me to the hospital to have a rape kit done. We pressed charges. Later that night, they went to Ziyad's house. He told them it was consensual. I didn't want to do it. He forced me. It was RAPE! (Tracy, 2020)

What Is Rape and Sexual Assault?

Speaking ... slowly freed me from the shame I'd felt. The more I struggled to speak, the less power the rape and its aftermath seemed to have over me!
—Nancy Venable Raine, Author and Rape Survivor

When we describe crime, sometimes the concept of an offender taking something from the victim is tangible, related to an object like money, a wallet, stolen identity, or valuable items like jewelry and electronics. We can even describe an offender as taking the life of the victim. This chapter deals with a different type of "taking," one that is buried beneath the obvious value of property and the devastating effect on the surviving family of homicide victims. This crime is devastating to its victims and involves the utmost of personal dignity, safety, physical health, and psychological well-being when describing what is "taken" from the victim. According to the **Rape, Abuse & Incest National Network (RAINN)**, an organization that partners with over 1,000 sexual assault service providers nationwide to prevent sexual violence, raise awareness, and advocate to help survivors, as well as bring perpetrators to justice, the crime of **sexual assault** refers to sexual contact or behavior without explicit consent or using physical violence, threat, or intimidation (RAINN, 2020c). Sexual assault can take on many different forms and can include the following:

- Fondling or unwanted touching
- Forcing a victim to perform sexual acts, such as oral sex
- Attempted rape of the victim
- Penetration of the victim's body or rape

Sexual assault is distinct from **sexual harassment**, which includes unwelcome sexual advances, requests for sexual favors, and other forms of physical or verbal harassment of a sexual nature in a workplace or social setting (U.S. Equal Employment Opportunity Commission, 2020).

As noted earlier, **rape** is a form of sexual assault, the most serious, and is defined by the Federal Bureau of Investigation (FBI) in the Uniform Crime Report as "penetration, no matter how slight, of the vagina or anus with any body part or object, or oral penetration by a sex organ of another person, without the consent of the victim" (Federal Bureau of Investigation. Uniform

Crime Report, 2018). Some states also distinguish between **forcible rape** as defined by the FBI and **statutory rape**, sexual intercourse or sexual penetration that is committed upon a minor who is under the age of consent (in most states the age of consent is 16; in some, it is 18; Beck & Boys, 2019). In this chapter, we will examine the crime of rape as it evolves through various patterns of offending, the relationship between the victim and offender, as well as traits and characteristics of rapists.

Various Patterns of Rape

The crime of rape occurs in various contexts, and these contexts often surround the relationship between the victim and the offender. One very important distinction to make before developing typologies of rape based on a pattern of offending is the division between acquaintance rape and stranger rape. Studies show that the vast majority of rapes occur between victims and offenders who know each other, work together, are dating, or who have some type of relationship with one another, with as high as 4 out of 5 rapes being attributed to **acquaintance rape** (Lopez et al., 2019). With that said, acquaintance rape is also the least likely form of this crime to be reported to law enforcement, with victims often experiencing feelings of embarrassment and shame or unwilling to accuse somebody they know (Gravelin et al., 2019). For this reason, official crime data are often skewed, showing **stranger rapes**, those attacks that occur between victims and offenders who do not know each other and have no direct relationship, to be more common. With these dynamics in mind, let us take a look at the various contexts within which rape offenses take place, examining four categories: date rape, spousal rape, same-sex rape, and gang rape.

Date Rape

One growing trend in violence against women is the crime of **date rape**, a form of acquaintance rape that takes place between a victim and an offender who are in some type of romantic or potentially romantic relationship, who are getting to know each other in that context and are "dating" or "on a date" (Lopez et al., 2019) The most common context within which date rape occurs is among college and high school students, with parties and the presence of alcohol and other drugs creating a variety of situations for victims to be sexually assaulted and taken advantage of. According to RAINN, sexual violence on college campuses is pervasive, with nationwide statistics showing the following trends (RAINN, 2020a):

- An estimated 11.2% of all college students (undergraduate and graduate) experience a rape or sexual assault using physical force, violence, or incapacitation
- About 8.8% of females and 2.2% of males who are in graduate and professional degree programs experience rape or sexual assault through physical force, violence, or incapacitation
- Among undergraduate students, 23.1% of females and 5.4% of males experience rape or sexual assault through physical force, violence, or incapacitation

- Although female college-aged students (18–24) are 20% less likely than nonstudents of the same age to be a victim of rape or sexual assault, male college-aged students (18–24) are 78% more likely than nonstudents of the same age to be a victim of rape or sexual assault
- Only 20% of female student victims, aged 18–24, report to law enforcement

These trends are compounded by the growing use of "date rape drugs" such as GHB (gamma-hydroxybutyric acid) and Rohypnol or "roofies." These powerful odorless, colorless, and tasteless drugs are usually added to alcoholic drinks at fraternity parties, or on a date, and have a strong sedating effect. The intention of the assailant is to incapacitate the victim in order to force sexual intercourse without their consent and with little to no resistance. Because these drugs can often induce drowsiness, blackout, and loss of memory, the victim can have difficulty recalling the events leading up to their rape (Paul & Mahesan, 2019). College campuses nationwide have over the past decade or so begun to respond to the publicity of sexual assaults on campuses and a growing concern among various women's groups and organizations calling for change. This response has largely focused on educating both men and women about personal safety, creating an organized, proactive response to reports of sexual violence, as well as participating in campaigns and discussion groups raising awareness of campus culture and dynamics of drinking, peer pressure, and partying, that can contribute to sexual assault and rape (Hayes et al., 2020). Many of these programs are designed to create dialog and communication among college students to identify situations in which sexual assault and rape can occur and to also understand that the use of force, intimidation, alcohol or drugs to coerce someone to engage in a sexual act is considered a serious crime.

Spousal Rape

Laws protecting victims against the crime of rape have not always protected individuals who are in a marriage relationship. As a matter of fact, it was not until 1976 that the state of Nebraska became the first state to eliminate the marital exemption to rape laws (England, 2020). Today, all 50 states in the U.S. recognize spousal or marital rape as a crime. This is not the case worldwide, however (see Figure 5.1). **Spousal** rape is defined as unwanted sexual intercourse or sexual acts by a spouse committed without the consent of the other spouse, against their will, using force, threat, intimidation, or incapacitation (England, 2020). Studies show that spousal rape is one of the least reported types of sexual assault, as many women are reluctant to report their victimization fearing public shame and humiliation, as well as losing their marriage (Richards, 1995). Spousal rape is also difficult to establish in terms of proof in a court of law, often requiring evidence of violence or injury. This is another reason victims are hesitant to report their victimization, in addition to the fear of retaliation by the spouse, with no resulting protection, leading to a continued lack of intervention and social support system to help victims cope with the devastating and long-term impact on personal and psychological health and well-being resulting from feelings of betrayal, shame, and fear (Stirling et al., 2020).

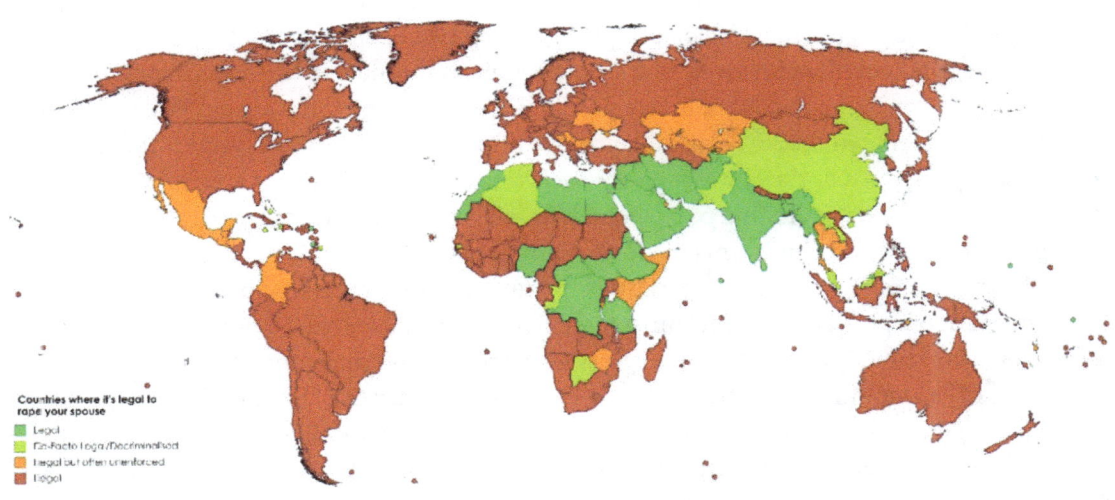

FIGURE 5.1 A Global Look at Spousal Rape Laws

Same-Sex Rape

Laws governing the crime of rape have a long-standing legal tradition and history limiting this form of sexual assault to attacks on women. This is largely due to the sociocultural misperception and stereotype that men cannot be raped and that females cannot be raped by members of the same sex. It was not until 2011 that FBI director Robert S. Mueller, III, approved the removal of the limited application of the crime of rape to the assault of women by men only. Social activism has, in recent years, raised awareness of the prevalence and impact of **same-sex rape**, defined as forced or coerced sexual acts perpetrated by an individual of the same sex, including oral sex, anal sex, and penetration of sexual organs of any sort (CPS, 2020). As with date rape, same-sex rape occurs most frequently between people who know each other or are in some type of intimate relationship, leaving victims feeling betrayed, ashamed, and reluctant to report (Javaid, 2018) their victimization out of fear of retaliation and humiliation.

Same-sex rape follows a similar pattern as heterosexual rape, with perpetrators attempting to control, dominate, and force the victim to submit to sexual acts using fear, intimidation, and violence. However, same-sex rape victims also go through a unique set of psychosocial dynamics not experienced by other types of rape victims. This is largely due to the stigma associated with sexual violence within the context of gender-specific sexual orientation. While victims of same-sex rape are not always gay or lesbian, this form of sexual violence can be a targeted hate crime against someone perceived to be gay, lesbian, bisexual, or transgendered. In addition, these victims may be particularly reluctant to come forward or report their victimization to law enforcement for fear of coming out to family, friends, and coworkers or being blamed for the assault based on their sexual orientation (Crofts et al., 2017).

Gang Rape

Some rapes occur where there are multiple assailants attacking the victim. This is referred to as **gang rape** or **group rape**, the rape of a single victim by two or more perpetrators. These rapes occur with some offenders involved in the actual rape and others used to facilitate the attack, restrain the victim, incite attackers, or act as onlookers encouraging the attack. The individuals not directly engaging in the sexual assault are also often collectively and severally charged with the crime of gang rape, as the law recognizes their role in the horrific act. Gang rapes can occur in a variety of contexts, including bars, nightclubs, alleys, parties, and college fraternities. They can be spontaneous and opportunistic, the product of males "egging each other on" or the result of some type of dare or joke. They can also be planned, targeted acts of violence intended for a specific goal or purpose such as punishment, retaliation, or during war (Randhawa, 2019). These attacks are also sometimes used as an expression of power and male dominance that is part of some type of "initiation" into a street gang, social club, or fraternity (Javaid, 2020).

The role of group behavior becomes a strong variable in the escalation of violence against the victim of a gang rape, which makes physical resistance more difficult and the use of force and violence more excessive. It also makes it more difficult for the victim to establish strong proof of the crime, as group rapists refuse to cooperate to testify against their own peers and friends. Their sense of belonging to the group, and their own feelings of masculinity by overpowering and dominating their victim supersedes their willingness to do the right thing and stand up for what is right.

THE REAL DEAL: "GOOD GUYS" RAPE TOO! — BOX 5.1

According to a recent study of sexual violence across 33 major universities in the United States, about 1 in 4 female college students, or about 25.9%, report having experienced some type of sexual assault or rape since starting college. The rate for male students experiencing victimization is 6.8%. Patterns of sexual violence have been growing at alarming rates on prestigious college campuses over the past decade, with attacks being perpetrated by groups of young men claiming to be "having fun" during sporting events, at parties, and inside fraternity houses. These individuals often feel that their behavior is beyond reproach, as they do not fit the typical image of a criminal but rather are looked upon with respect by members of the academic community. The denial of criminal responsibility for their actions is often associated with a misperception of the attack as "OK" given the reputation or condition of the victim as being heavily intoxicated and appearing to be consenting to the assault. Moreover, the culture of university groups can often associate this type of behavior with male bonding, connecting the aggression and violence with sexuality and male prowess.

These dynamics play a role in the victim's desire to report their victimization, with research data showing that a significant majority refrain from contacting offices on campus that are designed to handle such incidents. Among the reasons for not reporting, victims of campus sexual violence maintain that they felt embarrassed or ashamed, didn't think anyone would believe them, or didn't feel the incident was serious enough to report. They also felt that nobody would take them seriously given the popularity and good reputation of the assailants. For these reasons, college campuses nationwide have developed educational programs for students, faculty, and campus employees, raising awareness of what sexual assault is and training on how to identify and prevent sexual assault and violence on campus, as well as programs designed to provide support for survivors of sexual assault and rape.

Source: Anderson, N., Svrluga, S., & Clement, S. (2019, October 15). Survey finds evidence of widespread sexual violence at 33 universities. The Washington Post. https://www.washingtonpost.com/local/education/survey-finds-evidence-of-widespread-sexual-violence-at-33-universities/2019/10/14/bd75dcde-ee82-11e9-b648-76bcf86eb67e_story.html

As we have seen, patterns of rape and sexual assault vary significantly, and the context of the crime and the relationship between the victim and the offender or offenders define the outcome of the criminal event, its recurrence, and the likelihood of the victim reporting the attack. Let's take a closer look at how these dynamics also shape our understanding of the various characteristics of rape and sexual assault offenders and their victims.

Rape and Sexual Assault Offenders and Their Victims
Characteristics of Rape Offenders

People who commit sexual offenses come from all walks of life, with variations in socioeconomic background, educational level, religion, and culture (Yoder et al., 2018). However, while there is no particular "type" of person who commits rape and sexual assault, statistics show that the overwhelming majority of offenders are male (about 95%) with about half of them being under the age of 30 (RAINN, 2020b). Moreover, as previously noted, rapists and sexual offenders tend to target victims they know, often violating relationships of trust, positions of power, and circles of profession and friendships. Studies have also shown that males who commit the crime of rape are often socialized into accepting gender stereotypes about women being weak, less dominant, or considered to be property and show signs of hostility toward women in general, are sexually aroused by portrayals of sexual violence against women, or are part of peer groups that support such beliefs (Stirling & Wignall, 2020).

Sexual offenders vary significantly in their patterns of attack, with some planning out their crime, stalking their victim, and even fantasizing about it. Other offenders attack spontaneously with very little thought to target selection. Research on sexual assault and rape reveals that alcohol and drug use is prevalent among offenders, as well as high rates of exposure to violent pornography. Moreover, about half of rape offenders have prior arrest records for other violent crimes and sexual assault (NARSOL, 2018). These variable trends make it particularly challenging for researchers to study sexual offenders given the variety of motivations for this crime, including criminogenic attitudes, pathological personality traits, anger, sexual deficit, hypersexuality, and arousal from dominance, power, violence, and control. In a classic study of rape offenders, the following is a typology of rapists based on motivation for attacking their victims and the meaning attached to the crime:

WHO DID IT? A TYPOLOGY OF RAPE OFFENDERS — BOX 5.2

Rape is a complex crime that involves a complex interplay between psychosocial characteristics of offenders that interplay with environmental variables as well as criminal history to create a context within which an attack occurs on the victim. For years, criminologists have studied convicted rapists in order to develop a better understanding of the various elements of motive, target selection, and methods of executing their crimes in order to distinguish between attackers, their level of aggression, and their potential for future forms of sexual deviance. The following categories of offender profiles provide us with a more clear depiction of this crime based on systematic themes articulated by convicted rapists:

RAPIST	MOTIVE	PATTERN OF OFFENDING
Anger-Retaliatory	Rage against the victim or against a category of individuals represented by the victim; rape is an expression of anger	—Attack by surprise —Little or no planning —Spontaneous
Power-Dominance	Exercise control over the victim; rape is used as a means to assert power	—Plan attack on victim —Involves a great deal of force and violence —Can include an initial seduction of the victim
Sadistic-Excitement	Inflict harm upon the victim; rape is a means of sexual stimulation derived from harming the victim	—Plan out attack —Fantasize about details of the crime —Sometimes record the crime using video or photos
Masculine Identity Conflict	Assert masculinity; rape is a means of establishing sexual adequacy	—Stalk victim for a period of time —Some planning involved in target selection —Continue to pursue and harass victim after the attack
Pathological Personality	Inappropriate expression of sexuality; rape reflects a misperception of norms governing sexual relations	—Spontaneous attack on victims —Little to no planning —Opportunistic and often select targets that are acquaintances

Source: Groth, A. N., & Birnbaum, H. J. (2013). Men who rape: The psychology of the offender. Springer.

Characteristics of Rape Victims

The study of rape and sexual assault victimization is not a straightforward task. Measuring the extent and prevalence of these crimes is complicated by the dynamic of low reporting of victimization, especially when the perpetrator is an acquaintance of the victim. Data is therefore skewed toward characteristics of victims of rape and sexual assault crimes committed by strangers, as these are more likely to be reported to law enforcement. Thus, we rely on multiple data sources such as the National Crime Victimization Survey, as well as the **National Intimate Partner and Sexual Violence Study** to provide a more comprehensive picture of rape and sexual assault victimization (Centers for Disease Control and Prevention. U.S. Department of Health and Human Services, 2020). These and other research endeavors are conducted by institutions throughout the United States and have offered us valuable information on the context and impact of sexual violence on the lives of victims. This insight has affected how community resources and law enforcement agencies, as well as educational institutions, can implement strategies to help prevent such crimes. Moreover, research on rape and sexual assault has also helped us better understand the experiences of victimization, who victims are, and how society can become better equipped to help them heal and recover.

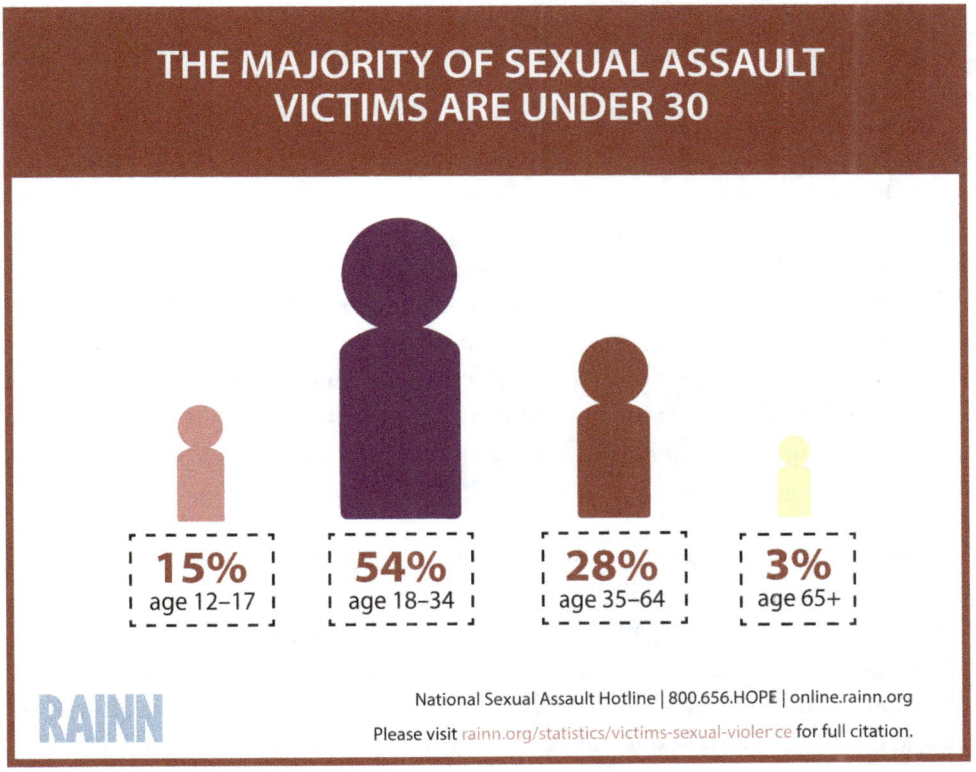

FIGURE 5.2 Age and Risk of Sexual Violence

Research shows that rape and sexual assault victims are overwhelmingly female, with women in their teens and early twenties being at a greater risk of victimization (see Figure 5.2). Moreover, studies show that single women living alone in urban residential, low-income neighborhoods also report higher rates of sexual assault and rape victimization (Konkel et al., 2019). While it is difficult to establish a full understanding of the magnitude and scope of rape and sexual assault victimization, self-report research surveys found the following (National Sexual Violence Resource Center, 2020):

- The self-reported incidence of rape or sexual assault more than doubled from 1.4 victimizations per 1,000 persons aged 12 or older in 2017 to 2.7 in 2018.
- Despite the increase in self-reports of rape and sexual assault, there was a decrease in reporting to police from 2017 to 2018. Forty percent of rapes and sexual assaults were reported to police in 2017, but only about 25% were reported to police in 2018.
- Approximately 1 in 5 (21.3% or an estimated 25.5 million) women in the United States reported completed or attempted rape at some point in their lifetime, including completed forced penetration, attempted forced penetration, or alcohol/drug-facilitated completed penetration.
- About 2.6% of U.S. men (an estimated 2.8 million) experienced completed or attempted rape victimization in their lifetime.
- Most female victims of completed rape (79.6%) experienced their first rape before the age of 25; 42.2% experienced their first completed rape before the age of 18 years.
- More than one quarter of male victims of completed rape (27.8%) experienced their first rape when they were 10 years of age or younger.
- The rate of revictimization for both male and female victims is high, with studies showing that as many as half of victims of sexual violence experience repeat victimization.
- There is a strong correlation between childhood sexual abuse and adult victimization.
- Victims experience a wide range of physical, emotional, and psychological effects of rape and sexual assault, including sexually transmitted diseases, urinary health problems, depression, anxiety, sleep disorders, post-traumatic stress disorder, eating disorders, guilt, fear, and intimacy and trust issues.

A widespread response to rape and sexual assault victimization must take into account these trends, with particular attention to the trauma and long-term impact of victimization, the low rate of reporting to law enforcement, and the correlations for repeat risk of victimization. Only then can we identify and implement a nationwide social movement to recognize sexual violence as an urgent and critical problem that needs to be addressed through social, cultural, and legal avenues that permeate various educational and institutional policies and practices.

Key Takeaways

Review the following list of bullet points for a quick overview of the key ideas and information in this chapter:

- Sexual assault offenses can take on many forms and are characterized by unwanted or nonconsensual sexual contact using physical violence, threat, or intimidation. These acts include sexual touching or fondling, forcing sexual acts upon a victim, attempted rape, and sexual penetration of a victim's body or rape. The crime of rape occurs in a variety of contexts, including date rape, spousal rape, same-sex rape, and gang rape.
- The vast majority of rapes and sexual assaults are perpetrated by individuals who are in some way acquainted with the victim. This, in turn, places particular categories of individuals such as those living on college campuses at a greater risk of victimization because of lifestyles that include partying, drinking, and attending sporting events. Studies show that an estimated 11.2% of all college students experience rape or sexual assault with physical force, violence, or incapacitation.
- While there is no particular type of sexual offender in terms of socioeconomic background, educational level, culture, religion, etc., studies show that the majority of offenders are male and about half of them are under the age of 30, with many of them possessing attitudes of hostility toward women, accepting gender stereotypes about women, or becoming sexually aroused by portrayals of sexual violence against women.
- According to various research and data sources, we can identify a significant majority of rape and sexual assault victims to be young women in their teens and early 20s. Moreover, studies show that single women living alone in urban residential, low-income neighborhoods also report higher rates of sexual assault and rape victimization. Rape and sexual assault impact victims in a significant way, with many victims reporting long-term physical, emotional, and psychological trauma.

Conclusion and Formal Summary Questions

In this chapter, we developed a typology of the different categories and types of rape and sexual assault. We learned that the context of this crime as well as the nature and characteristics of the offender and their relationship to the victim often define the distinct pattern of offense that emerges. Moreover, the motivation behind this crime of violence is diverse, and the manifestation of the sexual assault or rape offense is intricately connected to the meaning attached to the particular attack. Through our study of rape victimization, we see that this crime has the potential to affect victims in significant ways, and it is imperative to recognize the proactive role of education in preventing this crime, especially given the disproportionate number of victimizations that occur between offenders and victims who know each other.

- *Can you distinguish between the crimes of rape and sexual assault?*
- *Are you able to identify different patterns of rape and sexual assault offenses?*
- *Do you know what motivates sexual assault offenders and rapists?*
- *Who are the victims of rape and sexual assault?*

E-Resources

Visit the RAINN website at https://www.rainn.org/national-resources-sexual-assault-survivors-and-their-loved-ones to learn more about resources for survivors of rape and sexual assault.

Read the real-life horrors suffered by rape victims by getting to know their stories at https://www.healthyplace.com/abuse/rape/rape-victim-stories-real-stories-of-being-raped.

Check out this article that chronicles sexual assault in higher education and what is being done to prevent it: https://files.eric.ed.gov/fulltext/ED590263.pdf.

References

Beck, V. S., & Boys, S. K. (2019). Statutory rape laws. In F. P. Bernat, K. Frailing, L. Gelsthorpe, S. Kethineni, & L. Pasko (Eds.), *The encyclopedia of women and crime* (pp. 1–6). Wiley-Blackwell.

Centers for Disease Control and Prevention. U.S. Department of Health and Human Services. (2020). *Violence prevention: Sexual violence.* https://www.cdc.gov/violenceprevention/sexualviolence/index.html

CPS. (2020). Same sex sexual violence and sexual violence involving a trans complainant or suspect/defendant—toolkit for Prosecutors. *Legal Guidance.* https://www.cps.gov.uk/legal-guidance/same-sex-sexual-violence-and-sexual-violence-involving-trans-complainant-or

Crofts, M., Hill, K., Prokopiou, E., Armstrong-Hallam, S., Callaghan, J., & Barrick, R. (2017). *Safe spaces: Safeguarding students from violence and hate.*

England, Deborah. (2020). The history of marital rape laws. *Criminal Defense Lawyer.* https://www.criminaldefenselawyer.com/resources/criminal-defense/crime-penalties/marital-rape.htm

Federal Bureau of Investigation. Uniform Crime Report. (2018). *Crime in the United States.* https://ucr.fbi.gov/crime-in-the-u.s/2018/crime-in-the-u.s.-2018/topic-pages/rape

Gravelin, C. R., Biernat, M., & Bucher, C. E. (2019). Blaming the victim of acquaintance rape: Individual, situational, and sociocultural factors. *Frontiers in Psychology, 9,* 2422.

Hayes, B. E., O'Neal, E. N., & Hernandez, C. N. (2020). The sexual victimization of college students: A test of routine activity theory. *Crime & Delinquency,* https://doi.org/10.0011128720954347

Javaid, A. (2018). Out of place: Sexualities, sexual violence, and heteronormativity. *Aggression and Violent Behavior, 39,* 83–89.

Javaid, A. (2020). *Violence in everyday life: Power, gender and sexuality.* Zed Books Ltd.

Konkel, R. H., Hafemeister, A. J., & Daigle, L. E. (2019). The effects of risky places, motivated offenders, and social disorganization on sexual victimization: A microgeographic-and neighborhood-level examination. *Journal of Interpersonal Violence, 36*(17–18), 8409–8434. https://doi.org/10.0886260519849693

Lopez, E. C., Koss, M. P., & Kennon, K. (2019). Acquaintance rape. In F. P. Bernat, K. Frailing, L. Gelsthorpe, S. Kethineni, & L. Pasko (Eds.), *The encyclopedia of women and crime* (pp. 1–8). Wiley-Blackwell.

NARSOL. (2018). *Characteristics of sexual offenders*. https://narsol.org/2018/09/characteristics-of-sexual-offenders/

National Sexual Violence Resource Center. (2020). *Statistics*. https://www.nsvrc.org/statistics

Paul, A., & Mahesan, A. (2019). Date rape drugs in Las Vegas: Detection after the fact [11I]. *Obstetrics & Gynecology, 133*, 98S.

RAINN. (2020a). *Campus sexual violence: Statistics*. https://www.rainn.org/statistics/campus-sexual-violence

RAINN. (2020b). *Perpetrators of sexual violence*. https://www.rainn.org/statistics/perpetrators-sexual-violence

RAINN. (2020c). *Sexual assault*. https://www.rainn.org/articles/sexual-assault#:~:text=Some%20forms%20of%20sexual%20assault%20include%3A%201%20Attempted,of%20the%20victim%E2%80%99s%20body%2C%20also%20known%20as%20rape

Randhawa, K. B. (2019). Responses of resilience: The Delhi gang rape. In J. Rehman, A. Shahid, & M. Dickinson (Eds.), *The Asian yearbook of human rights and humanitarian law* (pp. 192–218). Brill Nijhoff.

Richards, V. R. W. A. L. (1995). *Intimate betrayal: Understanding and responding to the trauma of acquaintance rape*. SAGE Publications.

Stirling, J. L., Hills, P. J., & Wignall, L. (2020). Narrative approach to understand people's comprehension of acquaintance rape: The role of sex role stereotyping. *Psychology & Sexuality*, 1–18.

Tracy, N. (2020). Sexual assault, rape survivor stories. *HealthyPlace, Inc.* https://www.healthyplace.com/abuse/rape/sexual-assault-rape-survivor-stories

U.S. Equal Employment Opportunity Commission. (2020). *Sexual harassment*. https://www.eeoc.gov/sexual-harassment

Yoder, J. R., Leibowitz, G. S., & Peterson, L. (2018). Parental and peer attachment characteristics: Differentiating between youth sexual and non-sexual offenders and associations with sexual offense profiles. *Journal of Interpersonal Violence, 33*(17), 2643–2663.

Figure Credits

Fig. 5.1: Copyright © by Nederlandse Leeuw (CC BY-SA 4.0) at https://commons.wikimedia.org/wiki/File:Marital_rape_laws_by_country.svg.

Fig. 5.2: Copyright © by RAINN. https://www.rainn.org/statistics/victims-sexual-violence.

Chapter 6

Crimes of Interpersonal Violence

Robbery

Key Terms

Robbery
Institutional robbery
Transit robbery
Personal robbery
Mugging
Home invasion
Criminal subculture robbery
Market-related robbery
Status-related robbery
Personalistic robbery
Collective efficacy

Chapter Headings

1. Chapter opener
2. What is robbery?
3. Various patterns of robbery offenses
   3.1. Institutional robbery
   3.2. Personal robbery
   3.3. Home invasion
   3.4. Robbery for status
4. Robbery offenders and their victims
   4.1. Characteristics of robbers
   4.2. Characteristics of robbery victims
5. Chapter summary

Opening Questions

Before you begin the chapter, take a few minutes to reflect on the following questions:

1. *What images come to mind when you think of the term "robbery"?*
2. *Are there various different contexts in which robbery takes place?*
3. *Do the perpetrators of robbery have various motives and methods for their crimes?*
4. *Can victims of robbery have common characteristics?*

Chapter Objectives

After reading Chapter 6, students will be able to do the following:

- *Define the crime of robbery and describe what behavior it applies to*
- *Identify various typologies of robbery offenses*
- *Recognize who robbery offenders are and what motivates their crimes*
- *Create a typology of robbery victims and their various characteristics*

True Crime

Robbers steal, take, and threaten. They also assault, kill and commit other acts of harm. They are violent individuals whose crimes have the potential to escalate in a way that is unique to their actions. They target individuals and target buildings, homes, and banks. They are often masked but sometimes not masked at all. Robbery can be a mundane, everyday spontaneous crime involving snatching the purse off of a stranger on the street, or it can be a complex scheme to commit a bank heist involving elaborate planning. As such, a robbery offender can gain little to nothing at all in terms of money or reap millions of dollars in a matter of minutes. One interesting facet of robbery that is of a large scale is that it often involves an insider with some knowledge and information about the targeted location.

Such was the case in what is still the largest cash heist in American history. Masterminded by Allen Pace, a safety inspector for Dunbar Armored Trucking company in Los Angeles, the robbery took place on September 12, 1997. Pace manipulated the timing of security cameras and knew how they could be avoided. He used his keys to enter the armored car depot building, and he, along with five childhood friends recruited for the job, loaded millions of dollars into a U-Haul® truck awaiting them, after ambushing and assaulting and subduing several security guards one by one as they each took their lunch breaks right after midnight. Pace knew what he was doing and used his knowledge of the timing of security cameras, the date that the vault would be left open, and which bags of money contained the highest denominations and nonsequential bills to commit the heist, getting away with nearly $19 million. The gang of robbers eluded police for some time, concealing their millions through various schemes, property purchases, and phony businesses. However, they were all eventually caught when one of them used a stash of cash bound together with the original currency straps in a real estate deal. The broker became suspicious and called the police. This led to an arrest, confession, and the naming of his co-conspirators. Allen Pace was arrested, tried, and sentenced to 24 years in federal prison. The majority of the money continues to be unaccounted for (Malachi & Haswell, 2020).

What Is Robbery?

> *Sir Tristano spoke: "Stop! You are taking the great green pearl!" "Naturally!" said the voice from a point close behind. "That is the whole point of robbery: to acquire the victim's valuables!"*
> —John Vance, Author and Writer

Robbery is defined by UCR as the taking or attempted taking of anything of value from the care, custody, or control of a person or persons by force or threat of force or violence and/or by putting the victim in fear (Federal Bureau of Investigation. Uniform Crime Report, 2018). This definition sheds some important light on why this crime, apparently motivated by theft, is considered an interpersonal crime of violence, as the definition implies that there has to be a face-to-face confrontation between the victim and the offender. Thus, while the goal is to take something of monetary value, the law perceives that the harm to the victim is of greater importance, and therefore, the amount of punishment or the outcome of a case against a robbery offender is defined by the amount of force used and the resulting harm or jeopardy to the victim's life and well-being.

According to various data sources, robbers are more likely than any other type of violent crime offender to use a weapon, especially some type of firearm, with the UCR indicating strong-arm tactics used in 43%, firearms in 38.2%, knives or cutting instruments in 8.3% and other dangerous objects in 10.4% (Federal Bureau of Investigation. Uniform Crime Report, 2018). One very unique aspect of this crime is that unlike other crimes of interpersonal violence, such as homicide and assault, robbery offenders and their targeted victims are most likely to be strangers to one another and have no direct relationship (Kenny, 2020). Robbery is a crime that is often committed in a group context, with multiple offenders as described in our true crime chapter opener. Perhaps this is more so the case with large-scale offenses that are planned; nevertheless, a common aspect is for multiple offenders to be involved with differing roles played to execute the crime (Harding et al., 2019). For example, in the robbery of a convenience store, one offender may go into the store while another stays outside as a lookout or in a getaway car. Small-scale robberies can also escalate as the violent encounter between the victim and offender, the defense of self, and the presence of a weapon can produce a deadly outcome. With these multiple dynamics of difference within the context of robbery offenses, let's break this crime category down into different typologies of criminal behavior to better sort out its forms.

Various Patterns of Robbery Offenses

As we have noted before, the crime of robbery takes on many different forms depending on the situational context, the degree of planning and specialization, and the motive behind the crime, which, as we will see, is not always financial gain. While most robberies are spontaneous acts committed by offenders who engage in a variety of criminal activities, others are planned and sophisticated acts of professional thieves. According to the UCR, robbery offenses have declined over the past decade or so, with an estimated 282,061 robberies nationwide in 2018, down 31% from the 2009 estimate (Federal Bureau of Investigation. Uniform Crime Report, 2018). Let's take a closer look at these patterns of robbery offenses in some detail within the context of institutional robbery, home invasion, personal robbery, and robbery for status.

Institutional Robbery

The crime of robbery often conjures up images of individuals or groups of individuals entering some type of retail store or business, such as a bank, liquor store, jewelry, or pawn shop, and demanding money or something of value using force or threat of force. This type of robbery is referred to as **institutional robbery**, theft by force that takes place in commercial settings. Also included here is what we call **transit robbery**, an attack on a vehicle or armored truck that provides cash collection services. Targets selected are often businesses in secluded areas and underprivileged neighborhoods where there is less likelihood of security systems and measures for safety, as well as less customer traffic (Caplan et al., 2020). Moreover, robbers select commercial targets that they perceive as having easy and quick access to cash or other items of value.

Organized institutional robberies are less common than spontaneous acts committed by repeat chronic offenders and often involve more than one or two conspirators. They target larger cash outputs or other expensive items, such as jewelry, and have the potential to escalate in violence (Walsh, 2019). As mentioned earlier, robbery is the most likely violent crime category to involve the use of a weapon, and most large-scale institutional robberies involve offenders who use firearms, although less sophisticated offenders commonly have weapons such as knives, clubs, and baseball bats. Relative to other forms of robbery, institutional robberies comprise a fairly small percentage of all robberies (see Figure 6.1). This is an interesting dynamic given that this is probably the most likely form of robbery to be reported to police (Cook & Zhang, 2019). Let's turn now to a form of robbery that is often the least likely to be reported, personal robbery.

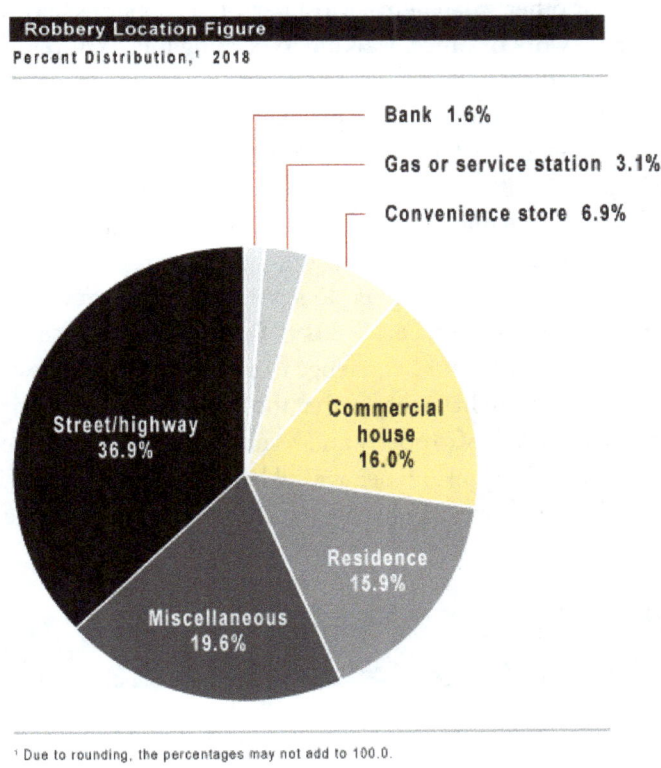

FIGURE 6.1   The Distribution of Different Types of Robbery

Personal Robbery

Studies show that the overwhelming majority of robberies that take place are what we refer to as **personal robbery**, a robbery that occurs in a neighborhood, public transportation, parking lot, or street setting. The Bureau of Justice Statistics defines personal robbery as the completed or attempted theft, directly from a person, of property or cash by force or threat of force, with or without a weapon, and with or without injury (Bureau of Justice Statistics, Office of Justice Programs, 2020). This is also sometimes called **mugging**, where an assailant or multiple assailants approach a victim and take their belongings by force or threat of force with or without the use or presence of a weapon. The key here is that the victim is placed in fear of danger or bodily harm if they do not comply with the assailant. According to research, robbers select victims who are perceived to be more vulnerable, offering less resistance and likely to be compliant (Adeyemi, 2020; Kenny, 2020). They also target victims who are likely to have something of value in their possession, such as a wallet, cash, jewelry, or other small items. Most personal robberies take place while a victim is walking to their car from work or office, walking in parking lots of stores and malls, at or near an ATM, and on public transportations such as metro and train stations (Li et al., 2019).

According to the UCR, the average value of property stolen in a personal robbery is around $1,739, representing a significant portion of overall robbery offenses (Federal Bureau of Investigation. Uniform Crime Report, 2018). This, however, does not represent the overall total of personal robberies committed, as this particular crime of violence is significantly underreported, especially when the victim is male. According to the NCVS, although men are more likely than women to be the victims of personal robbery, they are less likely to report their victimization, with as many as 50% of robberies going unreported (Zaykowski et al., 2019). Perhaps it is because the crime represents a failure to protect one's own property and a challenge to a male victim's sense of manhood. Studies conducted on robbery victimization have shown that the crime represents a frightening, traumatic experience that goes beyond the loss of property and results in long-term psychological distress and an enduring effect on the victim's social and behavioral health and well-being (Fuller & Ng, 2017). Box 6.1 illustrates the unfolding events of a robbery and its traumatic outcome:

WHO DID IT? A ROBBER AMONG US — BOX 6.1

It was an ordinary Sunday evening around 7:30 p.m. on a hot August day in Alexandria, Virginia, a very nice suburb just a few miles south of Washington, D.C. My neighborhood was on a major road off of a main highway, busy but still very quaint, safe, and friendly. I was about 7 years old, and my grandparents were visiting from Egypt, their native hometown, and staying with us for the summer. I remember we were always on the go, taking them places, visiting interesting sites, and accepting dinner invitations from friends and other relatives who lived close by. It was a big deal for them to be visiting us, their first time in the United States!

We were always out and about, especially on weekends, but one night, on a Sunday after an evening church service, my grandma was feeling sick, so we decided to go straight home instead of going out to eat. Our normal 10:00 p.m. arrival at home was much earlier, and my dad pulled into our driveway and noticed that there were some lights left on. That was a big deal in the late 1970s, as electricity was an expensive commodity, and you just didn't leave lights on for no reason. My brother, who was 2 years older than me, and I started arguing about who left the lights on; my mom was helping my grandparents get out of the car, and my dad was rushing ahead of us to open the door for everyone, and of course, turn off the extra lights. What happened next changed my life forever.

As we walked from our driveway to the front door, my brother and I still arguing, and my father opening the screen door and holding the door open for all of us to go in, I saw a very large man with a ski mask screaming and waving a knife in one hand, holding a gun and what looked like a pillowcase or sack in the other, running toward us from the top of the stairs in our house. He pushed my mom aside, who was going in first. I remember him running off, sort of running away from us, as if startled by our untimely arrival. I also remember my mom screaming for help, and my grandmother yelling, "He has a gun, he has a gun," and my grandfather, who was in his late 70s, chasing after the man. I was frozen, stunned, fearful, and couldn't even go in my house. Later that evening, we found out that the robber jumped a neighbor's fence down the street and broke his leg. Police dogs found him almost immediately, and we got back the items he had stolen, mostly jewelry and some cash that was in that pillowcase he had. Nothing was lost, not a single thing—except for the next decades of my own personal feelings of safety, security, and peace. Images of that day are so vivid in my mind, they keep me nervous and anxious almost always when I am alone, especially at night. I have a significant fear every time I enter my home, remembering the events of that day. Every single home or dwelling I have lived in since has had extensive security alarms systems. It has been personally and financially burdensome. Robbery is traumatic, and the trauma is permanent. This is my story and my name is Aida. I am a college professor, wife, mother, and coauthor of this textbook. I am also a robbery victim.

Source: Aida Y. Hass-Wisecup

Personal robbery is indeed a traumatic experience for victims. This crime often leads to long-term psychological effects, such as reliving the crime, flashbacks, anxiety, fear, and depression. We turn now to another form of robbery that also involves a significant amount of trauma to its victims, home invasion.

Home Invasion

Another, less common type of robbery that takes place, occurs when an intruder enters an individual's home or residence unlawfully or by force, restrains the occupants, and proceeds to steal items from the home or ransack the place. This type of robbery is known as a **home invasion.** This crime is defined as a separate type of robbery in various jurisdictions across the United States, while some jurisdictions consider it a subcategory of robbery. There are several common motives behind the crime of home invasion and not just the theft of goods or items of value. Very often, the intruder can be looking for something specific, such as drugs or money from a drug deal gone bad, weapons, incriminating evidence in a specific case, or other items of interest. In some cases, the home invasion is a form of retaliation against a domestic partner or rival gang member, targeting an individual for violence and robbing the dwelling during the criminal event (Klofas et al., 2019). Home invasions can also involve multiple intruders, and the robbery becomes incidental to other types of crimes, such as assault, rape, and homicide. For this reason, statistics on home invasions are difficult to determine as the crimes recorded are the more serious outcomes discovered by investigators and law enforcement officers on the scene (Byron et al., 2018). Moreover, the crime is sometimes undiscovered as both victims and offenders are part of an overall illegal crime ring or criminal transaction that led to the events of the home invasion.

Home invasion is a unique crime category that involves various elements of different crimes, including breaking and entering and burglary (discussed in our next chapter), as well as robbery since there is a face-to-face confrontation between the victim and offender or offenders. According to the Arizona State University's Center for Problem-Oriented Policing, home invasion robberies have the following five features (Heinonen & Eck, 2012):

- Offender entry is forced and/or unauthorized
- Offenders seek confrontation
- Confrontation occurs inside dwellings
- Offenders use violence and/or the threat of violence
- Offenders demand and take money and/or property

Home invasions are sometimes entangled with another form of robbery that is specific to the criminal subculture of violence that we discussed in Chapter 4. Let's take a look now at our final typology of robbery, robbery for status.

Robbery and the Criminal Subculture

Although the primary motive behind the various robbery typologies we have discussed so far has been the acquisition of tangible, material goods and possessions, a motive fueled by greed and the desire for quick and "easy" money, some robberies are motivated by a complexity of entanglements with the violation of the norms and rules of a street subculture (Kaufman, 2017). These robberies are often a response to situations created by criminal transactions involving street gangs, drug dealers, and other types of criminals, who, through various interactions, fail to adhere to the codes and regulations of a criminal subculture of violence, drug trafficking, and territorial wars (Harding et al., 2019). These types of violations can take on several different characteristics, including a challenge to one's sense of respect and street reputation, a challenge to one's position in the illegitimate economy, or a challenge to one's personal or family safety or honor. Table 6.1 provides an overview of these typologies of robbery offenses:

TABLE 6.1 **ROBBERY AND THE CRIMINAL SUBCULTURE**

Typology of Robbery	Elements of the Crime
Market-Related Robbery	• Robberies that occur to settle disputes arising between rival gang members, turf wars, etc. • Robberies that take place when drug deals go wrong, money is stolen, goods are not delivered, etc.
Status-Related Robbery	• Robberies that represent a means to restore reputation on the street when an individual has been disrespected or offended
Personalistic Robbery	• Robberies that result from incidents of personal injury or harm to oneself or to a family member as a method of retaliation and justice

Source: Jacobs, B. A., & Wright, R. (2006). Street justice: Retaliation in the criminal underworld. The British Journal of Sociology 58, 506–507.

Robbery is clearly a crime of interpersonal violence, regardless of the context, motive, or outcome, the presence of danger and threat is always there, and the resulting harm to victims can be devastating and long term. With that in mind, let's take a closer look at robbery offenders and their victims.

Robbery Offenders and Their Victims
Characteristics of Robbery Offenders

Once again, we must remember that offender profiles of criminal behavior must be approached with caution, as the information gathered is primarily based on arrest data and therefore reflects that trend rather than a complete picture of crime. With regard to the crime of robbery, the majority of offenders arrested are disproportionately male, disadvantaged members of minority groups. These statistics are very skewed, as previously stated, by reporting patterns of robbery and neighborhood profiling. Moreover, robbery offenders are fairly young, with approximately 60% between the ages of 15 and 24, and approximately 30% are under the age of 18 (Law Library—American Law and Legal Information, 2020).

Although a significant majority of robberies involve the use of a weapon as noted earlier in this chapter, most robbers are not offense specialists who engage in high-dollar commercial robbery as their sole criminal activity. Rather, most robbers are amateurs who actually commit a variety of other criminal offenses, such as shoplifting, burglary, and other forms of theft. Research studies show that the typical robber is a spontaneous offender who attacks as an opportunity presents itself (Connealy & Piza, 2019). This can be prompted by the need for quick cash to buy drugs or just a situational response to the presence of an opportunity to steal by force, with very little thinking about the consequences or getting caught (Connealy & Piza, 2019). Robbers can also become habitual offenders who steal by force as a lifestyle to make money. These are recurrent violent thieves who may follow a specific pattern of robbery, which can involve some planning and a repeat selection of similar targets, such as gas stations and convenience stores (Wüllenweber & Burrell, 2020). Professional robbers also commit robbery as a source of livelihood; however, their lifestyles are significantly more lavish and their crimes involve a great deal of planning in terms of target selection, timing, and the anticipation of the outcome (Scientific Articles Kazakhstan, 2020). With this diversity of robbery offender profiles, it becomes quite clear that robbery victimization is also subject to similar variations in terms of victim profile. Let's take a look at some of the characteristics of individuals and places targeted by robbery offenders.

Characteristics of Robbery Victims

Once again, we must remember to approach the study of robbery victimization with the understanding that the profile of robbery victims is based on the reporting of robbery to law enforcement and the collection of data on the victim. This dynamic is complicated by the fact that robbery, as previously mentioned, is significantly underreported. Relying on official data sources and victimization surveys can help us better develop a profile of robbery victims. With this in mind, one major trend in robbery victimization reveals that target selection is very often linked to both individual traits, as well as location traits. For this reason, we will examine the characteristics of robbery victims in the context of elements involving both physical features of place and attributes of individual victims. One consistent finding, however, is that robbers select targets who in some way appear vulnerable and who are expected to produce a better "yield" (Bernasco et al., 2017).

Studies of trends in robbery victimization reveal that those at greatest risk are African American and Hispanic males between the ages of 25 and 30 (National Center for Victims of Crime & United States of America, 2019). Moreover, single persons, those with lower incomes, and recent movers appear to be targeted for robbery more often than individuals who live in multiple dwelling homes in higher income neighborhoods. Robbery victimization is also higher in urban communities, especially in neighborhoods that are socially disorganized, have high rates of residential mobility, lower security measures in homes and buildings, and little **collective efficacy**, the ability of people in a community to band together to control the behavior of individuals and increase safety. According to the NCVS, robbery victims are more likely than other violent crime victims to encounter multiple offenders and offenders with weapons, as well as offenders who are strangers (U.S. Department of Justice, Office of Justice Programs, n.d.).

The outcome of robbery varies and can involve a variety of experiences that include physical and emotional harm, as well as psychological trauma and the additional loss of property and financial hardship. Robbery victims may underestimate their own feelings and sense of personal loss and security, as this crime can take place in one's own "safe space," such as home, workplace, or neighborhood. Box 6.2 features a U.S. Department of Justice spotlight on robbery victims in the workplace, some of the struggles they face, and some recommendations for coping with their victimization.

THE REAL DEAL: THE DYNAMICS OF ROBBERY VICTIMIZATION IN THE WORKPLACE — BOX 6.2

You've all seen a pebble drop into a pool of water and noticed the ripples which are produced by the impact of that pebble. A similar ripple occurs from person to person when a crime occurs. As an employee, you have been exposed to a crime in your work setting. Even if you were not directly confronted during the incident, you may experience reactions from your exposure to the robbery or attempted robbery. How people react to these events varies from person to person and is affected by individual factors such as how you usually handle stressful situations and what kind of support you have both inside and outside of work.

Your reaction may be immediate or may be delayed. You may experience symptoms that are physical, emotional, or cognitive (involving your thinking ability). It is important to realize that these are normal feelings, behaviors and reactions to an abnormal event. Employees and customers who have been through a robbery or an attempted robbery report having a variety of experiences.

> FEAR — They may be afraid of leaving a bank or office, being in public, or being re-victimized. They are afraid the robber will find them or will come back.
> HYPER-ALERTNESS — They find that they startle easily: they "jump" when suddenly approached by customers or when they hear loud sounds.
> GUILT — They feel that they could have done something differently; they wonder if they could have prevented the incident, or if they didn't do something they should have.
> ANGER — They are enraged that their life has been disrupted and that they no longer feel safe or in control.
> ISOLATION — They feel that they are the only ones who are having reactions to the event; they feel isolated from family and friends, and they feel no one can understand what they have been through.

EMOTIONAL AND PHYSICAL RESPONSES — Irritability, which may be directed at family and friends; loss of motivation—feeling blue or depressed; apathy and indifference; chronic fatigue and flashbacks.

Awareness and understanding are crucial in beginning to deal effectively with this event in your life. You can begin by being aware that you MAY react in some of the ways we have discussed. Remember that your reactions are normal. You may find that you react to sights, sounds, smells, and textures that were present at the time of the crime and which remind you of the incident. Sometimes being exposed to a traumatic event may trigger memories of past events in your life. Perhaps you have been victimized before, or have lost someone close to you. You may once again find yourself experiencing feelings related to these earlier events. Feelings of vulnerability and helplessness are frequent after victimization. One of the first things to pay attention to is your need to feel safe again. Take any precaution which will make you feel safer. Some examples might include:

(Continued)

- Having someone drive you to work and pick you up at the end of the day, until you are comfortable traveling yourself.
- Following procedures that will protect you from as much risk as possible at work or at home.
- Making your daily schedule as predictable and routine as possible for a while to return some control and stability in your life.

Co-workers and family can also help in these ways:
- Allow the victim to talk about the event long after you are tired of hearing about it. Don't minimize the fear or seriousness of the event as a way of "helping". This may lead the victim to feel that you don't understand the event or sympathize with fears that normally occur after such a traumatic event.
- Don't ask "why" questions. They put the blame on the victim. Even though you may want to "make it all better," understand that there is a healing process that victims must work through.
- Temporary sexual dysfunction is not an unusual reaction for victims.
- A desire for extra security precautions is normal. Examples may be locking house and car doors, using night lights, leaving radios and televisions on.

It is important to allow yourself time to heal at your own pace. It is important that you actively seek support from your family, friends, co-workers, and possibly professional counseling and victim support groups.

Source: U.S. Department of Justice, The United States Attorney's Office, Central District of California. Robbery victims. Retrieved from https://www.justice.gov/usao-cdca/victimwitness/robbery-victims

Key Takeaways

Review the following list of bullet points for a quick overview of the key ideas and information in this chapter:

- Robbery is a crime of interpersonal violence that involves a face-to-face confrontation between the victim and the offender. It involves the use of force or threat of force and violence to take something of value from the victim's possession. Robbery can involve an armed or unarmed assailant, and the property taken can either be of little or great value. The outcome of the crime in terms of seriousness has more to do with the harm to the victim rather than the amount or value of the property taken.
- Various typologies of robbery emerge through the defining nature of the context within which this crime takes place. Our study of motive, selection of target, pattern of criminal offending, and degree of sophistication of the crime have yielded categories based on institutional robbery, home invasion, personal robbery, and robbery for status.
- Studies show that the majority of robbery offenders are not specialists who engage in robbery as their sole criminal activity but rather amateurs who actually commit a variety of other criminal offenses and are spontaneous offenders who attack as an opportunity presents itself.
- Robbery victimization is characterized by target selection involving offender traits, as well as the physical features of the location. Robbery risk is greatest for young, minority males,

as well as those who appear to be vulnerable and have a high yield probability. Robbery is also more prevalent in areas that are marked by high rates of social disorganization and low neighborhood collective efficacy.

Conclusion and Formal Summary Questions

This chapter helped us develop a better understanding of the crime of robbery. We learned that the nature and characteristics of this crime place it in the category of interpersonal violence because of its potential for harm to victims as well as its confrontational qualities. Moreover, although the primary motivation behind this crime of violence is financial or monetary gain, robbery offenders have a variety of methods, degrees of planning and sophistication, and elements of criminal status associated with their offenses. Through our study of robbery victimization, we see that this crime has the potential to affect people in a variety of ways and that robbery victimization takes place in various contexts including the streets, homes, neighborhoods, workplaces, and commercial settings. These places all involve the presence of individuals, and therefore, the effect of robbery can be very traumatic, and victims can experience the need for long-term physical and emotional care and support.

- *Do you have a better understanding of robbery as a crime of interpersonal violence?*
- *Can you identify the specific elements that characterize robbery?*
- *Are you able to describe the various contexts within which robbery takes place?*
- *Can you tell what robbery offenders have in common?*
- *Who are robbery victims and how does this crime affect them both socially and psychologically?*

E-Resources

For more resources on how to help victims of robbery, visit the U.S. Department of Justice Office of Justice Programs, *Office for Victims of Crime* website at https://ovc.ojp.gov/sites/g/files/xyckuh226/files/pubs/helpseries/HelpBrochure_Robbery.html.

Get to know a professional bank robber a little better by reading about his story at https://www.independent.co.uk/news/world/americas/successful-bank-robber-who-never-got-caught-explains-his-modus-operandi-in-fascinating-ama-10312893.html.

Check out this article to learn more about serendipity and its role in robbery target selection: http://www.d-ddaily.com/images/6-1-15_Serendipity%20in%20Robbery%20Target%20Selection%20Jacobs%202010.pdf.

References

Adeyemi, O. E. (2020). Gender and victimization: A global analysis of vulnerability. In J. O. Ayodele (Ed.), *Global perspectives on victimization analysis and prevention* (pp. 114–133). IGI Global.

Bernasco, W., Ruiter, S., & Block, R. (2017). Do street robbery location choices vary over time of day or day of week? A test in Chicago. *Journal of Research in Crime and Delinquency, 54*(2), 244–275.

Bureau of Justice Statistics, Office of Justice Programs. (2020, August 18). *Home page.* https://www.bjs.gov/index.cfm?ty=tp&tid=313

Byron, R. A., Molidor, W. S., & Cantu, A. (2018). US newspapers' portrayals of home invasion crime. *The Howard Journal of Crime and Justice, 57*(2), 250–277.

Caplan, J. M., Kennedy, L. W., Piza, E. L., & Barnum, J. D. (2020). Using vulnerability and exposure to improve robbery prediction and target area selection. *Applied Spatial Analysis and Policy, 13*(1), 113–136.

Connealy, N. T., & Piza, E. L. (2019). Risk factor and high-risk place variations across different robbery targets in Denver, Colorado. *Journal of Criminal Justice, 60*, 47–56.

Cooke, E. M., & Zhang, Y. (2019). A multilevel analysis of factors related to business robbery clearance rates in a large city in Texas. *Policing: An International Journal, 43*, 213–228.

Federal Bureau of Investigation. Uniform Crime Report. (2018). *Crime in the United States.* https://ucr.fbi.gov/crime-in-the-u.s/2018/crime-in-the-u.s.-2018/topic-pages/robbery

Fuller, G., & Ng, S. (2017). Returning to work after armed robbery in the workplace. *Trends and Issues in Crime and Criminal Justice,* (529), 1.

Harding, S., Deuchar, R., Densley, J., & McLean, R. (2019). A typology of street robbery and gang organization: Insights from qualitative research in Scotland. *The British Journal of Criminology, 59*(4), 879–897.

Heinonen, J.A. & Eck, J.E. (2012). *Home invasion robbery.* Arizona State University. Center for Problem-Oriented Policing. https://popcenter.asu.edu/content/home-invasion-robbery-0

Kaufman, J. M. (2017). *Anomie, strain and subcultural theories of crime.* Routledge.

Kenny, J. F. (2020). Lurking in the shadows: Stranger danger and target selection. In S. Kendzior (Ed.), *Hiding in plain sight* (pp. 45–58). Palgrave Macmillan, Cham.

Klofas, J., Altheimer, I., & Petitti, N. (2019). *Retaliatory violent disputes.* CNA Corporation.

Law Library—American Law and Legal Information. (2020). *Robbery: Characteristics of offenders.* https://law.jrank.org/pages/1986/Robbery-Characteristics-offenders.html

Li, Y. S., & Qi, M. L. (2019). An approach for understanding offender modus operandi to detect serial robbery crimes. *Journal of Computational Science, 36*, 101024.

Malachi, B. & Haswell, J. (2020, March 26). *The greatest bank heists in history.* https://lulz.com/the-greatest-bank-heists-in-history-9262/

National Center for Victims of Crime & United States of America. (2019). *OVC help series for victims of crime: Robbery.*

Scientific Articles Kazakhstan. (2020, August 25). *Characteristics of robbery perpetrators.* https://articlekz.com/en/article/14431

U.S. Department of Justice, Office of Justice Programs. (n.d.). *National Crime Victimization Survey: Robbery.* https://www.bjs.gov/index.cfm?ty=tp&tid=313

Walsh, D. (2019). *Heavy business: Commercial burglary and robbery.* Routledge.

Wüllenweber, S., & Burrell, A. (2020). Offence characteristics: a comparison of lone, duo, and 3+ perpetrator robbery offences. *Psychology, Crime & Law,* 1–18.

Zaykowski, H., Allain, E. C., & Campagna, L. M. (2019). Examining the paradox of crime reporting: Are disadvantaged victims more likely to report to the police? *Law & Society Review, 53*(4), 1305–1340.

Figure Credits

Fig. 6.1: Source: https://ucr.fbi.gov/crime-in-the-u.s/2018/crime-in-the-u.s.-2018/topic-pages/robbery.

Property and Drug Crime Profiles

MODULE 3

Chapter 7

Property Crime

Key Terms

Antwerp World Diamond Centre (AWDC)
Property crime
Burglary
Larceny-theft
Motor vehicle theft
Arson
Arson investigation
Station Fire
National Crime Victimization Survey (NCVS)

Opening Questions

Before you begin the chapter, take a few minutes to reflect on the following questions:

1. *How is property crime defined?*
2. *What are the major types of property crime?*
3. *How do property crime offenders target potential victims?*

True Crime

In the middle of Antwerp, Belgium's, diamond district sits the **Antwerp World Diamond Centre (AWDC)**—the central organization at the core of the world's diamond trade. Antwerp's diamond district is one of the densest concentrations of wealth in the world and regularly generates billions of dollars in revenue each year. Among other activities, the AWDC housed numerous offices for hundreds of diamond vendors and safeguarded hundreds of millions of dollars

Chapter Headings

1. Chapter opener
2. What is property crime?
3. The scope and scale of property crime
4. Property crime subtypes
    4.1. Burglary
    4.2. Larceny-theft
    4.3. Motor vehicle theft
    4.4. Arson
5. Property crime characteristics
6. Chapter summary

Chapter Objectives

After reading Chapter 7, students will be able to do the following:

- *Define property crime*
- *Understand the scope of the property crime*
- *Describe the characteristics of property crimes*

of diamonds, gold, silver, precious gems, and jewelry in a vault complete with seismic sensors and infrared detectors, which was housed two stories underground.

Early the morning of Monday, February 17, 2003, guards at the AWDC made the shocking discovery that the ultra-high-security vault—thought to be one of the world's most complex and impenetrable—had been broken into, with the door left ajar and the floor strewn with cash, jewelry, and over 100 now empty or ransacked safe deposit boxes. A thief, or thieves, had broken into the vault sometime over the weekend and stolen over $100 million in loose diamonds, gold, and other jewelry without setting off any alarms or sensors (in fact, the alarm still showed as "fully functional" at the monitoring company's headquarters) or attracting any attention from security guards, citizens, or the police (Davis, 2009). It was a nearly perfect forcible entry burglary, with one exception. In their haste to dispose of a trash bag full of incriminating evidence, the thieves had tossed the trash into a thicket of brush in an area where they supposed it would never be noticed rather than burn it. Unfortunately, a property owner discovered the suspicious-looking trash and called the police. Antwerp's special Diamond Police immediately realized the thieves had provided them with a huge break; contained within the trash were documents that eventually incriminated Leonardo Notarbartolo, an Italian citizen, and several of his associates in what was dubbed the "crime of the century." Notarbartolo had in fact rented an office in the AWDC several years prior to the burglary to establish his cover as a low-level diamond merchant. By the time of the AWDC theft, Notarbartolo was a well-established career thief and ringleader of a group of thieves known as the School of Turin. While Notarbartolo was eventually sentenced to just 10 years in prison, and several of his associates received 5-year terms, none of the stolen diamonds, gold, or jewelry has ever been recovered.

What Is Property Crime?

Property crime is one of the two major categories of crime that law enforcement agencies collect data on and closely track on an annual basis, the other category being violent crime. Property crimes are those acts that involve the unlawful "taking of money or property" or the unlawful "destruction of property" (Federal Bureau of Investigation, 2018). Importantly, property crimes where money or property is unlawfully taken do not involve force or the threat of force—differentiating them from the violent crimes of robbery or extortion in which property is taken via force or the threat of force. You should note that the FBI's UCR only collects data on four major property crimes: burglary, larceny-theft, motor vehicle theft, and arson. For that reason, our focus in this chapter will be confined to those four property crime subtypes. However, you should note that there are other property crimes, such as vandalism, and property crimes that occur virtually, which are covered in more detail in the chapter on cybercrime (Chapter 9).

The Scope and Scale of Property Crime

Like violent crime, property crime is closely tracked in the United States, which allows us to examine things like the total volume of property crime, the number of victimizations and arrests, and year-over-year trends and rates. The breadth and quality of the official property crime data set the study of property (and violent) crime apart from other crime types detailed in this book, such as green crimes, state crime, organized crime, and cybercrime, which are not officially tracked and are thus much more difficult to analyze and compare.

In 2018, there were 7,196,045 property crime offenses recorded in the FBI's official UCR report. This compares to just 1.2 million violent crimes (Federal Bureau of Investigation, 2018). Thus, on an annual basis, it is common for the total amount of property crime to exceed violent crime by at least a factor of five if not more; in other words, property crime occurs far more frequently in the United States than violent crime, and you are much more likely to be a victim of a property crime at some point in your life than a violent crime. Importantly, you should note that the "official" data is not a complete accounting of ALL crime that occurs; each year, there is a significant percentage of property (and violent) crimes that are never reported, not recorded, etc. Thus, official data *undercounts* the total amount of crime that occurs. Take, for example, the violent crime of robbery (which involves taking property or money via force or threat of force); although this is not a property crime, the underreporting that takes place exemplifies the underreporting that goes on for nearly all types of crime. For every 1,000 robberies that take place, it is estimated that only about 619 are reported (RAINN, n.d.). One would imagine people would be *more* not less likely to report a violent crime like robbery than a nonviolent property crime.

REAL DEAL: THE ANATOMY OF DECLINING PROPERTY CRIME RATES — BOX 7.1

Importantly, the 7.1 million property crimes reported in 2018 reflected a 6.3% decrease from 2017 and a 22% decline from 2008 (Federal Bureau of Investigation, 2018). The 2018 property crime rate was 2,199 per 100,000 inhabitants, lower by nearly 7% from the prior year and more than 27% lower than in 2008. These trends are positive: overall property crime is decreasing—or at least it appears to be. But it's important to recognize that over the past 10 years, our reliance on, and use of, Internet technologies to conduct business, communicate, share information, and engage in commerce has grown exponentially as has the amount of cybercrime and the number of cybercrime victimizations. It is far easier and more lucrative today for criminals to engage in cybercrimes, many of which are variations of traditional property crimes (i.e., cyber theft, identity theft). As detailed in the chapter on cybercrime, it is harder to detect, investigate, and prosecute cybercrimes; a significant number go unnoticed and are never detected; even if they are detected, cybercrimes are highly likely to go unreported to the police, especially by individual victims. All of this is to say that while property crime incidents and rates appear to be decreasing, it may be because more and more criminal activity is moving online and escaping our notice. It's worth noting as well that we do an extremely poor job of collecting official data on cybercrime incidents.

Thus, it is fairly safe to bet that the trend in unreported thefts and burglaries is far higher than in the robbery example.

The financial harm caused by property crimes in the United States in 2018 was estimated to be north of $16 billion, again, this sum is lower than the actual total value of all property crimes, which is ultimately unknowable but highlights the significant burden these crimes place on individuals and businesses. It should be noted that there were only 1,167,296 arrests of property crime offenders in 2018 (arrest rate 361 per 100,000)—meaning only 17% of property crimes were officially cleared by arrests (or exceptional means) in 2018 (Federal Bureau of Investigation, 2018).

Comparing the amount of crime in the United States to other countries is difficult. The United States has a much larger population than most nations, and of those nations that are comparable in terms of population (or that are larger), such as China, Russia, India, and Brazil, their data is often not adequate or reliable (or may be nonexistent). Differences in legal systems and investigative techniques also complicate comparisons. We can look at some European Union member nations—but they are so much smaller in terms of their populations than the United States that comparisons often don't mean much. For example, Spain reported only 168,000 thefts in all of 2018—a small fraction of the amount in the United States. One might argue a comparison of rates would be fairer, but Spain calculated a reported 360 thefts per 1,000 inhabitants (Eurostat, n.d.). versus the United States' rate of 1,594 per 100,000 people—different rate calculations (1,000 v. 100,000) make comparisons difficult. The takeaway is that the United States has far more crime than other countries for which we have data, but it is also a significantly larger country in terms of population, with far more opportunities for offenders to engage in criminal activity.

Property Crime Subtypes

The four major property crimes are burglary, larceny-theft, motor vehicle theft, and arson. We turn to each of them for closer examination now.

Burglary

Burglary is defined as the "unlawful entry of a structure to commit a felony or theft" (Federal Bureau of Investigation, 2018). The FBI UCR clarifies further that "to classify an offense as a burglary, the use of force to gain entry need not have occurred" (Federal Bureau of Investigation, 2018). The UCR further identifies three subtypes of burglaries: those involving forcible entry (e.g., breaking a window to access a business), those involving unlawful entry with no force (e.g., walking into a warehouse through an unlocked door), and burglaries with an "attempted forcible entry" (Federal Bureau of Investigation, 2018). As you continue your studies, you may enroll in law classes and will learn the intricacies of definitions and legalese; for now, it is important only to note that the word "structure" within the definition of burglary has very specific meanings within the law, which have been developed over time via various criminal court cases (some of which are quite interesting). The FBI UCR defines a "structure" as any "house, apartment, barn, house trailer, or houseboat *when used as a permanent dwelling* (emphasis added), office, railroad car (but not automobile), stable, or vessel (i.e., ship)" (Federal Bureau of Investigation, 2018).

There were approximately 1,230,149 recorded burglaries in 2018—representing 17% of all property crimes. Nearly 65% of all burglaries were of residences (i.e., houses, apartments). The number of burglaries was down 11% from 2017 and 44% from 2009—a stunning decline given how many burglars target homes. What accounts for this decline? One possibility is linked to the increasing prevalence over the past decade of high-quality, super-affordable home security video cameras and security systems (i.e., Ring doorbells, Nest cameras). These may be acting as a deterrent given how many people now own some version of them—and the fact that they can be monitored remotely in real time and record high-definition video and still images to the "cloud." Another factor contributing to the decline may be changes in how people work: more people working remotely from home means fewer unoccupied residences. Finally, a third potential contributor to the decline in burglaries is—as noted earlier—the opportunity to engage in cyber forms of theft.

Of the burglaries that did occur in 2018, 33% of them were daytime burglaries; 56% were of the forcible entry variety; 36% were unlawful entries; just 6.6% were attempts at forcible entry (Federal Bureau of Investigation, 2018). The financial harm from burglaries in 2018 was $3.4 billion, with the average loss per incident of $2,799.00 (Federal Bureau of Investigation, 2018).

Larceny-Theft

Larceny-theft is defined as the "unlawful taking, carrying, leading, or riding away of property from the possession or constructive possession of another" (Federal Bureau of Investigation, 2018). When you take your criminal law class, you'll learn all about the evolution of this definition of larceny-theft, which is full of interesting cases and stories. Examples of larceny-theft include bicycle theft, stealing motor vehicle parts/accessories (but not the whole car), shoplifting, and pickpocketing. Generally, larceny-theft is a huge category of offenses, covering pretty much any form of theft of property or articles without using "force, threat of force, or fraud" (Federal Bureau of Investigation, 2018). Not included in this crime are types of acts such as embezzlement, forgery, or check fraud.

As noted, the larceny-theft crime type is huge, accounting for nearly 72% of all property crimes in 2018—totaling north of 5.2 million offenses (Federal Bureau of Investigation, 2018). Like the other types of crime detailed in this chapter, larceny-theft in 2018 declined by 5.4% from 2017 and over 17% from 2009 (Federal Bureau of Investigation, 2018). Importantly, larceny-theft, in addition to accounting for a significant portion of all property crimes, is the third-largest contributor to arrests each year: in 2018, police made over 887,000 arrests for larceny-theft (Federal Bureau of Investigation, 2018). Larceny-theft produced an estimated $6 billion in financial losses/harm in 2018, with an average loss per incident of $1,153—lower than the per-incident loss for burglary. About one fourth of all thefts in 2018 were of items valued at $50 or less, with 39% involving thefts of items worth $200 or more (Federal Bureau of Investigation, 2018).

Looking closer at subtypes of larceny-theft, it's valuable to know that more than one fourth (27%) of all incidents involved thefts from vehicles (e.g., smash/grab or opening unlocked doors to steal property inside the car; Federal Bureau of Investigation, 2018). In fact, one of the authors of this book was the victim of three such incidents in the same year while living in a heavily populated urban area! Table 7.1 gives a breakdown of the total thefts in 2018 across several theft subtypes; it's worth noting that the two largest subcategories of reported/recorded thefts were shoplifting and stealing from coin-operated machines—what most would consider pretty minor or petty offenses. This is worth thinking about, as one of the key ways many people find themselves on the wrong side of the law and immersed within the criminal justice system is by engaging in some form of larceny-theft (or drug crime, detailed in Chapter 8). This also highlights where the bulk of law enforcement's and the court's time and resources are being directed.

TABLE 7.1 TOTAL THEFTS BY VARIOUS SUBTYPES IN 2018

Category of Theft	Total Reported/Recorded Incidents in 2018
Shoplifting	937,012
Theft from coin-operated machines	448,439
Bicycle theft	131,777
Pocket picking	22,930
Purse snatching	16,877

Motor Vehicle Theft

Motor vehicle ("car" or "auto") theft is defined as any "theft or attempted theft of a motor vehicle," which can include any "self-propelled vehicle that runs on land surfaces and not on rails" (Federal Bureau of Investigation, 2018). This is an important distinction to remember. Motor vehicle theft as defined by the FBI UCR and for our purposes therefore includes thefts of cars, SUVs, trucks, buses, motorcycles, scooters (including electric scooters), ATVs, and snowmobiles. It does NOT include thefts of any farm equipment (tractors, combines, etc.) construction equipment (bulldozers, backhoes, skidders), airplanes, or any watercraft (boats of any type, houseboats, kayaks, canoes, or jet skis).

Motor vehicle theft may be a crime of opportunity for some, but is also a bit of a niche crime type, with more sophisticated auto-theft rings, gangs, and organized crime groups accounting for a large percentage of the total crimes. This was the case in 2019 when over 20 people from Montreal, Canada, were arrested for running an auto-theft ring that targeted Lexus, Toyota, and Ford SUVs and trucks (CBC News, 2019); likewise, in 2018, the FBI and local police arrested six people in Georgia who were targeting and stealing millions of dollars' worth of luxury vehicles, including Bentley's, Audis, Mercedes-Benzes, and more from across several southern states (Fox 5 Atlanta, 2018).

Motor vehicle theft accounted for just 10% of property crime offenses in 2018 (748,841 recorded incidents; Federal Bureau of Investigation, 2018). Unlike other types of crime, this crime type has not witnessed dramatic declines in overall volume or rates, declining just 6% since 2009 (Federal Bureau of Investigation, 2018). Still, this form of property crime hits above its weight in terms of financial harm, resulting in over $6 billion in losses in 2018, with an average loss per incident of close to $8,500.00 (Federal Bureau of Investigation, 2018). This fact tells us that the bulk of all auto thefts occur at the lower end of the vehicle value spectrum—and not the high-end luxury car price point as most movies or TV shows would portray.

Looking deeper at the data on this crime type, we can also see that three fourths of all motor vehicle thefts in 2018 were of automobiles (cars, trucks, SUVs), which intuitively makes sense (how many people would want to steal or be able to resell or reuse a big bus after all?). Motor vehicle theft occurred most frequently in the northeastern United States, likely because of the concentration of people and large urban and suburban areas—a theory supported by the fact that motor vehicle theft is also concentrated in places with more than 250,000 inhabitants (Federal Bureau of Investigation, 2018).

Arson

Arson is defined as the "willful or malicious burning or attempting to burn, with or without intent to defraud, of a dwelling house, public building, motor vehicle or aircraft, or personal property of another" (Federal Bureau of Investigation, 2018). Data on arson is limited to only those fires determined to be "willfully set" and does not include any suspicious or unknown origin type fires. Thus, we likely have only a partial picture of arson's extent or destructiveness because it is difficult (and sometimes impossible) to conclusively determine the cause of a fire (for more see Box 7.2).

You might wonder why arson is considered a property and not a violent crime? The best answer to this is that arson always involves the destruction of property, thus centering squarely within the realm of property crimes. Certainly, some arsons may be used to intimidate, harass, or even harm or kill people, but this is not the defining characteristic of the crime. The unlawful destruction of property is.

WHO DID IT? A CLOSER LOOK AT ARSON INVESTIGATION | BOX 7.2

Arson investigation is a complicated endeavor—most arsons occur at night and most normal physical evidence is destroyed by the fire. As a result, **arson investigation**—the systematic analysis of suspicious fire causation—is conducted by highly trained fire and law enforcement professionals. Arson investigators must look for patterns, unusual occurrences, and sometimes microscopic evidence to determine if a fire was intentionally set using accelerants (e.g., gas, kerosene) and/or by damaging or tampering with utilities (National Institute of Justice, n.d.). They may look for specific burn patterns that are often linked to intentional fire setting (National Institute of Justice, n.d.).

California—which seems to experience far more than its fair share of destructive and tragic wildfires—estimates that about 7% of wildland wildfires result from acts of arson (Arango, 2018). The 2009 **Station Fire**—so named because it started near a fire station—killed two firefighters and burned more than

160,000 acres of land in Los Angeles County (Bloomekatz et al., 2019) while also destroying over 200 structures (Los Angeles Times, 2012). It remains Los Angeles County's single largest wildfire and cost over $93 million. And it was all caused by an act of arson. Arson investigators went to the scene of the fire's origination and in examining the area noticed signs of accelerants and incendiary materials (Bloomekatz et al., 2019). It is likely they employed investigative techniques similar to what archaeologists use to find small bits of ancient dinosaurs or civilizations, a "grid" and sifting method. They would also be looking for any evidence such as "puddle burn patterns caused by an accelerant—or the remains of a cigarette ... footprints or tire marks, and any stray bits of metal that might have been part of a time-delayed incendiary device" (Slate, 2009). Evidence collection at the Station Fire was complicated, as the site where the fire started was burned over twice. Still, investigators were able to piece together enough evidence to determine the fire was intentionally set. Unfortunately, on an annual basis, only about 22% of arsons are ever cleared by arrest—highlighting how difficult it is to investigate and prosecute these offenses. The Station Fire is no different; although it killed two people and destroyed countless land and property, no person has ever been arrested or prosecuted for the crime.

According to our official data, there were just 36,127 arsons in the United States in 2018 (11 per 100,000 people; Federal Bureau of Investigation, 2018). Of course, this does not reflect all arsons—just those destructive fires we know were willfully set. Nevertheless, 36,000+ intentional, destructive fires is a lot! One of the authors of this book has a sister whose small northeastern city was terrorized by a serial arsonist (a single person who repeatedly and maliciously engages in destructive fire setting), resulting in dozens of fires to homes, garages, and other buildings in the city. Even the sister's home was impacted when the arsonist set fire to a neighboring garage, which partially caught their home on fire!

According to our data, most (43%) of arsons in 2018 targeted structures—homes, apartments, businesses, etc.—while a little more than one fifth (23%) targeted mobile property; about one third (33%) of arsons were willfully set to timber, crops, etc. (Federal Bureau of Investigation, 2018). Unsurprisingly, arson results in a far higher average dollar loss per incident than other types of property crime ($17,406.00 per incident); a closer look reveals that arsons of industrial and manufacturing structures averaged $100,000 per incident! (Federal Bureau of Investigation, 2018).

Property Crime Characteristics

Additional property crime data and insights can be gleaned from the **National Crime Victimization Survey (NCVS)**. This nationally representative survey is based on interviews with a random sample of persons in U.S. households—it asks questions about crime victimization and involvement in crime. Thus, it collects data from the victim's or offender's perspective and does not rely on official counts of crimes reported by law enforcement agencies, as does the FBI UCR.

The NCVS is conducted each year. The most recent report found that property crime victimization declined between 2014 and 2018, which aligns with our understanding of the overall decrease in property crimes, as indicated by the UCR (Morgan & Oudekerk, 2019). In 2018, the report found a total of 13.5 million property crime victimizations (Morgan & Oudekerk, 2019). The property crime victimization rate was 108 victimizations per 1,000 households (note the change here from the UCR, which calculates rates based on 100,000 per population).

Keeping in mind that this does not represent ALL victimizations, it is striking to see how the volume of property crime grows when approaching the issue from a different angle rather than relying only on officially reported or known crimes. Recall that the UCR reported just over 7.1 million property crimes in 2018. Thus, by using the UCR and NCVS data, we can illustrate the underreporting/undercounting phenomenon described earlier. The NCVS data gives us a better glimpse as to the true extent of property crime victimization.

Table 7.2 presents the total victimizations and victimization rates for three of the four property crimes described in detail earlier in the chapter. It should be noted that based on the NCVS data, it is estimated that about 7% of all U.S. households experienced one or more property crime victimizations in 2018 (Morgan & Oudekerk, 2019).

TABLE 7.2   **PROPERTY CRIME VICTIMIZATION COUNTS AND RATES, 2018**

Property Crime Type	Total Reported Victimizations	Victimization rate (per 1,000 Households)
Burglary	1,724,000	13.8
Larceny-theft	10.3 million	82.7
Motor vehicle theft	534,000	4.3

Note: Content sourced from Morgan & Oudekerk (2019)

Mirroring violent crimes, data show that almost two thirds of property crime offenders and arrestees are White males over 18 years old. In general, males are overrepresented as property crime perpetrators; the difference between male and female criminality balances out more in certain property crime subtypes like shoplifting. Property crime offenders often select "soft" targets—or what they perceive to be soft targets: unlocked or unguarded property or valuables, businesses with outdated or missing security systems, homes with windows or doors that can be accessed without being seen by neighboring houses, etc. As a result, target-hardening measures—installing security systems, outdoor lighting, ensuring doors/windows are locked, cutting back bushes and trees that provide convenient hiding places, etc.—could all potentially deter property crime offenders.

As noted earlier, time of day does play a role in some property crime types, as offenders may seek the cover of darkness to help hide their activities as well as help them evade detection; businesses closed for the night are more tempting targets for burglars than those open and full of customers and employees. Yet certain types of property crime show the inverse is true: shoplifting is a crime often committed during normal business hours in daylight; still other crime types show no real pattern for day/night preference among offenders, such as vandalism or destruction of property. Police are often trained to notice people, places, the things people do, and the times they do them as a way to help train and heighten their sense of people and activities that are out of place or unusual. Criminals often know this, and so the cat-and-mouse game between criminals and law enforcement is always evolving.

Key Takeaways

Review the following list of bullet points for a quick overview of the key ideas and information in this chapter:

- Property crime includes the crimes of burglary, theft, motor vehicle theft, arson, and more.
- In general, the rates (volume and frequency) of property crimes have declined over the last 10 years or more, as measured through official data sources like the UCR and NCVS.
- Property crime is tied to other types of crime, including cybercrime and drug crime; it is one of the primary crime categories that is measured and is the subject of significant law enforcement attention and resources.

Conclusion and Formal Summary Questions

This chapter helped us learn about property crimes. We learned that property crime is one of the two major categories of crime that we collect official data for in the United States through such efforts as the UCR and NCVS. For many people, property crime offending or victimization (of some kind and to some degree) is likely during their lifetimes since property crime includes such things destruction of property, larceny-theft, burglary, motor vehicle theft, and arson. While many people may not consider themselves property criminals, anyone who has "taken" supplies or items from work or school, "borrowed" someone's property without asking, shoplifted, sprayed graffiti, or intentionally damaged any property has engaged in a property crime. Importantly, however, overall, the official property crime rate trends are positive, with declines across all the major property crime subtypes (burglary, theft, motor vehicle theft, arson) over the past 5 years and 10 years.

- *Can you describe how property crime rates might be influenced by the development of new technologies and the rise of cybercrime?*
- *Official data on property crime often undercounts the extent of the problem. Can you summarize how data from the NCVS expands our understanding of the scale and scope of property crime?*

- *Property crime shows some patterns and routinization (e.g., nighttime burglaries are more common than daytime ones). Can you describe some of the property crime characteristics, as well as what steps citizens or police might take to deter property crimes from occurring?*

E-Resources

1. Link to the FBI's Uniform Crime Reporting site for property crimes: https://ucr.fbi.gov/crime-in-the-u.s/2010/crime-in-the-u.s.-2010/property-crime.
2. YouTube/ABC Nehhws video, *Inside the Mind of an Arsonist*: https://www.youtube.com/watch?v=qJq1UolgPBw.
3. FBI Crime Data Explorer—an interactive tool for learning about crime types in the United States: https://crime-data-explorer.fr.cloud.gov/pages/explorer/crime/property-crime.

References

Arango, T. (2018, August 20). Behind most wildfires, a person and a spark: 'We bring fire with us'. *The New York Times*. https://www.nytimes.com/2018/08/20/us/california-wildfires-human-causes-arson.html

Bloomekatz, A. B., Blankstein, A., and Dimassa, C.M. (2019, September 4). Blaze an 'unacceptable crime.' *Los Angeles Times*. https://www.latimes.com/archives/la-xpm-2009-sep-04-me-fire4-story.html

CBC News. (2019, December 17). *Police bust high-tech auto theft ring* [Video]. YouTube. https://www.youtube.com/watch?v=EpiR5kC3Ch0

Davis, J. (2009, March 12). The untold story of the world's biggest diamond heist. *Wired*. https://www.wired.com/2009/03/ff-diamonds-2/

Eurostat. (n.d.). *Recorded offences by offence category—police data (crim_off_cat)* [Data set]. https://ec.europa.eu/eurostat/data/database

Federal Bureau of Investigation. (2018). *Uniform crime report*. https://ucr.fbi.gov/crime-in-the-u.s/2018/crime-in-the-u.s.-2018/topic-pages/property-crime

Fox 5 Atlanta. (2018, July 14). *Multi million dollar car theft ring bust* [Video]. YouTube. https://www.youtube.com/watch?v=mJfsH8Ybf4U

Los Angeles Times. (2012, August 16). *Station Fire: A misjudged threat*. https://www.latimes.com/local/la-station-fire-sg-storygallery.html

Morgan, R. E., & Oudekerk, B. A. (2019). *Criminal victimization, 2018*. Bureau of Justice Statistics, U.S. Department of Justice. https://bjs.ojp.gov/content/pub/pdf/cv18.pdf

National Institute of Justice. (n.d.). *Fire and arson investigations*. https://nij.ojp.gov/law-enforcement/investigations/fire-and-arson-investigations

RAINN. (n.d.). The criminal justice system: Statistics. https://www.rainn.org/statistics/criminal-justice-system

Slate. (2009, September 3). *Explainer: How did the Station Fire start?* https://slate.com/news-and-politics/2009/09/how-did-the-station-fire-start-and-other-questions-about-the-2009-wildfires-in-southern-california.html

Chapter 8

Drug Crime

Key Terms

Drug Crime
Controlled Substance Act of 1971
War on drugs
The Harrison Narcotics Act of 1914
National Institute of Drug Abuse
Fentanyl

Chapter Headings

1. Chapter opener
2. What is drug crime?
3. The scope and scale of drug crime
4. Drug crime subtypes
    4.1. The cocaine trade
    4.2. The heroin trade
5. Drug crime characteristics
    5.1. Drug crime and violent crime
    5.2. Drug crime and property crime
6. Chapter summary

Chapter Objectives

After reading Chapter 8, students will be able to do the following:
- *Define drug crime*
- *Understand the scope of the drug crime*
- *Describe the characteristics of drug crimes*

Opening Questions

Before you begin the chapter, take a few minutes to reflect on the following questions:

1. *How is drug crime defined?*
2. *What are the major types of drug crimes?*
3. *How does drug crime intersect with other forms of crime?*

True Crime

In 1996, "Freeway" Rick Ross (Figure 8.1) was arrested. His charge: conspiracy to buy 100 kilograms (220 pounds) of cocaine from an undercover agent. Thus, ended—at least for the time—Rick Ross's career as a drug kingpin and his legacy as one of the crack cocaine epidemic's key players.

According to his own account, Ross got involved in the drug trade in 1979, buying a small amount of cocaine for $50 and reselling it for $100. The easy money captured his fascination. From that point forward, Ross expanded his involvement in the drug trade in Southern California—moving from $50 purchases to buying kilos,

FIGURE 8.1 Freeway Rick Ross

and then hundreds of kilos, of cocaine, which he, at least in part, helped refine into crack cocaine—helping to ignite the crack epidemic in Los Angeles in the early 1980s. Ross is alleged to have grossed about $1 billion in proceeds from his cocaine empire in the 1980s—and by his own admission, his net earnings were about $300 million in tax-free profits. Ross's involvement in the drug trade isn't unique, though his success and ability to avoid the degree of violence that normally follows such involvement, as well as his flair for bouncing back, all set him apart from many of his peers. After an early release from federal prison in 2009, Ross released several books and was a central figure in a Netflix documentary about the Los Angeles drug trade. He also became an advocate for legal marijuana and the vice president of community outreach and relations for the National Diversity and Inclusion Cannabis Alliance. He even filed a lawsuit against rapper Rick Ross for illegally profiting from his name and likeness, which he lost!

What Is Drug Crime?

The phrase "**drug crime**" encompasses a wide range of activities, including violations of laws "prohibiting or regulating the use, distribution, or manufacture of illegal or banned substances" (Bureau of Justice Statistics, 1994), as well as the plethora of illegal activities that flow from, or relate to, the use or sale of drugs (e.g., thefts, burglaries, robberies, homicides). To understand the extent of drug crimes, we can look at data on arrests, overall drug usage and substance abuse, and other estimates on the underlying motivations or factors contributing to criminal behavior.

In comparison to other nations, such as some of those in Europe like Portugal, the United States takes a hardline stance against illegal drug manufacture, distribution, and personal use. It is this latter aspect of American drug policy—personal use—that produces the greatest resource strain on the criminal justice system, as well as the greatest debate.

Since the 1970s, America has waged a "**war on drugs**," funneling billions of dollars annually toward campaigns, strategies, and tactics to curb drug consumption, while at the same time supporting, or in some cases turning a blind eye to, the actions of drug cartels in foreign nations that funnel massive quantities of drugs into the American market (Drug Policy Alliance, n.d.-a). Total spending by the United States on the "war on drugs" now exceeds $1 trillion in aggregate (Pearl, 2018). Drug crime is thus a complex, multilayered issue linked to the political economy of nations and the global marketplace (Figure 8.2).

Importantly, the American stance toward drug possession and use has evolved over time; many articles and books recount how drugs like cocaine were once widely used as key ingredients in pain tonics, serums, and elixirs and consumed by many white, middle- and upper-class citizens. Likewise, for marijuana. These historical analyses of drug laws unanimously highlight how antidrug campaigns and new laws prohibiting drugs have deep ties to efforts to delegitimize, marginalize, or control racial, ethnic, or religious minorities. Thus, at the core of American drug laws and antidrug policies are deep-seated issues of power and control.

Table 8.1 outlines the federal government's stance toward illicit drugs and substances. The **Controlled Substances Act of 1971** created a series of categories, with those substances considered most dangerous and/or with the lowest acceptable medical use in "Schedule I" (Drug Enforcement Administration, n.d.). Take

FIGURE 8.2 The War on Drugs Has Long Been a Contentious Issue, With Many People Protesting Both the Costs and Outcomes of Enforcement

note that marijuana, lysergic acid diethylamide (LSD), and peyote (a variety of cactus with hallucinogenic properties) are all Schedule I banned substances at the federal level. Criminal enforcement is heavily focused, and criminal penalties are the highest for trafficking and possession, for those substances in Schedule I, Schedule II, and so on. States often take their cue for how to enforce drug laws from the Controlled Substances Act.

TABLE 8.1   CONTROLLED SUBSTANCES ACT SCHEDULE OF BANNED SUBSTANCES

Schedule	Prohibited Substances
I – dangerous drugs with no currently accepted medical use and high potential for abuse	heroin, LSD, marijuana (cannabis), 3,4-methylenedioxymethamphetamine (MDMA, ecstasy), methaqualone, and peyote
II – dangerous drugs with high potential for abuse, potentially leading to severe psychological and/or physical dependence	combination products with less than 15 milligrams of hydrocodone per dosage unit (Vicodin), cocaine, methamphetamine, methadone, hydromorphone (Dilaudid), meperidine (Demerol), oxycodone (OxyContin), fentanyl, Dexedrine, Adderall, and Ritalin
III – moderate to low potential for physical and psychological dependence	products having less than 90 milligrams of codeine per dosage unit (Tylenol with codeine), ketamine, anabolic steroids, testosterone
IV – low potential for abuse and low risk of dependence	Xanax, Soma, Darvon, Darvocet, Valium, Ativan, Talwin, Ambien, Tramadol
V – lowest potential for abuse and limited quantities of certain narcotics	cough preparations with less than 200 milligrams of codeine or per 100 milliliters (Robitussin AC), Lomotil, Motofen, Lyrica, Parepectolin

There is widespread debate about the inclusion of marijuana, LSD, and peyote as Schedule I banned substances; in particular, many people take issue with the idea that those three substances have no "accepted medical use," despite an abundance of research indicating the opposite. For that reason, many states have loosened their enforcement of some of these substances, especially marijuana. As of 2020, 11 states have made marijuana fully legal—meaning it is decriminalized and available for medicinal use; another 13 states have decriminalized marijuana and made it legal for medicinal use, but have not made it fully legal; 15 states have allowed marijuana to be used for only medicinal purposes, but it is not decriminalized; in three states, marijuana is decriminalized only but not available for medicinal use. Only eight states continue to treat marijuana as an entirely illegal substance. Nevertheless, the fact that marijuana is still illegal at the federal level places the states at odds with the federal government and federal law enforcement agencies with respect to marijuana enforcement.

The Scope and Scale of Drug Crime

In 2018, there were more than 10.3 million arrests in the United States. The single-highest category of arrests was for drug abuse violations, with more than 1.6 million people arrested (note the second-highest category of arrests was for DUI; Federal Bureau of Investigation, 2018). The trend of drug abuse violations representing the largest category of arrests holds true on an annual basis each year. Thirty-six percent of those drug abuse violation arrests were for marijuana possession, with another 25% for possession of other dangerous non-narcotic drugs.

Table 8.2 provides a glimpse of the breakdown of arrests in 2018 for drug sales or manufacturing:

TABLE 8.2   ARRESTS IN 2018 BY DRUG TYPE AND % OF ARRESTS (FEDERAL BUREAU OF INVESTIGATION, 2018)

Drug Type	% of Arrests
Heroin, cocaine, or derivatives (including crack)	4.4%
Marijuana	3.3%
Synthetic drugs	1.8%
Other	0.4%

Note: Content sourced from the Federal Bureau of Investigation (2018)

As you see from the data, arrests for possession of drugs far outpace arrests of those manufacturing or trafficking in drugs. This is partly explained by the high volume of drug users. Data from National Institute on Drug Abuse (NIDA) show that drug usage is widespread and starts at an early age. An annual survey of high school students recently found that 35% of 12th graders had used marijuana at some point in the past year and about 3% had used narcotics (about 30% had also used alcohol; National Institute on Drug Abuse, n.d.-a). As people age, the likelihood they have, or will, experiment with or will become regular drug users continues to rise: a separate study of 19- to 22-year-old, college-age students found that 42% of young adults in college and not in college had used marijuana in the prior 12 months, and about 3% had misused opioid prescription drugs (National Institute on Drug Abuse, 2019). The data indicated that about 6% of adults in college and 11% of noncollege adults admitted to being daily marijuana users (National Institute on Drug Abuse, 2019). As you expand the data and look solely at adults, over age 26, recent NIDA data highlights that 16% admitted using an illicit drug in the past month, and more than 51% had used some illicit drug in their lifetime (Substance Abuse and Mental Health Services Administration, n.d.). Table 8.3 shows the usage data for various drugs among people aged 26 or older:

TABLE 8.3   LIFETIME DRUG USAGE AMONG ADULTS 26 AND OLDER

Drug Type	% of People Indicating Some Abuse in Their Lifetime
Marijuana	47%
Cocaine	17%
Crack cocaine	4%
Hallucinogens	17%
LSD	11%
Inhalants	9%
MDMA	7%
Meth	6%
PCP	3%
Heroin	2%
Opioid medications/prescriptions	21%–29% misuse; 8%–12% develop abuse disorder

Note: Content sourced from Substance Abuse and Mental Health Services Administration (n.d.)

Thus, drug use—and therefore possession—is high in the United States and when compared to other countries. It makes sense then that arrests for possession would be high. Arrests data also show, though, that with possession arrests being so high, a large portion of law enforcement, court, and correctional system resources are being used to deal with low-level drug users or abusers. Since 1990, the number of annual arrests for drug abuse violations has increased by 123% from 741,600 to the 2018 tally of over 1.6 million (Snyder, 2012).

Commensurately, the number of prisoners incarcerated for drug violations has climbed significantly. As of 2018, about half of all federal prisoners were incarcerated for drug offenses—the majority for drug trafficking, not possession (McVay, 2021). According to the Prison Policy Initiative, of the 1.29 million people locked up in state prisons in 2020, 191,000 (15%) were incarcerated for drugs, while 19% of those held in county jails were there for drug offenses. This data does not count all the people who are arrested each year, or incarcerated, for committing crimes tied to their involvement or use of drugs (Sawyer & Wagner, 2020). The true extent of the drug abuse and drug crime problem is slightly clearer when you realize that the financial costs of a drug crime, drug use–related health care, and lost productivity are north of $310 billion per year (National Institute on Drug Abuse, n.d.-b). Globally, the trade in illegal drugs likely generates profits for those involved at over $870 billion per year—if not more—according to the United Nations (United Nations Office on Drugs and Crime, 2011a).

Several other data points are worth exploring as they relate to the influence of drugs on other criminal behavior, especially the role that drug dependency or addiction plays in pushing people toward criminal conduct.

According to one study from the Bureau of Justice Statistics, 17% of state prisoners and 18% of federal prisoners admitted they committed their crimes to obtain money for drugs (Bureau of Justice Statistics, n.d.). Further, in 2002, the Bureau of Justice Statistics estimated that one fourth of property crime offenders in local jails committed their crimes to obtain money for drugs (Bureau of Justice Statistics, n.d.). And in 2004, they estimated that about 30% of property crime and 10% of violent crime offenders in state prisons engaged in their crimes out of a quest for drugs or drug money (Bureau of Justice Statistics, n.d.). In a report released in 2017 that looked at crimes from 2007 to 2009, data showed that 21% of inmates in state prisons and local jails were "incarcerated for crimes committed to obtain drugs or money for drugs" (Sawyer, 2017). That study also supports earlier research in finding that 40% of property crime offenders and 14% of violent crime offenders committed their "most serious offense for drug related reasons" (Sawyer, 2017).

Another way to consider the role of drugs on other types of crime is to look at something like drugged driving: In 2017, 13 million people were estimated to have driven or operated a vehicle after taking illicit drugs—certainly a criminal act with potentially serious repercussions (National Institute on Drug Abuse, 2018). Among people killed in driving accidents in 2016, 43% were tested for drugs and came back with positive results (National Institute on Drug Abuse, 2018). Of those, fully one half (50%) tested positive for two or more drugs (National Institute on Drug Abuse, 2018).

Drug Crime Subtypes
The Cocaine Trade

Cocaine was once commonly found in cough drops, hair tonics, Coca-Cola, Vin Mariani, and other tonics and beverages (History.com, 2018). Consumed by middle- and upper-class Whites, it was not until the drug was associated (wrongly) with newly freed African Americans and the myth of the "Negro Cocaine Fiend" was created and disseminated by anti-black, racist politicians, newspapers, and others that efforts to criminalize and delegitimize its use jumped off (Hart, 2014). Since that point, cocaine has been criminalized, enforcement action has been heavy, and the rest, as they say, is history!

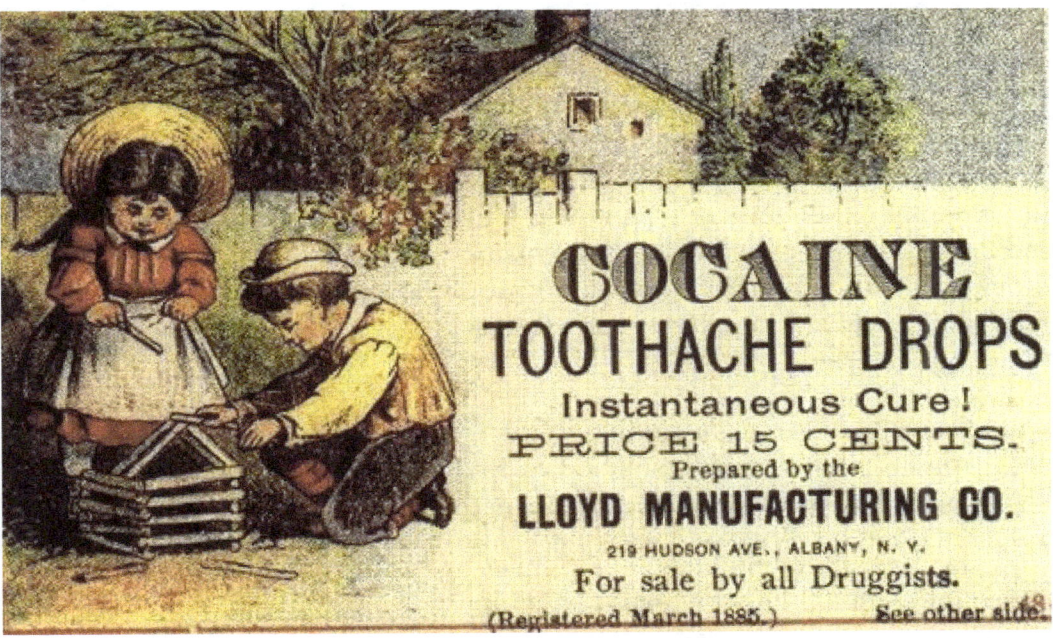

FIGURE 8.3 Cocaine Was Once a Widely Accepted "Cure" for a Variety of Medical Issues, Including Toothaches and Hair Loss

One study from 2011 placed the value of the American and European cocaine trades at $70 billion annually combined (United Nations Office on Drugs and Crime, 2011b). The money from the sale of cocaine accumulates primarily to those cartels and gangs that control large segments of the illegal industry. As one article explained the economics of the cocaine trade,

> According to figures from the U.N. ... coca farmers in Colombia receive $1.30 for each kilogram of fresh coca leaf. In Peru and Bolivia, where the leaf is air dried before being sold, farmers receive $3.00 per kilogram. For the fresh leaf used in processing in Colombia, it takes somewhere between 450 and 600 kilograms of coca leaf to produce 1 kilogram of cocaine base, depending on the variety of coca plant used. At $1.30 per kilogram, that means that it costs somewhere between $585 and $780 to purchase the coca leaf required to produce one kilogram of cocaine base. One kilogram of cocaine base can then be converted into one kilogram of cocaine hydrochloride, which is commonly referred to as: cocaine. As cocaine progresses from ... production ... to end users it increases in value. ... A kilogram of cocaine can be purchased for $2,200 in the jungles in Colombia's interior and for between $5,500 and $7,000 at Colombian ports ... the price increases ... once it leaves the production areas. ... In Central America, cocaine can be purchased for $10,000 per kilogram, and in southern Mexico, that same kilogram sells for $12,000 ... in the border towns of northern Mexico ... it is worth $16,000 ... and it will fetch between $24,000 and $27,000 wholesale ... in the

> United States. The prices are even higher in Europe, where they can run from $53,000 to $55,000 per kilogram, and prices exceed $200,000 per kilogram in Australia. The retail prices per gram of cocaine (1,000 grams to 1 kilogram) are ... $100–150 in the United States, $130–185 in Europe, and $250–$500 in Australia. (Snyder, 2012)

Thus, as cocaine moves along the supply chain, the costs increase, in effect compensating for the labor and risk of bringing the product closer to consumers. While a coca leaf farmer may only make a few hundred dollars for a large supply of coca leaves, a cocaine trafficker could easily net several hundred thousand dollars by selling a few kilos of cocaine to street-level dealers. The article goes on to note:

> Along the supply chain there is also quite a bit of "cutting", which is when substances are added to the cocaine to dilute its purity and stretch profit ... the purity of cocaine leaving [Colombia] is about 85%. By the time it reaches somewhere like the United Kingdom, for example, purity may be only 60%, and it drops further to about 30% at the retail level.

A downturn in the price of powdered cocaine due to an oversupply of the product led, in the early 1980s, to the development and subsequent sale of crack cocaine, a derivative of powdered cocaine. Even more addictive and far cheaper (a single crack "rock" might sell for $5–$10), crack's arrival in American cities and towns created an epidemic of drug abuse, not unlike that which we are now seeing with opioid painkillers and heroin. Between 1985 and 1989, the number of regular or "daily" cocaine users skyrocketed from 4.2 million to over 5.8 million people (History.com, 2018). Attempts to curb the crack epidemic led directly to mass incarceration of mostly low-level drug users—further destabilizing urban areas and negatively affecting those individuals. For example, at crack's height, the federal government passed the Anti-Drug Abuse Act of 1986 with penalties for crack cocaine that were 100 times harsher than penalties for powdered cocaine: possession of just 5 g of crack (about 1 teaspoon) could result in the same sentence as possession of 500 g of powdered cocaine. Crack possession also carried a minimum mandatory 5-year sentence. It was not until the passage of the Fair Sentencing Act of 2010 that the weight ratio between crack and powder sentencing was reduced (but not made equivalent) to 18:1 and the 5-year mandatory minimum sentence for possession was eliminated.

Accompanying the crack/cocaine markets in the United States, and in the countries where the product is produced and trafficked, has been a rise in associated forms of crime. For example, at the peak of the crack epidemic, one study from the Bureau of Justice Statistics estimated that 32% of all homicides and 62% of all drug-related homicides in New York City were linked to crack cocaine (History.com, 2018). Another study examining the impact of crack cocaine on urban crime rates in the 1980s found that had crack not been introduced into those urban areas, those places would likely have seen a 10% reduction or more in their crime rates (Grogger & Willis, 2000).

Cocaine is synonymous with both organized and the more random street-level violence in countries like Colombia and Mexico, as well as many other Central and South American countries, which collectively are at the epicenter of the global cocaine trade (Stewart, 2013). The immense wealth generated by the cocaine trade creates power vortices and imbalances—which undermine the rule of law and law enforcement—in all countries, including the United States, which also has witnessed (and continues to see) a high proportion of violent crime whose origins trace back to the drug trade.

Miami, Florida, is a perfect case study for how drugs and the drug trade lead to both violence and corruption, which fuel further violence and distrust in societal institutions. During the 1980s, Miami was the epicenter of the cocaine trade and became America's murder capital. Drugs, primarily powdered cocaine, flowed north from South America, up through the Caribbean, and into the southern tip of Florida—where Miami became the flashpoint and hotspot for drug-related crime, violence, and corruption.

In 1980, Miami had 573 murders, in 1981, 621—there were so many murders occurring in Miami due to the influx of drugs and drug traffickers, and escalating turf battles, that the city had to rent refrigerated trucks to store the corpses (Alvarado, 2011). That same year *Time* magazine proclaimed Miami as "Paradise Lost" in a front-page cover story (Time, 1981). Those refrigerated trucks remained in use until 1988, by which time Miami had become the center of the U.S. war on drugs. During that time, the corrosive and corrupting effects of millions of dollars of drug money had already wreaked havoc on Miami's businesses, government, and law enforcement agencies. For example, 10% of the Miami police department was suspended or fired due to a cocaine-related drug scandal in the late 1980s—the cops were effectively protecting and profiting off the cocaine trade, even engaging in violence and murder (Lersch, 2001). As things often do, the cocaine trade in Miami eventually ebbed, and violence linked to it fell off, but in 2017, as Colombian cocaine production again reached record highs, the Drug Enforcement Administration (DEA) and other officials noted that Miami was already seeing a rise in drug-related deaths and other forms of crime (Velzer, 2017).

Violence and violent crime swirl around the cocaine trade. At his cartel's peak, Pablo Escobar was reliably rumored to be worth $30 billion—his Medellin cartel controlled 80% of the world's cocaine trade; they raked in so much money, they allegedly spent $2,500 per month on rubber bands to hold bankrolls of cash together (Amrani, 2018). The DEA estimates that 90% or more of cocaine seized in the United States traces back to Colombia (Velzer, 2017). Violence in Colombia because of the cocaine trade in the 1980s and 1990s was astounding in its breadth and severity: Avianca flight 203 was brought down with a bomb, killing all 107 aboard, in a failed attempt to assassinate a tough-on-drug crime presidential candidate; over 7,000 people estimated killed just by Escobar's cartel during the mid-1980s; cocaine became the lynchpin in an ongoing civil war between the Colombian government and rebels called the Revolutionary Armed Forces of Colombia (FARC), leading to more violence and death; between 1986 and 1991—the peak of the cocaine boom—homicide rates grew by 311% (Amrani, 2018; Human Rights Watch, n.d.). Although violence has been significantly reduced in Colombia since the 1980s and 90s, the country still produced 710 metric tons of cocaine in 2017 in response to the demand in countries like the United States (Holland, 2016).

> ### REAL DEAL: THE ANATOMY OF NARCO-TRAFFICKING — BOX 8.1
>
> Drug trafficking—or "narco"-trafficking—involves moving illegal or banned substances across borders and it occurs all around the world, with major hubs in Southwest and Southeast Asia, South and Central America, the Middle East/Central Asia, and Europe. Narco-trafficking is closely tied to the production or manufacture of illegal drugs, especially cocaine (South and Central America), opium/heroin (South Asia and Central Asia), marijuana, and methamphetamine, although it may also involve the movement of substances like anabolic steroids, synthetic drugs, and illegally obtained prescription drugs, like opioid painkillers. Drug trafficking is often controlled by organized crime groups or drug cartels who employ a variety of methods to move their illegal "product" to where consumers and demand reside, including by using vehicles, tractor-trailer trucks, trains, planes, boats, improvised submarines, and human couriers (including the coffins of the deceased), as well as by hiding or disguising the drugs inside a variety of household and garden products, food products, and manufactured goods.
>
> The drug trade—particularly the enormous amounts of money it generates—infiltrates legitimate businesses and helps corrupt government agencies and law enforcement personnel. For example, in Mexico, an entire police force was arrested in 2019 on charges of corruption and assisting in the narco-trafficking cartels there, and in 2018, 200 police officers were suspended from their jobs in Tehuacana and 113 more fled their jobs to avoid prosecution (Jaramillo, 2019). The high stakes of the drug trade and the potential to become multi-millionaires or billionaires lead to heightened competition among gangs and cartels for territory and control, leading to violence and death. In Mexico, for example, the drug trade which was once divided among four dominant cartels has now fractured after years of infighting, Mexican and U.S. government crackdowns, and bloodshed into more than nine drug cells, led by the following dominant groups: the Sinaloa Cartel in the northwest, one of the "largest drug trafficking organizations in the world," (BBC News, 2019); the Jalisco New Generation Cartel in parts of the south and southwest; and the Gulf and Loz Zetas cartels in the northeast. The Mexican cartel wars, which have been raging since 2006 in Mexico, have killed at least 150,000 people (Council on Foreign Relations, n.d.) including 26 people massacred at a rehab clinic and a federal judge who were killed on July 1, 2020 (Grillo, 2020). The DEA has called the Mexican drug cartels the "greatest crime threat" to the United States" and has said they also have the "greatest drug trafficking influence" (Beittel, 2020). The violence and ancillary crimes that accompany drug trafficking—from homicidal violence to the overdose-related deaths and crimes of drug users—are directly traceable to the actions of the drug cartels and gangs around the world that manufacture, distribute, and profit from the vast majority of the world's drug users.

One aspect of drug violence people in America often overlook is the role that their own consumption of illicit drugs plays in the cycle of violence and crime; 29,000 people were murdered in Mexico in 2017 as the country was racked by continuous drug cartel violence (Amrani, 2018). Ciudad Juarez, on the U.S.-Mexico border, was named one of the 50 most dangerous cities in the world in 2018 (Young, 2018), with over 1,020 homicides in 2020—a shocking 140 killings in the month of July 2020 (Borunda, 2020). Other cities in Mexico, like Los Cabos, have experienced even higher per capita homicide rates: Los Cabos was experiencing one homicide per day in 2017–2018, which for a city of just 330,000 people is extraordinary (Young, 2018). Much, if not nearly all of this violence is in some way, shape, or form tied to the flow and control of illicit drugs in and through Mexico. Demand for drugs among Americans fuels much of this violence.

The Heroin Trade

Since the mid-2000s, America has been gripped by an "opioid" epidemic (see Box 8.2). Like the crack epidemic that came before, the opioid epidemic has deep roots in the global drug trade and the world of modern medicine. Prescription opioid medications—things like Vicodin, OxyContin, and **fentanyl**—are called synthetic (or man-made) opioids. Like natural opioids, such as morphine or codeine, they "act on the same targets in the brain to produce analgesic (pain relief) effects" (Drug Enforcement Administration, 2020). Unlike natural opioids, which are derived from the seed pods of opium poppies—the synthetic variants are made in labs. In pill or powder form, these synthetics can be much stronger than natural opioids—and can easily cause fatal overdoses. America's opioid epidemic is tied in large part to the ease of access to prescription opioid painkillers and the overprescribing by doctors—sometimes intentionally—of these drugs. While greater attention and control have helped curb the practice of overprescribing opioids, according to one study, "the amount of opioids in morphine milligram equivalents prescribed per person is still around three times higher than it was in 1999" (Centers for Disease Control and Prevention, 2019). As of 2017, there were still 58 opioid prescriptions being written for every 100 Americans—a startlingly high amount!

WHO DID IT? A CLOSER LOOK AT AMERICA'S OPIOID CRISIS | BOX 8.2

In August 2016, 26 people in the small town of Huntington, West Virginia, suffered opioid overdoses, with nearly half of the overdoses occurring around the same apartment complex—all 26 lived, which is nothing short of a miracle (Joseph, 2016). West Virginia has not been alone in dealing with a significant increase in opioid-related overdoses, and deaths, linked to the overprescribing of opioid prescription painkillers and the subsequent development of substance abuse disorders among those taking the drugs. Ohio, Vermont, Kentucky—states across the country have seen a surge in opioid-linked deaths as usage rates have risen across the country.

In 2017, 47,000 Americans died from opioid overdoses, while across the country another 1.7 million people suffered from substance use disorders linked to opioids. Between 1999 and 2018, almost 450,000 people in America died from an overdose involving an opioid, including prescription and illicit opioids (Centers for Disease Control and Prevention, n.d.). The DEA considers fentanyl to be involved in more deaths than any other drug (Drug Enforcement Administration, 2019). Often mixed with heroin and sometimes with cocaine, in 2018, Tucson police discovered a small bindle of fentanyl mixed with sugar to resemble "black tar"

(Continued)

heroin—the first noted observation of this form, which could easily kill an unsuspecting drug user (Drug Enforcement Administration, 2019). Much of the modern opioid crisis stems from the overprescription of opioid pain meds (National Institute on Drug Abuse, n.d.-c). For example, 80% of people who abuse heroin start by abusing opioid medications, according to the National Institute on Drug Abuse (National Institute on Drug Abuse, n.d.-c). Data also show that 21% to 29% of people who are prescribed opioids for pain management end up abusing or misusing them, with 8% to 12% developing opioid abuse disorders and 4% to 6% of those people then transitioning to heroin use. In 2018, 652,000 suffered from heroin use disorders—some also abused painkillers or synthetic opioids like fentanyl (National Institute on Drug Abuse, n.d.-c). The net result is that in 2018, 128 people were dying each day from overdosing on opioids (pills like OxyContin or Vicodin, heroin, or fentanyl-type synthetics), at a financial cost to the health-care system, criminal justice system, and local communities like Huntington of near $78.5 billion per year (National Institute on Drug Abuse, n.d.-c).

Synthetic opioids, as with natural ones like heroin, are part of a complex illicit drug trade, with deep historical roots. **The Harrison Narcotics Act of 1914** outlawed cocaine and opium in the United States. Up to that point, both cocaine and opium were consumed and used as various medicinal cures. Throughout the 18th and 19th centuries, opium was central to a lucrative international trade between Great Britain and China and China and the United States. However, opium was a major trade good for hundreds of years before the East India Trading Company and major modern world powers got involved.

Many people are familiar with opium from TV or movies—opium can be smoked—but is most obviously turned into heroin, which can come in the form of black tar, brown, and white powder versions (Drug Enforcement Administration, 2019). Today, most heroin in the United States enters via Mexico (and most fentanyl enters via Mexico or China); internationally, Afghanistan and Southwest Asia (Burma-Laos-Thailand) are also substantial producers of raw opium poppy, which then flows into the global drug market. Opium and heroin are stable products for organized crime, drug cartels, and gangs around the world. The price per pure gram of heroin was $1,168 in 2018 (Drug Enforcement Administration, 2019). At the street level, heroin is increasingly being cut with synthetic opioids, reducing its purity and upping its lethality.

As with cocaine, opioids and heroin are closely linked with crime. First, prescription fraud, theft, and intentional overprescribing or selling prescription drugs are crimes. In 2018, three different doctors or pharmacists were convicted in high-profile cases for illegally selling opioid prescription pills, receiving sentences of 2–5 years each (Department of Justice, 2017). In 2017, a pharmacist in Berea, California was sentenced to 30 years for prescription drug fraud and money laundering while a doctor in Michigan received a 23-year sentence for similar crimes (Department of Justice, 2017). Overall in 2018, the Office of the Inspector General and law enforcement partners charged 601 defendants with prescription drug fraud. Of particular concern to law enforcement officials is Medicare Part D fraud in relation to opioid prescription drugs—which in several reports appears rampant throughout the United States (Department of Health and Human Services, 2021).

Drug Crime Characteristics

In general, men are more likely than women to be represented as offenders and victims in drug-related violent and property crimes and are also more likely to be incarcerated for drug-related crimes. An exception is with the crime of prostitution which skews female. Research indicates that drug and substance abuse may play a key role in why many women (and men) get engaged in selling sex. According to one study of 200 prostitutes, 55% reported being addicted to drugs prior to getting involved in prositiution, and another 30% became addicted after getting into prositiution (Silbert et al., 1982). Further, data show that women and children may be at higher risk of physical abuse and domestic violence when male members of the household abuse drugs or other substances. For example, one study followed 3,000 women for two years and found that "interpersonal assault increased" after "use of alcohol and drugs even in those women without prior history of substance abuse" (Kilpatrick et al., 1997).

People under age 40 are more likely to be represented among drug abusers, drug offenders, perpetrators and victims of drug crime, and arrestees. Over one million arrests for drug abuse violations in 2018 were of people over 18, which was up 13% from 2009 (Federal Bureau of Investigation, 2018). When comparing adult men to adult women, adult men were four times more likely to be arrested for drug offenses in 2018, with over 800,000 arrests compared to 269,000 arrests of women (Federal Bureau of Investigation, 2018).

In terms of race, while overall Whites represent the majority of those people arrested for drug offenses (and related crimes), Blacks and Hispanics are disproportionately represented among those arrested and incarcerated for drug offenses and related crimes: approximately "80% of federal prisoners and 60% of state prisoners incarcerated for drug offenses are Black or Latino" (Drug Policy Alliance, n.d.-b). It is important to recognize, as the Drug Policy Alliance stated, "Higher arrest and incarceration rates for these communities are not reflective of increased prevalence of drug use, but rather of law enforcement's focus on urban areas, lower income communities and communities of color" (Drug Policy Alliance, n.d.-b). The racial disparities among minorities in terms of arrests and incarceration for drug offenses are one of the critical contemporary social justice issues facing the United States.

Key Takeaways

Review the following list of bullet points for a quick overview of the key ideas and information in this chapter:

- Drug crime is connected to drug use and abuse and to the global illicit drug economy. Drug use and abuse include the use or abuse of drugs like cocaine, heroin, methamphetamine, and marijuana, as well as the use or abuse of controlled substances: things like prescription drugs, anabolic steroids, etc.

- Drug crime includes crimes connected to violations of laws against manufacturing, distributing or selling, or consuming illegal (e.g., cocaine, heroin, methamphetamine) or controlled substances (e.g., prescription drugs) and the crimes that are linked to the drug trade, which includes a variety of violent (e.g., homicide, robbery), property (e.g., burglary, theft), and public order crimes (e.g., prostitution, DUI/DWI).
- Illegal drug production is tied to consumer demand; like other forms of the legitimate economy, the fluctuations and dynamics of the drug trade are tied to fundamental economic concepts like supply and demand.
- Often, drug consumption in developed nations like the United States fuels drug production in less developed countries around the world, such as in Central and South America. Drug consumption habits in some countries lead to drug-related crimes (especially violence) in others.
- Increasingly, the use and abuse, including the overprescription, of synthetic opioid prescription drug medications (like OxyContin, or Vicodin) have been at the root of a massive surge in overdose deaths in the U.S., and a growing number of heroin users.

Conclusion and Formal Summary Questions

This chapter helped us learn about drug crime. We learned that drug crime is tied to drug use and abuse, as well as that drug consumption habits in some places fuel drug production in others (thus creating a global illicit drug economy). Moreover, we explored how drug crime includes not just violations of laws against illicit drug production, distribution, and consumption but also the myriad crimes linked to the drug trade and drug use/abuse, including many forms of violent, property, and public order offenses. Lastly, we took an in-depth look at the cocaine and heroin trades to learn more about how crime develops and accompanies those forms of illicit drugs.

- *Can you describe how drug abuse is connected to violent and property crimes?*
- *Can you explain how drug abuse and addiction are linked to other issues like socioeconomic status, class, race, age, and gender?*
- *Are you able to describe how drug crime in the United States is connected to the global economy and to drug-related issues in other nations?*

E-Resources

1. *What Is the Drug War YouTube Video*: https://www.youtube.com/watch?v=HSozqaVcOU8
2. Link to the Drug Policy Alliance for numerous policies and other resources related to drug use: https://drugpolicy.org/about-us

3. The Crack Epidemic—A Short History: https://www.drugfreeworld.org/drugfacts/crackcocaine/a-short-history.html

References

Alvarado, F. (2011, August 10). 1981: Miami's deadliest summer. *Miami New Times*. https://www.miaminewtimes.com/news/1981-miamis-deadliest-summer-6565290

Amrani, I. (2018, August 1). Here in Columbia, the hypocrisy of western cocaine users is laid bare. *The Guardian*. https://www.theguardian.com/commentisfree/2018/aug/01/colombia-hypocrisy-western-middle-class-cocaine-users-violence

BBC News. (2019, October 24). *Mexican cartels: Which are the biggest and most powerful?* https://www.bbc.com/news/world-latin-america-40480405

Beittel, J. S. (2020). *Mexico: Organized crime and drug trafficking organizations*. Congressional Research Service. https://crsreports.congress.gov/product/pdf/R/R41576

Borunda, D. (2020, July 30). Juárez murders top 1,000 as violence continues despite COVID-19 pandemic. *El Paso Times*. https://www.elpasotimes.com/story/news/local/juarez/2020/07/30/juarez-mexico-murders-top-1000-drug-violence-despite-covid-19-pandemic/5535755002/

Bureau of Justice Statistics. (n.d.). *Drug use and crime*. U.S. Department of Justice. https://bjs.ojp.gov/drugs-and-crime-facts/drug-use-and-crime

Bureau of Justice Statistics. (1994). *Fact sheet: Drug-related crime*. U.S. Department of Justice. https://bjs.ojp.gov/content/pub/pdf/DRRC.PDF

Centers for Disease Control and Prevention. (n.d.). *Understanding the epidemic*. https://www.cdc.gov/opioids/basics/epidemic.html

Centers for Disease Control and Prevention. (2019). *Prescribing practices*. https://www.cdc.gov/drugoverdose/deaths/prescription/practices.html

Council on Foreign Relations. (n.d.). *Criminal violence in Mexico*. Global Conflict Tracker. https://www.cfr.org/global-conflict-tracker/conflict/criminal-violence-mexico

Department of Health and Human Services. (2021, August 12). *Combating the opioid epidemic*. Office of the Inspector General. https://oig.hhs.gov/reports-and-publications/featured-topics/opioids/

Department of Justice. (2017, June 15). *Former doctor sentenced to 23 years in prison for distributing prescription drugs, health care fraud and money laundering* [Press release]. Eastern District of Michigan, U.S. Attorney's Office. https://www.justice.gov/usao-edmi/pr/former-doctor-sentenced-23-years-prison-distributing-prescription-drugs-health-care

Drug Enforcement Administration. (n.d.). *Drug scheduling*. https://www.dea.gov/drug-information/drug-scheduling

Drug Enforcement Administration. (2019). *National drug threat assessment*. https://www.dea.gov/sites/default/files/2020-01/2019-NDTA-final-01-14-2020_Low_Web-DIR-007-20_2019.pdf

Drug Enforcement Administration. (2020). *Synthetic opioids*. https://www.dea.gov/sites/default/files/2020-06/Synthetic%20Opioids-2020.pdf

Drug Policy Alliance. (n.d.-a). *A history of the drug war*. https://drugpolicy.org/issues/brief-history-drug-war

Drug Policy Alliance. (n.d.-b). *Race and the drug war*. https://drugpolicy.org/issues/race-and-drug-war

Federal Bureau of Investigation. (2018). *Uniform crime report*. https://ucr.fbi.gov/crime-in-the-u.s/2018/crime-in-the-u.s.-2018/topic-pages/property-crime

Grillo, I. (2020, July 7). How Mexico's drug cartels are profiting from the pandemic. *New York Times*. https://www.nytimes.com/2020/07/07/opinion/sunday/mexico-drug-cartels-coronavirus.html

Grogger, J., & Willis, M. (2000). The emergence of crack cocaine and the rise in urban crime rates. *The Review of Economics and Statistics, 82*(4), 519–529. http://www.jstor.org/stable/2646648

Hart, C. L. (2014, January 29). How the myth of the 'Negro cocaine fiend' helped shape American drug policy. *The Nation*. https://www.thenation.com/article/archive/how-myth-negro-cocaine-fiend-helped-shape-american-drug-policy/

History.com. (2018, August 21). *Cocaine*. https://www.history.com/topics/crime/history-of-cocaine

Holland, L. (2016, August 27). 'The Michael Jordan of criminals': How Narcos found a true villain in Pablo Escobar. *The Guardian*. https://www.theguardian.com/tv-and-radio/2016/aug/27/narcos-netflix-pablo-escobar-wagner-moura

Human Rights Watch. (n.d.). *Medellín*. https://www.hrw.org/reports/1994/colombia/gener2.htm

Jaramillo, J. C. (2019, August 21). Entire police forces continue to be arrested in Mexico. *InSight Crime*. https://insightcrime.org/news/brief/entire-police-forces-continue-arrested-mexico/

Joseph, A. (2016, August 22). *26 overdoses in just hours: Inside a community on the front lines of the opioid epidemic*. Stat. https://www.statnews.com/2016/08/22/heroin-huntington-west-virginia-overdoses/

Kilpatrick, D. G., Acierno, R., Resnick, H. S., Saunders, B. E., & Best, C. L. (1997). A 2-year longitudinal analysis of the relationships between violent assault and substance use in women. *Journal of Consulting and Clinical Psychology, 65*(5), 834–847. https://doi.org/10.1037//0022-006x.65.5.834

Lersch, K. M. (2001). *Drug related police corruption: The Miami experience (from police misconduct: a reader for the 21st century, P 132–144, 2001, Michael J. Palmiotto, ed.—See NCJ-193774)*. Office of Justice Programs, U.S. Department of Justice. https://www.ojp.gov/ncjrs/virtual-library/abstracts/drug-related-police-corruption-miami-experience-police-misconduct

McVay, D. (2021). *Drugs and the prison, jail, probation, and parole systems*. Drug Policy Facts. https://www.drugpolicyfacts.org/chapter/drug_prison

National Institute on Drug Abuse. (n.d.-a). *Monitoring the future study: Trends in prevalence of various drugs* [Data set]. https://www.drugabuse.gov/drug-topics/trends-statistics/monitoring-future/monitoring-future-study-trends-in-prevalence-various-drugs

National Institute on Drug Abuse. (n.d.-b). *Costs of substance abuse*. https://archives.drugabuse.gov/trends-statistics/costs-substance-abuse

National Institute on Drug Abuse. (n.d.-c). *Opioid overdose crisis*. https://www.drugabuse.gov/drug-topics/opioids/opioid-overdose-crisis

National Institute on Drug Abuse. (2018). *Drugged driving infographic*. https://www.drugabuse.gov/drug-topics/trends-statistics/infographics/drugged-driving-infographic

National Institute on Drug Abuse. (2019). *Drug and alcohol use in college-age adults in 2018*. https://www.drugabuse.gov/drug-topics/trends-statistics/infographics/drug-alcohol-use-in-college-age-adults-in-2018

Pearl, B. (2018). *Ending the war on drugs: By the numbers*. Center for American Progress. https://www.americanprogress.org/article/ending-war-drugs-numbers/

Sawyer, W. (2017). *BLS report: Drug abuse and addiction at the root of 21% of crimes*. Prison Policy Initiative. https://www.prisonpolicy.org/blog/2017/06/28/drugs/

Sawyer, W. & Wagner, P. (2020). *Mass incarceration: The whole pie 2020*. Prison Policy Initiative. https://www.prisonpolicy.org/reports/pie2020.html

Silbert, M. H., Pines, A. M., & Lynch, T. (1982). Substance abuse and prostitution. *Journal of Psychoactive Drugs, 14*(3), 193–197. https://doi.org/10.1080/02791072.1982.10471928

Substance Abuse and Mental Health Services Administration. (n.d.). *National survey on drug use and health (NSDUH)* [Data set]. https://www.samhsa.gov/data/data-we-collect/nsduh-national-survey-drug-use-and-health

Snyder, H. N. (2012). *Arrest in the United States, 1990–2010*. Bureau of Justice Statistics, U.S. Department of Justice. https://bjs.ojp.gov/content/pub/pdf/aus9010.pdf

Stewart, S. (2013, January 3). *Mexico's cartels and the economics of cocaine*. Stratfor. https://worldview.stratfor.com/article/mexicos-cartels-and-economics-cocaine

Time. (1981, November 23). Paradise lost? http://content.time.com/time/covers/0,16641,19811123,00.html

United Nations Office on Drugs and Crime. (2011a). *Estimating illicit financial flows resulting from drug trafficking and other transnational organized crimes*. https://www.unodc.org/documents/data-and-analysis/Studies/Illicit_financial_flows_2011_web.pdf

United Nations Office on Drugs and Crime. (2011b). *The transatlantic cocaine market*. https://www.unodc.org/documents/data-and-analysis/Studies/Transatlantic_cocaine_market.pdf

Velzer, R. V. (2017, May 26). Cocaine comes roaring back to South Florida—and then some. *Sun Sentinel*. https://www.sun-sentinel.com/news/florida/fl-reg-cocaine-surge-fueling-overdoses-20170523-story.html

Young, A. (2018, July 17). Juarez among the 50 most dangerous cities in the world. *El Paso Times*. https://www.elpasotimes.com/story/news/world/2018/07/17/juarez-50-most-dangerous-cities-world/791543002/

Figure Credits

Fig. 8.1: Patrick Bastien Photography, "Freeway Rick Ross," https://commons.wikimedia.org/wiki/File:Ricky_Donnell_Ross.jpg. Copyright © 2010 by . Reprinted with permission.

Fig. 8.2: Copyright © by Neon Tommy (CC BY-SA 2.0) at https://www.flickr.com/photos/necntommy/6316413344.

Fig. 8.3: Source: https://www.pharmacytimes.com/view/vintage-pharmacy-ad-promoted-cocaine-toothache-drops.

Cyber and Environmental Crime Profiles

MODULE 4

Chapter 9

Cybercrime

Key Terms

Ransomware
Cybercrime
Cyber deviance
Cyberstalking
Hackers
Hacktivism
Cyberterrorism
Exponential scaling
Internet Crime Complaint Center (IC3)
Cyberspace
Cyber vandalism
Cyber theft
Identity theft
Phishing, vishing, smishing
Cyberbullying
Sexploitation
The deep web
Silk Road

Opening Questions

Before you begin the chapter, take a few minutes to reflect on the following questions:

1. What are the three primary ways that technology impacts modern crime?
2. How is cybercrime defined?
3. What are the major types of cybercrime that occur today?
4. How are law enforcement agencies responding to and controlling cybercrime?

Chapter Headings

1. Chapter opener
2. What is cybercrime?
3. The scope and scale of cybercrime
   3.1. How much cybercrime is there?
   3.2. The evolution of cybercrime
4. Cybercrime subtypes
   4.1. Computer intrusions
   4.2. Identity and cybertheft
   4.3. Cyberbullying and stalking
   4.4. Virtual black markets
   4.5. Cyberviolence
5. Cybercrime characteristics
   5.1. Cybercrime offenders
   5.1. Cybercrime victims
6. Chapter summary

Chapter Objectives

After reading Chapter 9, students will be able to do the following:

- Define cybercrime
- Understand the evolution of cybercrime
- Understand the scope of the cybercrime problem and the meaning of the term "exponential scaling"
- Describe the characteristics of cybercrime subtypes and offenders

True Crime

Riviera Beach is a sleepy oceanside community on Florida's east coast, just a few miles north of the retirement haven of West Palm Beach. In late May 2019, a police officer opened a seemingly harmless email and clicked on an attached file. The file was a virtual trojan horse. In one click, anonymous hackers infiltrated the city's computer system, locking it down and crashing nearly all online systems, including those that controlled local water utility pump stations. The hacker's demand: pay up and we'll let you have your computer systems and files back. Just a few weeks later, Riviera Beach officials made the difficult choice to give in and pay the hackers $600,000.

Riviera Beach joins a long and growing list of governments, corporations, and individuals that have fallen victim to a dangerous new type of cybercrime called **ransomware**, where hackers create and deploy software that enables them to access and control computer systems, hard drives, and user files. Hundreds of millions of ransomware attacks occur each year, with hackers making millions of dollars in ransom as victims confront the choice of paying or seeing their systems and sensitive files destroyed or made public. In an age where nearly everyone spends some time online or uses a computer system, this type of cybercrime is only likely to continue increasing in its scale and severity.

What Is Cybercrime?

> *Technology is remaking what is possible for individuals and institutions and for the international order.*
> —President Barack Obama, January 17, 2014

> *We are building our lives around our wired and wireless networks. The question is, are we ready to work together to defend them?*
> —Quote appearing on the FBI cybercrime web page 2016

Cybercrimes are any acts or events committed by, or against, any individual, group, organization, government, or their property using the Internet, computers, computer networks, computer hardware, software, and applications, networked devices, or related technologies, including mobile phones, that produce significant social harms or violate a local, state, national or international criminal statute. Many cybercrimes are committed by **hackers**, individuals who secretly and without authorization access computer systems or networks, as well as by organized criminal groups. Cybercrime is a broad category, encompassing computer crimes and what are sometimes called "high-tech" crimes, but it is a narrower idea than **cyber deviance**. Cyber deviance entails using the Internet or a networked device to engage in behavior or activities that, while not criminal, might be considered offensive, abnormal, or strange to some people.

Cybercrimes occur along a diverse spectrum of sophistication and harm. Just as there are significant differences between liquor store robbers and high-end jewel thieves, so, too, are there differences between cybercriminals. Hacking into government network servers or the accounts of financial institutions, for example, requires a high degree of sophistication and technological savvy. Posting a false ad on Craigslist or engaging in **cyberstalking**, however, require an Internet connection and far less sophistication (Bocij, 2004). Cybercrimes thus come in many forms, mirroring the diversity of crimes occurring in the terrestrial, "real" world. Some of those real-world crimes (e.g., thefts, stalking, harassment, espionage, narcotics trafficking), can now easily become cybercrimes once the perpetrator involves a computer and/or the Internet to facilitate them. Other cybercrimes are truly unique events, for example planting malicious code or cyber-trespass.

Researchers have proposed several taxonomies to clarify the landscape of cybercrime types. For example, Wall (2001) identifies four broad categories of cybercrime within which most cybercrime acts fit: (1) cyber-trespass, (2) cyber-deceptions and thefts, (3) cyberpornography, and (4) cyberviolence. Alkaabi et al. (2010) produced a simplified classification system modeled after the Federal Bureau of Investigation (FBI) Uniform Crime Report (UCR), involving Type I and Type II cybercrime offenses. Type I offenses are those where the computer or networked device is the target of criminal activity. Examples include hacking, planting malicious code, denial of service attacks, and identity theft. Type II offenses involve any offense in which the computer or computer network is the tool for committing some other crime, such as facilitating/distributing child pornography, cyber fraud, cyberstalking, terrorism, or murder. Importantly, neither the Wall (2001) nor Alkaabi et al. (2010) classifications are exhaustive or all-inclusive, leaving room for further clarification and refinement as cybercrime continues evolving.

The Scope and Scale of Cybercrime

Cybercrime's impact is felt at all scales, with victims ranging from individuals to corporations, organizations, and governments. Physical, emotional, and psychological harms can stem from cybercrimes, but their most widely cited consequence is their collective financial impact on the global economy, estimated to be in excess of $600 billion a year, a figure that highlights their scale and global reach (Lewis, 2018).

In fact, we are currently at the earliest evolutionary stages of the cybercrime problem. Thanks to rapid advances in related technologies (e.g., microprocessors, or "chips", Internet service) that have led us in just a short time from clunky flip phones to powerful, pocket-size mini-computers (think: iPhone or Galaxy type devices), cybercrime is experiencing unbelievable growth in terms of frequency of occurrence and sophistication. Rather than slow, linear growth over decades, cybercrime is experiencing **exponential scaling** where the scope, scale, and sophistication of cybercrimes are nearly off the charts, changing and evolving so fast that law enforcement can barely keep up. Goodman (2012) alluded to this issue of "scale" against the backdrop of the 2012 Sony PlayStation Network hack by asking "when in the history of humanity has it ever been possible for one person to rob 100 million [people at once]?"

The steady evolution of cybercrime is making it one of modern society's global social problems: traditional obstacles to crime commission like geographic separation and international borders are rendered inconsequential by the Internet. As a result, transnational collectives of cybercriminals and organized crime groups are increasingly engaging in cybercrime (Alkaabi et al., 2010). The United Nations estimates that more than 80% of cybercrime originates from the "organized activity" of a group of connected offenders (United Nations Office on Drugs and Crime, 2013). For example, over a 2-year period (2013–2015), one organized group of cybercriminals hailing from Eastern Europe, Russia, and China stole $1 billion from more than 100 banks located in 30 countries, including Japan, Switzerland, and the United States (Lennon, 2015).

How Much Cybercrime Is There?

Efforts to quantify the scope and scale of the cybercrime problem are done at the local, state, national, and international levels. Importantly, within the United States, neither the Bureau of Justice Statistics (BJS) National Crime Victimization Survey nor the FBI's UCR collect regular annual data on cybercrime offenses, arrests, or number of victimizations.

The lack of reliable, official cybercrime data is itself a significant issue that creates an obstacle to developing a complete understanding of cybercrime in America (Wolff, 2018). As with traditional violent and property crimes, cybercrime data mostly rely on "known" offenses (e.g., an arrest or prosecution has occurred) or self-reported offending or victimization. Much cybercrime occurs deep within the "dark" web or "darknet", on websites and on discussion boards not reachable by traditional search engines, hidden behind cloaked Internet Protocol addresses, resulting in a dark figure of cybercrime—the real amount that occurs—that is unknown and likely significantly underestimated.

BOX 9.1 — THE REAL DEAL: THE ANATOMY OF THE CYBERCRIME PROBLEM

The FBI-maintained Internet Crime Complaint Center (IC3) was established in May 2000. Its purpose is to receive and process cybercrime complaints; data are self-reported by cybercrime victims. IC3 is not widely publicized; the complaints come from victims who either find the site themselves or are directed to it: www.IC3.org. The IC3 records an average of 284,000 distinct cybercrime complaints per year; between 2013 and 2017, IC3 received 1,420,555 complaints with associated financial losses exceeding $5.5 billion. IC3 data show that cybercrime complaints have increased each year for the past five years (see Figure 9.1) across 33 different types of cybercrime (including thefts, frauds, scams, etc.).

(Continued)

FIGURE 9.1　Recent 5-Year Trend in Cybercrime Complaints Collected by the IC3

The IC3 has collected more than four million cybercrime complaints since 2001. However, the FBI estimates that only 15% of all Internet crime victims report their victimization to law enforcement, and less than 10% report to the IC3 (Wolff, 2018). The actual number of crime victims would probably be closer to 40 million—a low-end estimate. IC3 data on cybercrime thus provide only a small glimpse of all cybercrimes occurring in the United States. A 2017 report by Cybersecurity Ventures and the Herjavec Group estimated the global annual cost of cybercrime will rise to $6 trillion by 2021 (Morgan, 2017). The report highlights the fastest growing and most significant cybercrime category is cyberattacks/data breaches. For example, the Yahoo and Equifax client data hacks collectively produced three billion potential cybercrime victims (a high-end estimate). Data collected by Internet security provider Norton indicates that as many as 978 million people may have become cybercrime victims in 2017, with 44% of people who engage in cyber commerce impacted, resulting in $172 billion in financial losses.

At the international level, official cybercrime data are collected by the United Nations, the International Criminal Police Organization (Interpol), Europol, and individual countries. The United Nations reports that 14 adults become cybercrime victims every second—about one million per day (United Nations, 2011). According to a United Nations Office of Drugs and Crime Report, more than half of all cybercrime incidents have an "international dimension" to them (United Nations Office on Drugs and Crime, 2013), meaning the victim and offender were not in the same country, a trend first predicted in a 1979 Interpol report (Schjolberg, 2008).

The Evolution of Cybercrime

Computing technology predates the Internet. The earliest computers were huge, cumbersome machines. For example, the University of Pennsylvania's ENIAC (Electrical Numerical Integrator and Calculator; Figure 9.2) weighed 30 tons and occupied 1,800 square feet of space but could only perform basic mathematical calculations (Swaine & Freiberger, 2014).

In 1958, the integrated circuit boosted computing power, complexity, and enabled the size of computers to shrink. Computers became widely adopted in industrial, government, and corporate settings. Then, in early 1971, the Intel Corporation produced the first microprocessor, or "micro" chip, about the size of a postage stamp and with as much computing power as the entire ENIAC machine. The microchip led directly to the first personal computer—and sparked a wave of innovation among people like Bill Gates (founder of Microsoft) and Paul Allen and Steve Wozniak (cofounders of Apple).

FIGURE 9.2   The ENIAC Computer

Internet technology intersected the development of computing technology in the late 1950s and early 1960s. Researchers at the Massachusetts Institute of Technology (MIT), University of California Los Angeles (UCLA), and the federal government's Defense Advanced Research Projects Agency (DARPA) began conceptualizing a globally interconnected set of computers capable of communicating with each other. In 1969, DARPA created a coast-to-coast network of large, mainframe computers housed on college and university campuses dubbed ARPANET (for Advanced Research Projects Agency Network; Figure 9.3). ARPANET allowed connected computers to share packets of information. It is the basis for today's modern Internet.

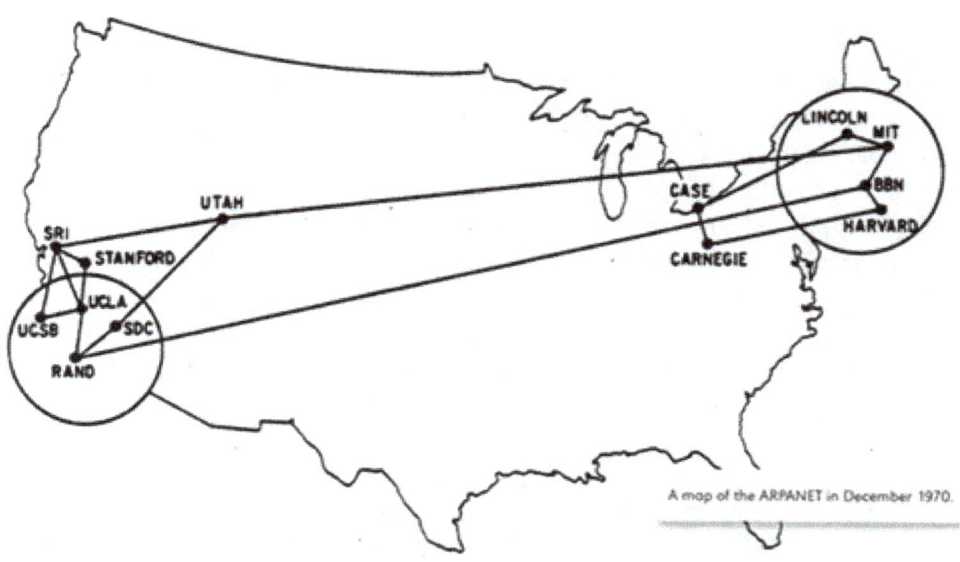

FIGURE 9.3   The ARPANET Network Circa 1970

A major advancement, coinciding with the creation of the microprocessor, occurred in the early 1970s when Vinton Cerf developed the Transmission Control Protocol/Internet Protocol (TCP/IP), which allowed computer communications to occur among geographically isolated mini-networks of connected computers. Quickly, in 1972, ARPANET was revealed to the public, and later that year the first email communication program was developed for it.

According to a history of the Internet compiled by the Internet Society, "widespread development of LANS (local area networks) and personal computers ... in the [early and mid-1980s] allowed the nascent Internet to flourish" (Leiner et al., 1997, p. 8). Cerf's TCP/IP protocol was crucial, helping "transform the Internet into a worldwide" communication network. By the early 1980s, ARPANET was being used by large defense and other organizations; by 1985 it was increasingly leveraged by communities of networks at research centers and universities and government organizations, playing the important role of facilitating daily communications. However, the Internet remained a utilitarian method for transmitting data and information from one point (or network) to another.

Things changed in 1991 when the World Wide Web ("www") was introduced. The creation of the World Wide Web moved the Internet forward, transforming it from a utilitarian data-sharing platform to a worldwide open network capable of storing information that anyone with access to the Internet could use. The World Wide Web revolutionized and helped commercialize the Internet as a **cyberspace** where information could be created, hosted, shared, and discussed. The introduction of the first web browser followed in 1992 (called Mosaic, later renamed Netscape) furthered the potential usability of the Internet for everyday communication and interaction.

In 1995, the Federal Networking Council officially defined the term Internet as:

The global information system that (i) is logically linked together by a globally unique address space based on the Internet Protocol (IP) or its subsequent extensions/follow-ons; (ii) is able to support communications using the Transmission Control Protocol/Internet Protocol (TCP/IP) suite or its subsequent extensions/follow-ons, and/or other IP-compatible protocols; and (iii) provides, uses or makes accessible, either publicly or privately, high level services layered on the communications and related infrastructure described herein. (Leiner et al., 1997, p. 17)

Today, computers, networked devices (e.g., a device connected and able to communicate with other devices), microprocessor technology, and the Internet are ubiquitous and central to social life. Most places and people are now, to some degree, dependent on the Internet and computer technology. Most businesses and organizations make use of both the public Internet to carry out their affairs, as well as nonpublic networks called "intranets" where internal communications and other information are stored. Cybercrime is a natural outgrowth of this technological (r)evolution and our increasing reliance on computers and the Internet to carry out daily tasks. With the rise of the modern Internet in the 1990s, our lives changed forever, and so too did the nature of crime.

Cybercrime Subtypes
Computer Intrusions

Computer intrusions involve the unauthorized access of a computer, or network, for any purpose and are the virtual equivalent of a real-world burglary. Computer intrusions are so common that the FBI has listed them as a law enforcement priority, even forming 54 cybercrime investigative divisions, along with smaller cybercrime squads, and rapid response "action teams" to deal with them. Multi-agency partnerships and task forces to combat computer intrusions are also increasingly prevalent, with agencies like the National Security Agency (NSA), Central Intelligence Agency (CIA), Interpol, and Europol joining forces to control them.

Governments are worried about computer intrusions due to national security concerns and the fear that criminals and criminal networks will exploit vulnerabilities in networks and systems to gain access to sensitive government information. Many hackers follow up their illegal entry into computers and networks by engaging in **cyber vandalism**, which entails defacing websites, or systems, or altering content, or planting a computer virus, worm, bot, spyware, or malware (Federal Bureau of Investigation, 2016a).

The U.S. BJS surveyed over 7,000 businesses, with more than two thirds reporting a cyber intrusion incident over a 1-year period; many businesses were not aware of the intrusion until well after the fact, even when money or information was stolen (Rantala, 2008). It is likely that the number of known computer intrusions significantly underestimates the actual extent of the problem and the financial losses, which total well into the billions of dollars each year (Federal Bureau of Investigation, 2016a).

Identity and Cyber Theft

In February 2016, an unknown hacker or group of hackers secretly broke into the Central Bank of Bangladesh's computerized banking systems and stole $81 million (Gladstone, 2016). This sophisticated **cyber theft**—the unlawful obtaining of personal, financial, information, goods, or services via the Internet or a networked device—took place despite multiple safeguards. Cyber thefts like the one against Bangladesh's Central Bank are growing more frequent, even as advances are made to protect financial and other sensitive information. Particularly common targets of cyber thefts are financial institutions, including banks, as well as credit card companies. However, nearly any corporation or organization is vulnerable to this form of cybercrime. For example, most major corporations, and many smaller ones, including Sony Pictures Studios, Target, Anthem Health Insurance, and many more corporations and organizations have been the victims of large-scale cyber thefts in just the last few years.

Identity theft is a subtype of cyber theft and occurs when someone unlawfully obtains another's personal information and uses it to commit theft or fraud (Federal Bureau of Investigation, 2016c). Personal information could be anything from birthdates and social security numbers to account numbers, PINs, addresses, passport numbers, death certificates, and even fingerprints. Today, many identity theft crimes originate in cyberspace. Hackers may breach email accounts, computer hard drives, credit card agencies, or any number of other networked deviances or services to steal someone's identifying information.

Cybercriminals frequently **use phishing, smishing,** or **vishing** (Federal Bureau of Investigation, 2016d) scams to steal personal information. The difference between the three is that **phishing scams** generally target computers, while **smishing** and **vishing scams** target mobile phones. In all three instances, cybercriminals send out deceptive messages, via emails, phone calls/voicemails, and text messages. Regardless of how they arrive, these messages often claim that your bank account has experienced some suspicious activity. They then direct you to respond by writing or calling back or visiting a website, where you'll be asked to provide sensitive personal information, which is used to steal your money or identity.

The extent of cyber and identity theft is hard to measure accurately because many people may not even be aware their information has been stolen until long afterward and then may never report it to police. In 2019, more than 20 million people were victims of identity theft in the U.S. alone, according to data from the National Crime Victimization Survey. One of the gravest concerns of law enforcement, especially national and international law enforcement agencies like the FBI and Interpol, is that stolen personal information may be used to provide false identities and a "powerful cloak of anonymity" (Federal Bureau of Investigation, 2016d) to terrorists intent on causing harm to large numbers of people. While the FBI has successfully prosecuted more than 2,000 cyber and identity theft cases since 2008 (Federal Bureau of Investigation, 2016b), their efforts have hardly made a dent in the problem since many people and businesses never know, or only realize too late, that they have become a victim of this type of cybercrime.

Cyberbullying and Stalking

When 18-year-old Rutgers University freshman Tyler Clementi leaped to his death from the George Washington Bridge connecting New Jersey and New York, his family, friends, and classmates were shocked. A police investigation eventually revealed that Tyler Clementi's death was the tragic result of the cyberbullying and harassment he encountered at Rutgers University after his roommate and several others secretly recorded his sexual encounter with another man and shared the video with others (Federal Bureau of Investigation, 2016b). The Tyler Clementi case is an example of just how serious **cyberbullying**, stalking, harassment, and exploitation can be.

From a research standpoint, the cybercrimes of bullying, stalking, harassment, and exploitation exemplify how traditional forms of criminal behavior have made the transition to the cyber realm (Grabosky, 2001; Beran & Li, 2005; Beran & Li, 2008). In the case of cyberbullying and online harassment, research indicates that people who are bullied face-to-face are likely to be the same people bullied online. Likewise, the impacts of cyberbullying are equal to, if not worse than, those associated with traditional bullying—anger, frustration, depression, self-harm, and suicide. What often makes cyberbullying and harassment worse is the fact that so much of our social lives take place online and in public, through videos and photos that all become permanent fixtures in cyberspace.

The Internet and computer technologies make it easier to stalk, harass, and exploit people because so much personal information—from social media accounts to phone numbers and addresses—is stored online, not to mention photographs. In some cases, the Internet is used to facilitate even more heinous crimes, especially those involving the sexual exploitation of men, women, and children. Online child pornography and "**sexploitation**"—the sexual exploitation of children and adults—are serious state and federal crimes that are, unfortunately, becoming more frequent.

Since first becoming aware of the role that computers and the Internet play in enabling the sexual exploitation of children in 1993, the FBI, along with state and local law enforcement agencies, have become particularly concerned with this issue. Since beginning the task in 2002, the National Center for Missing and Exploited Children's "Child Victim Identification Program" has analyzed more than 322 million online images and videos depicting children and minors in illegal sexual activities (National Center for Missing and Exploited Children, 2021) in an effort to identify the victims and suspects. Child pornography is traded among child porn users, and the Internet is key for this file-sharing and exploitation process.

Virtual Black Markets

In the early 1990s, U.S. government workers created a device called TOR—The Onion Router—which made it possible for government agents to communicate in secret. In the early 2000s, TOR became publicly available. Essentially, the TOR device adds layers of anonymity to an Internet user's identity and location (i.e., the layers of an "onion") by disguising their unique Internet address (IP) and bouncing their location around to various places around the globe. This makes it virtually impossible to uncover the true location or identity of a person using the TOR device. Importantly, the TOR technology also allows access to what is called the "deep web" or dark net (Figure 9.4).

The deep web or dark net has been described as the "vast ocean of hidden websites" (Kushner, 2014). What most of us consider the "Internet"—Google, Yahoo, Facebook, news, business, and shopping websites—represents just a tiny fraction of the actual Internet universe, perhaps 1% or less. The other 99% of Internet content and websites—tens of trillions of them—reside on the deep web. Unless, of course, you have TOR. Contained within the deep web are thousands of websites, Internet message boards, and forums where illegal goods and services are bought, sold, and traded and where illegally obtained or produced content, like child pornography, is stored and shared. The deep web has gone from being a place where secret government communications can occur to a sprawling, virtual black marketplace—the modern world's largest criminal black market.

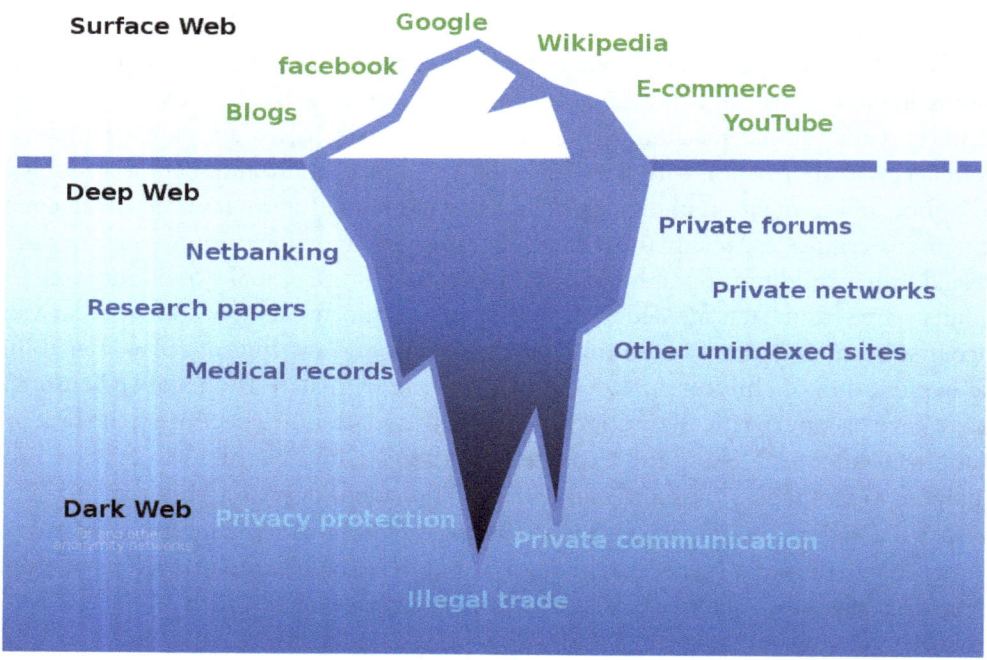

FIGURE 9.4 The Modern Internet Has Many Layers, Including the Deep Web and Dark Web, Which Most People Know Very Little About

In 2013, FBI agents arrested a 29-year-old Ross Ulbricht after a lengthy criminal investigation. Federal prosecutors charged Mr. Ulbricht with running the "most sophisticated and extensive criminal marketplace on the Internet" (Kushner, 2014) named **the Silk Road**, a massive illegal version of commerce websites like Amazon, E-Bay, and Craigslist (Kushner, 2014). Users accessing the Silk Road through their TOR devices could purchase drugs, including cocaine, MDMA (ecstasy), heroin, marijuana, and more from sellers around the world (Kushner, 2014). They could buy fake IDs, including driver's licenses, passports, and social security cards. They could shop for weapons and explosives, hacking tools, malicious software, and tutorials for committing cybercrimes like theft or hacking into an ATM machine. And they could even allegedly hire hitmen to kill on their behalf (Kushner, 2014). All of this illegal commerce occurred within an environment modeled after legitimate e-commerce websites. Users could leave ratings and reviews of the sellers they did business with.

In just two years, the FBI estimated that Ulbricht's Silk Road black marketplace generated over $1.2 billion in illegal revenue, likely a conservative estimate (Kushner, 2014). Even though the FBI arrested Ulbricht and saw him convicted and sentenced to life in prison for his crimes in 2015, this has not altered the role of the deep web in serving as a site for illegal transactions. There are dozens of similar dark net markets in operation at this moment and more being created each day, even as the FBI and other law enforcement agencies take them down.

Cyberviolence

Cyberspace facilitates the commission of serious violent crimes like robbery, murder, and terrorism. Not only does cyberspace make it possible to locate and stalk potential victims, but it can also serve as a place for recruiting or inspiring others to join violent groups or engage in violent acts. For example, Phillip Markoff, the "Craigslist Killer" (Biography.com Editors, 2020), used online classified ads to commit several robberies and murders. More recently, Ronnie Towns was arrested and charged with the double murder of an elderly Georgia couple after luring the couple to a secluded area with a fake ad about a 1966 Ford Mustang for sale. When the couple met with Towns, he shot and killed them, and stole their money (Kovac, 2015). In an even more disturbing case, an 8-month pregnant woman named Michelle Wilkins was brutally stabbed and left for dead at the home of a woman she'd gone to visit after seeing an ad the woman placed on Craigslist to sell baby clothes. Once at the home, Wilkins was attacked, stabbed, and had her unborn child cut from her womb using a knife and broken glass. The child died, and Wilkins survived, and the killer was charged with murder, attempted murder, and many other felonies.

Statistics on cyberviolence are virtually non-existent. But, we do know that in addition to interpersonal violent crimes, like robbery and murder, the Internet is increasingly being used by organized terror groups to facilitate their recruitment efforts, disseminate propaganda, and organize attacks. In 2008, the terrorists that attacked foreign hotels in Mumbai, India, received real-time updates from a terrorist command center via text messages on their mobile phones. Today, the terrorist group ISIS uses the Internet and social media sites like Twitter and YouTube to post messages, videos, and recruit followers to its ranks.

Other organized terrorist groups, including those working on behalf of governments, are leveraging the power of the Internet to engage in **cyberterrorism**. The goals of cyberterrorists are much like those of any terrorist group—to influence the policies and/or actions of a government, organization, or group of people through threat or fear.

However, rather than effect this influence via outright violence, cyber terrorists work behind the scenes to access and steal sensitive and protected information in the forms of "government and trade secrets, ideas and technologies" (Federal Bureau of Investigation, 2014a), which they can leverage to achieve their goals. Additionally, cyberterror groups may attempt to access networked technologies critical to the functioning and safety of a nation. For instance, many critical infrastructure technologies, from traffic lights to power plants, use networks. Any network can be hacked by an individual or group with the skill and time. Thus, a terrorist group could potentially access and hack a city's traffic control system or an electric plant or any number of other important systems. They could thus cause even more disruptions and, potentially, deaths, through these sorts of actions than traditional bombings or shootings.

Cybercrime Characteristics

Both in the United States and globally, the most important characteristic of cybercrime is that it is rapidly increasing in frequency and severity. Thus, unlike U.S. violent and property crime rates, which have been decreasing or stable since their peaks in the 1980s and early 1990s, cybercrime rates are consistently rising. Another defining characteristic of cybercrimes is their financial impact. This is not to say that some cybercrimes, including cyberviolence and cyber terrorism, do not have physical impacts. But the financial costs and losses stemming from cybercrimes set them apart from other criminal activities. Estimates put the financial losses resulting from cybercrimes in the United States at nearly $1 billion annually (Federal Bureau of Investigation, 2014b), while the global cost is in excess of $1 trillion per year (Federal Bureau of Investigation, 2014b; Wiederhold, 2014).

Cybercrimes, like traditional street and property crimes, occur along a diverse spectrum of sophistication and harm. Just as there are significant differences between liquor store robbers and high-end jewel thieves, so too are there differences between cybercriminals. Hacking into government servers or financial institutions, for example, requires a significant degree of sophistication and technological savvy. Posting a false ad on Craigslist or engaging in cyberbullying requires only technological competence and an Internet connection. Likewise, while crimes on the streets produce many types of harms, those harms are not all equivalent: theft of a slice of pizza is far less harmful than aggravated rape. This logic holds true in cyberspace as well. The harm from Internet-facilitated violence, like murder, is far more notable than the harm from planting a malware program inside a single computer.

Cybercrime today is expanding and diversifying so fast that law enforcement is struggling to combat and control it. New types of cybercrime arise more quickly than new laws that can criminalize and control them. Consider also that traditional crimes possess a real physical component (e.g., a specific neighborhood, type of business, address). They are fairly easy for police to respond to and have well-established strategies to control them. Shootings or robberies may yield actual physical evidence that can be easily collected at a pace that suits law enforcement and then be used as the basis for a subsequent prosecution. But the connection between cybercrimes and the physical world is tenuous; they occur in a virtual world, which seriously alters how law enforcement agents can respond to, investigate, and prosecute them, and how and what types of evidence we can collect. All of these factors give cybercrime and cybercriminals the advantage over legal systems and law enforcement officers whose mission is to combat and control them.

Lastly, one of the most important characteristics of cybercrime is that it is increasingly international. In fact, it is so easy for someone in, say, Ukraine, to commit a cybercrime against a business based in Argentina that this pattern of offending has become the rule rather than the exception to it. According to a United Nations Office of Drugs and Crime Report, more than one half of all cybercrime incidents today have an "international dimension" (United Nations Office on Drugs and Crime, 2013) to them, a trend first predicted in 1979 by Interpol, the international police agency based in France (Interpol, n.d.). This trend has serious implications for how we respond to cybercrime and negatively impacts our abilities to control it (Figure 9.5).

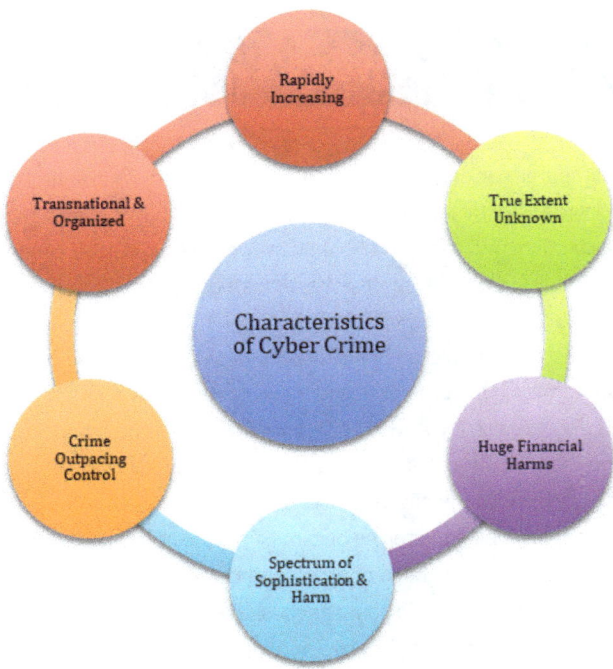

FIGURE 9.5 Primary Characteristics of Cybercrime

Cybercrime Offenders

As cybercrime is becoming an offense that knows no borders, it is also increasingly being committed by transnational organized crime groups and collectives of cybercriminals (Interpol, n.d.). The United Nations estimates that 80% or more of cybercrimes originate from an "organized activity" among a group of offenders (United Nations Office on Drugs and Crime, 2013). These organized cybercrime groups are capable of committing crimes on a massive scale. Over a 2-year period (2013–2015), an organized group of criminals from Russia, Eastern Europe, and China stole $1 billion from more than 100 banks in 30 different countries, including Japan, Switzerland, and the United States (Lennon, 2015).

Organized cybercrime groups see great opportunities for profit by engaging in cybercrimes, and they are leveraging their resources to commit crimes within the virtual space of the Internet. They may commit these offenses for profit or to generate profits that can be used to fund more traditional criminal activities that have a real physical dimension, like drug, weapons, human, and wildlife trafficking. Other cybercriminal groups engage in **hacktivism**, a form of cybercrime as resistance, or political protest, against the policies or practices of a government or organization. Still others use cyberspace to engage in **cyberterrorism**—as a way to influence real-world political outcomes and recruit new members to join their form of cyber terrorism.

WHO DID IT? EDWARD SNOWDEN — BOX 9.2

Hacktivism, using computer hacking capabilities and the platform of the Internet to engage in activism about economic, social, and political issues, is a new 21st-century phenomenon; in fact, dictionaries pre-2001 wouldn't even have contained the word. Hacktivism, however, is quickly becoming a powerful tool and method for raising awareness about certain events and issues; it is a modern method of leveraging cyber technology to produce greater transparency in the world.

Groups like Anonymous, for example, an online collective of computer-savvy hackers, take pride in engaging in hacktivism, often targeting governments and individuals they view as corrupt or disingenuous. Anonymous has focused its efforts against the Motion Picture Association of America, the local prosecutors and law enforcement in Steubenville, Ohio; Facebook; the NSA; the Ku Klux Klan; and more.

Individuals have also gotten into the hacktivism game. The most notable case is that of Edward Snowden. Snowden formerly worked for the CIA. Later, he became a private computer professional and contracted to work for Dell and Booz Allen Hamilton, both of which had contracts with the NSA. It was while working on behalf of the NSA that Snowden learned of that agency's covert domestic surveillance and spying program. He secretly copied tens of thousands of sensitive and classified files and then fled the United States. He divulged many of the files to journalists, who subsequently brought the issues of NSA domestic spying on American citizens to the public's attention. It should be noted that the NSA domestic spying program was both unconstitutional and illegal.

At first glance, hacktivism might not seem like such a negative thing. Clearly, it is important for powerful organizations and governments to be kept in check. Committing crimes against your own citizens and exploiting your power to oppress or exploit people are bad things. At the same time, hacktivism is, by definition, illegal. The members of Anonymous and people like Edward Snowden have all violated multiple criminal laws—from online theft to espionage—in carrying out their hacktivism agendas.

The question is, should we view them as criminals?

The broader issue here is who gets to define what is criminal. Policing and prosecuting hacktivism may be in the best interests of governments and corporations, but is it in the best interests of the people? There are no clear or black and white answers to these questions. Each person has to decide for themselves where they stand with regard to hacktivism and its illegality.

Research shows that cybercriminals mirror their real-world counterparts on most major characteristics. Young, White, males are overrepresented cybercriminals. Research consistently shows that those who engage in cyberviolence, a subtype of cybercrime, are also more likely to engage in violence in the real world. Individuals who engage in cyberviolence—bullying, stalking, murder—also tend to mirror their peers on most major characteristics. Notably, the Craigslist Killer, Phillip Markoff, was a young, White male who used Craigslist to lure young women to hotels where he could murder them. Ronnie "Jay" Towns was only 28 when he also used a false Craigslist ad to lure an elderly Georgia couple to their death.

Motivations for engaging in illegal or criminal behavior are notoriously difficult to discern. Some hackers, like Edward Snowden, commit their crimes out of a sense of social or political justice. Others like Ross Ulbricht, creator of the Silk Road website where users could buy and sell drugs, weapons, and other illicit merchandise, engage in cybercrime for the money. As with traditional street and property crimes, motives tend to vary as much as the types of cybercrimes that occur. We do know from research studies that low self-control and associating with deviant peers are common factors shared by many cybercriminals. Interestingly, many hackers have high levels of self-control because of the nature of their crimes, which require significant knowledge and time to become skilled at committing. Hackers also tend to teach others how to engage in criminal behavior, often thriving in hacker subcultures.

Cybercrime Victims

The FBI estimates that only 15% of all Internet crime victims ever report their victimization to law enforcement, and less than 10% report anything to the Internet Crime Complaint Center. The United Nations reports that as many as 14 adults become cybercrime victims every second—about one million per day (United Nations, 2011). When we discuss cybercrime victims, we include both individuals and organizations, corporations, and governments.

Unlike with street crimes, individual cybercrime victims tend not to know the offender—given how cyberspace works, it's common for victims of identity theft, fraud, and hacking attacks to be separated by vast geographic distances. Victims tend to span a far larger range of ages; with the elderly especially likely to fall victim to certain types of cyber fraud, like phishing attacks. Importantly, research shows that our routine activities (the things we do in the normal routine of our lives) have a direct link to our likelihood of becoming victims of cybercrime. In particular, visiting pornographic websites, sites on the dark web, and downloading or sharing music, videos, or other content online, raise our vulnerability and likelihood of victimization. While both males and females can become victims of cyberviolence, females tend to be overrepresented as victims of cyberbullying and cyberstalking—again mirroring the trends we see within more traditional violent crimes in the non-virtual world.

Key Takeaways

Review the following list of bullet points for a quick overview of the key ideas and information in this chapter:

- Cybercrime, which includes crimes committed via the Internet, networks, or electronic devices is one of the newest categories of crime. It is expanding in scale (i.e., number of offenses) exponentially and changing or evolving rapidly.
- Cybercrime data presents special challenges; we do not adequately collect data about cybercrime offenses or victim or offender data, and the special circumstances of cybercrime make it hard for us to truly understand the scope, scale, or trends of this type of crime.
- Cybercrime offenses present special challenges for law enforcement agencies and investigators. The lack of physical interaction between victims and suspects (including "organizational" victims), the unique nature of cybercrime digital evidence, and the physical distance between victims and offenders (they can be separated by thousands of miles) all create unique challenges for law enforcement agencies trying to respond to and control this type of crime.
- Cybercrimes occur along a diverse spectrum in terms of sophistication, harm, and offender characteristics.

Conclusion and Formal Summary Questions

This chapter helped us learn about cybercrime. We learned that cybercrime, which is one of the newest forms of crime and is growing at an exponential scale and changing or evolving at a rapid pace; the evolution of cybercrime is moving quicker than law enforcement's capacity or capability to deal with the problem. Moreover, we focused on the unique challenges cybercrime presents to law enforcement and to researchers. Good data on cybercrime are hard to come by and likely incomplete; cybercrimes don't involve the typical victim-offender interactions, typical types of evidence, and can be committed across vast differences, bringing up a host of jurisdictional issues. We examined some types of cybercrime, noting that cybercrimes occur along a diverse spectrum in terms of sophistication, harm, and offender characteristics. Some forms of crime require special technological expertise and skill, while others do not. In some cases, new technologies have simply opened up new opportunities for traditional offenders to engage in traditional forms of crime more efficiently or in new ways—for example, using fake classified ads to lure people into situations where they can be robbed or murdered.

- *Cybercrime is increasing in its scale and scope around the world. Can you describe the role that organized criminal groups are playing in the global growth of cybercrime?*

- *Many types of cybercrime mirror crimes in the real world. Can you identify the primary characteristics of cybercrime and come up with two examples of how cybercrimes and real-world crimes intersect?*
- *Good data on cybercrime is hard to find because few people report being cybercrime victims. Can you describe some characteristics of cybercrime victims and come up with two ways that the public could reduce the chance of becoming a cybercrime victim?*

E-Resources

1. Link to *Cybercrime Magazine*—an online repository for all things cybercrime: https://cybersecurityventures.com/
2. *The Dark Web* (YouTube)—how the unseen Internet is accessed: https://www.youtube.com/watch?v=ngT2Aq1VBFc
3. "Inside the Mind of a Hacker"—interactive learning module via the *Washington Post*: https://www.washingtonpost.com/brand-studio/raytheon/inside-the-mind-of-a-hacker/

References

Alkaabi, A., Mohay, G. M., McCullagh, A., & Chantler, N. (2010). Dealing with the problem of cybercrime. In I. Baggili (Ed.), *Digital forensics and cyber crime* (pp. 1–18). Springer. https://doi.org/10.1007/978-3-642-19513-6_1

Beran, T., & Li, Q. (2005). Cyber-harassment: A study of a new method for an old behavior. *Journal of Educational Computing Research, 32*(3), 265–277. https://doi.org/10.2190/8YQM-B04H-PG4D-BLLH

Beran, T., & Li, Q. (2008). The relationship between cyberbullying and school bullying. *Journal of Student Wellbeing, 1*(2), 15–33. https://doi.org/10.21913/JSW.v1i2.172

Biography.com Editors. (2020). *Philip Markoff biography*. Biography.com. https://www.biography.com/crime-figure/philip-markoff

Bocij, P. (2004). *Cyberstalking: Harassment in the internet age and how to protect your family*. Praeger.

Federal Bureau of Investigation. (2014a, September 10). *Statement of Robert Anderson, Jr., executive assistant director, Criminal, Cyber, Response, and Services Branch, Federal Bureau of Investigation, before the Senate Committee on Homeland Security and Government*. https://www.fbi.gov/news/testimony/cyber-security-terrorism-and-beyond-addressing-evolving-threats-to-the-homeland

Federal Bureau of Investigation. (2014b). *Internet crime report*. Internet Crime Complaint Center. https://www.ic3.gov/Media/PDF/AnnualReport/2014_IC3Report.pdf

Federal Bureau of Investigation. (2016a). *Computer intrusions*. https://www.fbi.gov/about-us/investigate/cyber/computer-intrusions

Federal Bureau of Investigation. (2016b). *Identity theft*. https://www.fbi.gov/about-us/investigate/cyber/identity_theft

Federal Bureau of Investigation. (2016c). *Identity theft overview*. https://www.fbi.gov/about-us/investigate/cyber/identity_theft/identity-theft-overview

Federal Bureau of Investigation. (2016d). *Smishing and vishing scams to be aware of this holiday season*. https://www.fbi.gov/news/stories/2010/november/cyber_112410

Gladstone, R. (2016, March 15). Bangladesh bank chief resigns after cyber theft of $81 million. *New York Times*. https://www.nytimes.com/2016/03/16/world/asia/bangladesh-bank-chief-resigns-after-cyber-theft-of-81-million.html

Grabosky, P. N. (2001). Virtual criminality: Old wine in new bottles? *Social & Legal Studies, 10*(2), 243–249. https://doi.org/10.1177/a017405

Interpol. (n.d.). *Cybercrime*. https://www.interpol.int/Crimes/Cybercrime

Kovac, J. (2015). Prosecutor: Alleged Craigslist killer tried to prey on others. *Macon Telegraph*. https://www.macon.com/news/local/article30225942.html

Kushner, D. (2014, February 4). Dead end on the Silk Road: Internet crime kingpin Ross Ulbricht's big fall. *Rolling Stone*. https://www.rollingstone.com/culture/culture-news/dead-end-on-silk-road-internet-crime-kingpin-ross-ulbrichts-big-fall-122158/

Leiner, B. M., Cerf, V. G., Clark, D. D., Kahn, R. E., Kleinrock, L., Lynch, D. C., Postel, J., Roberts, L. G., & Wolff, S. (1997) *Brief history of the internet*. Internet Society. https://www.internetsociety.org/internet/history-internet/brief-history-internet/

Lennon, M. (2015, February 15). Hackers hit 100 banks in 'unprecedented' $1 billion cyber heist: Kaspersky lab. *Security Week*. https://www.securityweek.com/hackers-hit-100-banks-unprecedented-1-billion-cyber-attack-kaspersky-lab

Lewis, J. (2018). *Economic impact of cybercrime—no slowing down*. McAfee & Center for Strategic and International Studies. https://csis-website-prod.s3.amazonaws.com/s3fs-public/publication/economic-impact-cybercrime.pdf

Morgan, S. (2017, May 18). *Global ransomware damage costs predicted to exceed $5 billion in 2017*. Cybercrime Magazine. https://cybersecurityventures.com/ransomware-damage-report-2017-5-billion/

National Center for Missing and Exploited Children. (2021). *Child sexual abuse material*. https://www.missingkids.org/theissues/csam

Rantala, R. R. (2008). *Cybercrime against businesses, 2005*. Office of Justice Programs, U.S. Department of Justice. https://bjs.ojp.gov/content/pub/pdf/cb05.pdf

Schjolberg, S. (2008, December). The History of Global Harmonization on Cybercrime Legislation—The Road to Geneva. https://cybercrimelaw.net/documents/cybercrime_history.pdf

Swaine, M., & Freiberger, P. (2014). *Fire in the valley: The birth and death of the personal computer*. Pragmatic Bookshelf.

United Nations. (2011, December 12). *Cybersecurity: A global issue demanding a global approach*. Department of Economic and Social Affairs. https://www.un.org/en/development/desa/news/ecosoc/cybersecurity-demands-global-approach.html

United Nations Office on Drugs and Crime. (2013). *Comprehensive study on cybercrime*. https://www.unodc.org/documents/organized-crime/UNODC_CCPCJ_EG.4_2013/CYBERCRIME_STUDY_210213.pdf

Wall, D. S. (2001). *Cybercrimes and the internet* (D. Wall, Ed.). Routledge.

Wiederhold, B. K. (2014). The role of psychology in enhancing cybersecurity. *Cyberpsychology, Behavior, and Social Networking, 17*(3), 131–132. https://doi.org/10.1089/cyber.2014.1502

Wolff, J. (2018, February 12). The real reasons why cybercrimes may be vastly undercounted. *Slate*. https://slate.com/technology/2018/02/the-real-reasons-why-cybercrimes-are-vastly-underreported.html

Figure Credits

Fig. 9.1: Source: https://pdf.ic3.gov/2017_IC3Report.pdf.

Fig. 9.2: Source: https://commons.wikimedia.org/wiki/File:World%27s_First_Computer,_the_Electronic_Numerical_Integrator_and_Calculator_(ENIAC).gif.

Fig. 9.3: Source: http://mercury.lcs.mit.edu/~jnc/tech/arpageo.html.

Fig. 9.4: Copyright © by Flori4nK (CC BY-SA 4.0) at https://commons.wikimedia.org/wiki/File:Iceberg_of_Webs.svg.

Chapter 10

Green Crimes and Harms

Key Terms

Green criminology
Green crime
Environmental justice movement
Environmentalism
Greenwashing
Prosecution gap
Air pollution
Great Smog of 1952
Air Quality Index (AQI)
Fracking
Water pollution
E-waste
Hazardous waste
Great Pacific Garbage Patch
Wildlife trafficking
Poaching
Environmental racism
Global illegal wildlife trade

Chapter Headings

1. Chapter opener
2. What is "green" criminology?
3. The scope and scale of green crimes and harms
4. Subtypes of green crimes and harms
    4.1. Air pollution and water pollution
    4.2. Disposal of hazardous and "e"-waste
    4.3. Poaching and illegal wildlife trafficking
5. Green crime characteristics
    5.1. Green crime offenders
    5.2. Green crime victims
6. Chapter summary

Opening Questions

Before you begin the chapter, take a few minutes to reflect on the following questions:

1. How widespread and what types of harms do you think result from environmental or "green" crimes?
2. What do you think the connection is between the environmental movement and the field of green criminology?
3. How do you think law enforcement and prosecutors prioritize the investigation and punishment of environmental crimes and harms?
4. How do you think the study of green crimes and harms overlap with other types of crime?

Chapter Objectives

After reading Chapter 10, students will be able to do the following:

- Define social harm, green crimes, green criminology, and environmental justice
- Describe the scope and impacts of green crimes on individuals and society
- Describe what is meant by the phrase "green crime prosecution gap"
- Identify specific subtypes of green crime and their characteristics

True Crime

Methyl isocyanate (MIC) is one of the most lethal by-products of manufacturing pesticides. Union Carbide, an American chemical corporation, began operating a chemical production plant in the small city of Bhopal, India in the 1960s. On the night of December 2, 1984, a MIC storage tank at the plant began leaking after water entered the tank and began a chemical chain reaction that forced open a pressure release valve. Escaping MIC gas—30 to 45 tons in all—spread quickly from the plant into surrounding areas. Drifting slowly through streets, doorways, and open windows, the MIC gas cloud killed indiscriminately: men, women, children, animals—some 3,800 in the first few hours (Taylor, 2014). Those not killed immediately suffered chemical burns to their eyes, noses, throats, and skin. Over the following weeks, thousands more died—nearly 15,000 killed in all (Taylor, 2014; Figure 10.1). Many survivors were left permanently scarred, crippled, and blinded from their exposure to the gas. Decades later, physical birth defects, higher rates of illness, disease, and death persist among residents.

Union Carbide was immediately accused by many of running a shoddy operation without concern for the health and safety issues that were reported prior to the gas leak, which could have contributed to it. The company shifted responsibility for the tragedy to its Indian subsidiary, which it claimed had complete and sole responsibility for the design, maintenance, and operation of the Bhopal plant. Eventually, Union Carbide, which was purchased by Dow Chemical in 2001, settled various lawsuits related to the gas leak in 1989, paying $470 million to the victims of the tragedy, amounting to just over $500 per person (Mackenzie, 2002). Union Carbide agreed to clean up the many acres of contaminated land and the plant itself, however, that cleanup has yet to occur in any meaningful sense. For its part, the Indian government charged various Union Carbide officials, including then-CEO Warren Anderson, with various crimes, including homicide and assault. In 1992, the Indian government issued an arrest warrant for Anderson, though that symbolic gesture was never expected to result in any actual arrest.

FIGURE 10.1   The 1984 Bhopal Disaster Killed Thousands and, Unfortunately, Is Only One of Many Examples of Preventable Environmental Crimes That Occur Each Year

What Is "Green" Criminology?

Green criminology is the study of "harms against humanity … the environment … and non-human animals committed by both powerful institutions and ordinary people" (Beirne & South, 2007). It may be easiest to think of green criminology as an umbrella category where we collect data and explore crimes and harms that impact the environment, humans, and other species (Lynch, 1990). A key assumption within green criminology is that most ecological problems produce social problems (i.e., desertification leading to food insecurity), and many social problems produce ecological ones (i.e., poverty leading to wildlife trafficking or illegal poaching). Thus, green criminology is actively engaged in debunking the myth that the world's ecological and social problems can be understood independent of one another (Dillard-Wright, 2009; Goedeke, 2004; Jerolmack, 2008).

Green criminology uses a broad critical perspective and definition of crime, where crime also includes "social and ecological harms." These harms may not technically be "illegal", but because they produce significant economic, social, cultural, and environmental damage, green criminologists argue we should still pay equal attention to them. **Green crimes** thus encompass environmental crimes and illegal acts, things like air pollution; crimes against other species, like poaching; and socially harmful but not necessarily criminal, activities that impact humans, the environment, and other species. Research in green criminology therefore closely overlaps with research into other "crimes of the powerful" since power—who has it and what they choose to do with it—plays a key role in the causation of environmental harm and crime. Likewise, studying environmental harm and crime without examining the actions of powerful individuals, organizations, corporations, and governments would lead to an incomplete understanding of the ways green crimes and harms connect to other types of crime.

You might be wondering why we have named the study of crimes and harms that affect the natural environment "green" criminology and not simply environmental crime. The answer is that the name "environmental crime" was already being used in the 1990s to identify the field of criminology that looks at the spatial nature and distribution of criminal events (e.g., where and when crime physically happens). Thus, in criminology, most people know that environmental crime refers to where, when, and under what conditions crime events happen (i.e., day/night, specific location, etc.) *not* to crimes *against or involving* the environment. To solve this problem, we came up with the name green criminology! This means that we will refer to crimes against nature, ecosystems, and other species as "green" crimes and harms (Table 10.1).

TABLE 10.1 **EXAMPLES OF GREEN CRIMES AND HARMS**

Illegal Dumping	Air pollution
Poaching	Illegal logging
Hazardous waste disposal	Electronic (e) waste disposal
Resource extraction: oil, methane, fracking	Overfishing
Deforestation	Ecoterrorism
Animal abuse	Ecological disasters
Global warming	Wildlife trafficking and sale
Water pollution	Mining (strip, open pit, etc.)

Green criminology has strong connections to the American environmental movement, which came to prominence in the 1960s and resulted in many new environmental laws and regulations (Table 10.2), and to the **environmental justice movement**, which takes a critical look at how and why the victims of green crimes tend to disproportionately come from low-income, poor, or marginalized racial and ethnic groups and communities. **Environmentalism**—the belief in protecting and improving the environment for its own benefit and for the benefit of human life—thus is a key belief system at the core of green criminology. Key events throughout modern American and world history—the Centralia, Pennsylvania, coal mine fire; the Santa Barbara oil spill; the Cuyahoga River fire; and the Bhopal disaster have provided further evidence of the need for us to study and discuss green crimes, who is committing and being victimized by them, and how we can control and prevent them.

TABLE 10.2   ENVIRONMENTAL PROTECTION LEGISLATION CREATED IN THE 1960S AND 1970S

Policy or Regulation Name	Year
Solid Waste Disposal Act	1965
Clean Air Act	1967
National Environmental Policy Act	1970
Environmental Protection Agency	1970
Clean Water Act	1972
Toxic Substance Control Act	1976

The Scope and Scale of Green Crimes and Harms

Efforts to combat and control green crimes in the United States occur at local, state, and federal levels, with numerous agencies participating. At the international level, organizations like the United Nations, Interpol, and Europol take the lead, while within the United States, responsibility for controlling green crimes is partly related to where the offense occurs and what the offense is. Local police agencies, or state-level environmental law enforcement divisions, or fish and wildlife divisions may play a role. Depending on the nature and type of the green crime, the federal Environmental Protection Agency and its Criminal Investigation Division, or the Department of Justice Environmental Crimes Section, and/or the U.S. Fish and Wildlife Service may get involved (Department of Justice, Environmental Crimes Section, 2021). Collectively, these agencies are responsible for enforcing numerous local, state, and federal environmental laws and regulations, investigating offenses, filing charges, and prosecuting cases. However, enforcement and prosecution of green crimes are often not the top law enforcement priority of local, state, or federal governments. Budgetary constraints and limitations, political priorities, and agendas significantly influence whether, and what type, of green crimes actually get serious attention (if any) from law enforcement and the court system.

As a result, green crime investigations and enforcement may taper off significantly during periods when environmental protection laws are weakened, or enforcement is deprioritized, as is currently the situation in the United States (Harvard University, n.d.). As with cybercrimes and crimes committed by the powerful, green crimes and harms often escape public, media, political, and law enforcement attention. As a result, many go unnoticed and underpunished. Another reason for this is because of their close association with the actions of the powerful corporations, governments, and organized crime. When powerful organizations and individuals engage in ecologically and socially harmful behavior, they can leverage their resources (i.e., money, status, relationships) to hide their conduct or deflect public and law enforcement attention from it. **Greenwashing** occurs when an organization uses its power and influence to create an environmentally friendly or environmentally responsible public image of itself, despite engaging in environmentally criminal or harmful practices behind the scenes. Greenwashing campaigns can thwart the control and prosecution of green crimes and harms. The criminal actions of CITGO Petroleum in Corpus Christi, Texas, have been detailed by media outlets and researchers (Geman & National Journal, 2014). But despite evidence that CITGO knowingly and willfully failed to regulate the amount of cancer-causing benzene being released into the air from its East Plant Refinery in the mid-2000s, the company avoided significant negative publicity (Jarrell, 2009) because of its ability to manipulate the media and create an image of itself as a positive force in the local communities that were closest to the refinery (Jarrell, 2009, p. 23).

Many criminal and harmful activities that impact the environment have become a part of daily life, to the extent that we may fail to notice their impact or feel no obligation to do anything to change them. Littering is a good example of this phenomenon—despite laws against littering, we see trash and plastic along roads, fields, wetlands, and waterways, and many people seem disinclined to change their behavior to curb this issue. Thus, like cybercrime, the "gray area" of green crimes—the actual amount that occurs—is substantially greater than what we know about through formal enforcement mechanisms or actions.

THE REAL DEAL: THE ANATOMY OF THE GREEN CRIME PROSECUTION GAP — BOX 10.1

Data from the Department of Justice show that environmental crime prosecutions between 1998 and 2014 resulted in 774 years of incarceration and $825 million in fines (Department of Justice, 2021). However, it is rare for those committing green crimes to see their cases end in a jury verdict. Most often, especially with corporations, green crime offenders reach a plea deal or face only civil penalties. In 2018, for example, the DOJ Environment and Natural Resources Division prosecuted more the 3,800 cases in civil court, resulting in about $260 million in civil fines or penalties, but only won four criminal prosecutions. This pattern is typical at the state/local levels as well, where many green crimes are handled in civil courts,

(Continued)

with civil penalties, not in criminal courts. For example, in 2012, 2 years after 11 people were killed and millions of gallons of oil poisoned the Gulf of Mexico through a preventable oil spill, British Petroleum agreed to pay a civil fine of $4.5 billion; four company officials also pled guilty to reduced criminal charges (Kates, 2014). Unfortunately, civil enforcement actions and systems are ineffective at sending strong messages to green crime offenders, many of which continue with business as usual, becoming green crime recidivist (repeat) offenders.

According to data from the Environmental Protection Agency (EPA), over 64,000 companies or facilities are in violation of one, or more, environmental regulations in any given year, yet less than one half of one percent are criminally investigated; even fewer are actually prosecuted or held accountable for their actions (Kates, 2014). The **"green crime prosecution gap"** (Kates, 2014) in the United States may be explained in part by a lack of political will or desire to prioritize holding powerful organizations accountable for their green crimes. It wasn't until 1988 that the U.S. government even gave the EPA the authority to prosecute violations of environmental statutes resulting in harm to our nation's air, water, public land, and wildlife (Kennedy, 2004).

Subtypes of Green Crimes
Air Pollution and Water Pollution

Air Pollution. The industrial revolution changed and is changing, our planet and the lives of every living thing on it. **Air pollution** is primarily caused by burning fossil fuels: things like coal, oil, and natural gas (National Geographic, 2015). As industry and manufacturing ramped up in the 19th century, factories relied on cheap, very dirty coal as energy to power their smelters, looms, and other machines that would sometimes run 24 hours per day to meet product demands. With the invention of the automobile and the airplane, we began burning gasoline and aviation fuel. As the world's population continues growing, many people still rely on home heat derived from burning fuel oil, coal, or natural gas. The combustion of these dirty fuels releases huge quantities of carbon dioxide ($CO2$) and other particulates into the air, creating "smog," which is harmful to human health and a key contributor to global climate change.

The air quality in London, England, was so bad from the 1850s through the 1950s that days of heavy, lingering smog were nicknamed "pea-soupers" (Cleaner Air for London, 2015). So much coal was burned in London that buildings were left covered in black coal soot (Cleaner Air for London, 2015). London's Great Smog of 1952 is directly responsible for killing between 4,000 and 12,000 citizens and injuring over 100,000 more (Cleaner Air for London, 2015). Of course, there was nothing technically illegal about the Great Smog because it was the result of perfectly legal actions. Yet, the magnitude of the harm caused is worthy of note and is exactly what green criminologists are interested in: during just that one event, nearly as many people died as are killed each year by homicide in the United States. Likewise, the largest natural gas leak ever, which occurred in Aliso Canyon, California, at a well owned by Southern California Gas Company over a period of 5 months in 2015–2016, released an estimated 99,000 tons of methane gas, which is 84 times more potent than CO2 gas (California Air Resources Board, 2016). During the incident's peak, an estimated 44,000 kilograms of methane, benzene, and other noxious, toxic, and carcinogenic compounds were being released into the air per hour (California Air Resources Board, 2016). This is the equivalent of the emissions from over 200,000 vehicles (California Air Resources Board, 2016).

Today, we measure and track air quality for public health purposes using the **Air Quality Index (AQI),** which measures and reports pollution levels for "ground-level ozone, particle pollution (also known as particulate matter), carbon monoxide, sulfur dioxide, and nitrogen dioxide" (Environmental Protection Agency, n.d.). The AQI reports air quality levels that range from 0 (completely clean) to 500. The higher the score, the worse the air quality. Developing countries and countries that burn a lot of dirty fossil fuels typically have very poor AQI ratings. Many Chinese manufacturing cities like Beijing and Chengdu regularly experience unhealthy to very unhealthy air quality measurements, meaning people should stay indoors, avoid exertion, and wear masks, or even respirators. Record AQI readings have been taken in Beijing, including what many consider the worst-ever recorded AQI reading of 755, literally off the charts, in 2013 (Wong, 2013). Across the United States, AQI levels average between 25 and 35.

Image 10.1

Water Pollution. **Water pollution** is caused by the intentional and unintentional, direct and indirect, release of substances that negatively modify the water. Sewage, waste in the form of trash or debris, and agricultural and industrial chemicals are also substances that can negatively modify the health of a water body or system. The direct release of pollutants into water bodies would involve, for example, pumping wastewater straight into a river, or allowing wastewater to overflow into rivers (as still happens in many places during heavy rain), or draining chemicals into the ocean. Because of stronger laws, regulations, and oversight, this form of pollution is becoming less common in the United States today than it used to be in the past when people used rivers and streams like open sewers. However, in many developing nations around the world, direct water pollution is very common.

For example, some Chinese rivers run indigo blue when dyes from denim factories are discharged into them. In many African nations, the release of human waste into rivers used for bathing, cooking, and drinking continues to cause lethal outbreaks of disease. **The Great Pacific Garbage Patch (GPGP)**—a floating miasma of junk from around the world that coagulates into an island of trash twice the size of Texas—famously attracts tourists from around the world each year, despite being only one of several such floating trash islands in our oceans. Thanks to the abundance and longevity of plastics, sites like the GPGP will only continue to grow.

Water pollution in all its forms, as with air pollution, has stemmed from the commission of serious crimes and harms that have subsequently killed and seriously injured millions of people, and negatively impacted many non-human species.

For example, **fracking**—a controversial method for extracting natural gas from deep inside the Earth by using high-pressure water—is raising new legal and public health concerns. For example, in 2013, California officials required oil companies to test the wastewater from fracking operations for chemical and toxic compounds. The results confirmed some people's worst fears. Levels of benzene, a lethal, cancer-causing chemical, were on average 700 times higher than state and federal regulations permitted or considered safe (Cart, 2015). Worse still, California officials allowed this "flow back fluid" to be reinjected into groundwater, meaning it could have ended up in drinking water, given to livestock, or sprayed onto agricultural crops. This, of course, represents a serious violation of state regulations, which the EPA called "shocking."

American citizens are fortunate that, in comparison to millions of people living in other places around the world, they don't usually need to worry about the quality, or cleanliness, of the water they drink or bathe in. That has not always been the case. Indeed, one of the key catalysts for the modern American environmental movement was when Ohio's Cuyahoga River became so polluted with chemicals that it actually caught on fire.

And, depending on where you live today, water quality in the United States is still a serious concern. The indirect release of pollutants into water remains a serious concern anywhere that industrial, mining, or manufacturing activities occur. This form of pollution is harder to detect and control than more direct forms since the substances may seep or leech into aquifers, wells, municipal water supplies, and rivers and streams over many years and great distances.

WHO DID IT? UNSAFE TO DRINK—A CLOSER LOOK AT THE WOBURN AND FLINT, MICHIGAN CASES — BOX 10.2

Between 1965 and 1980, 19 children in the small town of Woburn, Massachusetts, were diagnosed with childhood leukemia, a type of cancer that is often deadly (Cutler et al., 1986). Six of the children were next-door neighbors (Cutler et al., 1986). The rate of childhood leukemia in small-town Woburn was 3 times higher than the national average (Cutler et al., 1986). Other people in the town reported developing strange skin rashes and other ailments (Seattle University School of Law, n.d.). A campaign to find out what was going on and a subsequent investigation into the quality and chemical content of Woburn's drinking water revealed that 184 barrels containing toxic chemicals and chemical "sludge" had been illegally buried near the city at a site not far from where two drinking water wells that the children and adults who got sick received their drinking water from (Seattle University School of Law, n.d.). The EPA discovered high levels of the cancer-causing chemical trichloroethylene in the drinking water supply.

Flash forward to 2014 and the down-on-its-luck former automotive and manufacturing City of Flint, Michigan. In April 2014, to cut costs, city officials began drawing drinking water from the Flint River rather than the City of Detroit's drinking water system. Residents immediately began complaining about the water's taste and reported rashes and other strange health issues, but the city issued a statement saying, "Flint water is safe to drink" (New York Times, 2016). Over the ensuing months, residents were advised to boil their water to kill harmful bacteria and an automotive plant stopped using it because it "corroded their car parts" (New York Times, 2016). In early February 2015, the City of Flint continued to dismiss concerns about the water quality and refused an offer to reconnect to Detroit's system for free (New York Times, 2016). Just a few weeks later, testing revealed excessive amounts of lead in the drinking water. One test showed 104 parts per billion (ppb) of lead in the water; the EPA limit for "safe" water is just 15 ppb! A follow-up test showed lead levels in excess of 395 ppb! Lead exposure and poisoning can cause serious health effects, such as brain and nervous system damage, kidney damage, and even death, especially in small children (World Health Organization, 2021).

In the Woburn case, outside pressure from concerned citizens resulted in a civil lawsuit against two companies, W.R. Grace and Beatrice Foods, which each had industrial factories and used potent chemicals within close proximity to the drinking water wells that were contaminated and closed in 1979. After a lengthy civil trial, detailed in the book *A Civil Action* by Jonathan Harr, a jury found insufficient evidence against Beatrice Foods and returned a contradictory verdict against W.R. Grace. Eventually, W.R. Grace settled its case for just $8 million in 1986 (World Health Organization, 2021). In Flint, a similar process is unfolding, where pressure from local citizens and nonprofit groups, researchers, and some health officials has forced investigations and lawsuits. In Flint, it was subsequently learned that when the city began drawing corrosive water from the polluted Flint River, it ate away at the interior of the city's old water pipes, allowing lead and other heavy metals to enter the city's water supply. Both cases highlight the important role non-law-enforcement, non-governmental organizations play in ensuring that green crimes and harms get the attention and victims get the help they deserve.

Disposal of Hazardous and "E" Waste

Green criminologists are focused on the illegal or harmful disposal of hazardous and electronic "e"-waste. **Hazardous waste** is any liquid, solid, gas, or sludge that is harmful or dangerous to the environment and/or human health (Environmental Protection Agency, 2016). Examples of hazardous wastes include household cleaning fluids, pesticides, paints, batteries, radioactive materials, and many by-products from industrial and manufacturing processes. Electronic "e"-waste is a newer but rapidly growing problem. The term **e-waste** is used to describe the nearly 65 million tons of electronics that are discarded each year—anything that is "nearing the end of its useful life," including televisions, computers/tablets, cell phones, stereos, and more (CalRecycle, 2021). E-waste often contains many hazardous materials and components.

Over 400 million tons of hazardous waste (The World Counts, n.d.) is produced each year around the world along with enough e-waste to fill 1.15 million tractor-trailer trucks full (41 million metric tons of e-waste) (Causes International, n.d.)! Some e-waste ends up discarded into the trash and in our landfills but most is "recycled." Indeed, in the United States, most municipal governments now require that electronic items be sorted from the regular trash and recycled. What this often means in practice, however, is that our e-waste is recycled by being legally exported to places like China, India, Nigeria, or Ghana. Worse still is that the United Nations Environment Program estimates that as much as 90% of the world's e-waste is illegally traded or dumped each year (Figure 10.2).

Once it arrives in a foreign country, it typically becomes the job of the poorest, least educated, least protected workers to sort through it. Many of those workers engage in dangerous practices to extract the precious metals: gold, silver, platinum, palladium, copper, coltan, etc.—from inside the devices. The fastest way to do this is for workers to burn the electronics or use cyanide to retrieve the metals. This process can release mercury, lead, and cadmium into the air, ground, and their bodies. While each device yields incremental amounts of these precious metals, when you consider the volume of e-waste generated, it becomes more obvious why workers would risk their lives mining these metals.

Researchers have long noted that the locations of waste-producing industrial and manufacturing facilities, along with waste disposal sites, are not evenly distributed (Mata, 1994). Indeed, these facilities are often constructed in the poorest, most disorganized communities, with large minority populations (Lynch & Stretesky, 2014). These communities often lack the political, economic, and social capital to organize and resist or oppose the construction of these facilities in their neighborhoods, and, often, they come to rely on these places as vital sites of employment. This means that exposure to the risks from hazardous and toxic wastes, as well as air and water pollution, is higher among particular groups of people living in specific places, both in the United States and around the world (Massey, 2004). The term attached to this phenomenon is **environmental racism,** and it is a key issue within the larger **environmental justice movement** that seeks to promote fairness and justice in terms of exposure to environmental risks, as well as the investigation, prosecution, and punishment of criminal and civil offenders (Bullard, 1990).

FIGURE 10.2 Many of Us Use and Discard Our Electronic Devices Without Thinking About the Impact the Toxic Substances and Heavy Metals Contained Within Them Wreak on Our World and Lives

A significant issue in the illegal and/or harmful disposal of hazardous and e-waste is the role played by organized criminal groups. In 1985, two sociologists, Alan Block and Frank Scarpitti, published a book exposing the role of organized criminal groups in the disposal of toxic waste in the United States (Block & Scarpitti, 1985). *Poisoning for Profit* revealed how organized crime groups had infiltrated many "legitimate" waste disposal companies in order to gain access to the lucrative, high-value contracts awarded to those hauling away America's unwanted waste.

The problem with organized criminal involvement in hazardous waste disposal is that they have no incentive to follow regulations or abide by waste disposal laws—their interest is solely in making a profit. Moreover, the presence of organized crime in the waste disposal industry undoubtedly results in the corruption of the waste disposal oversight system, as regulators and police are bribed or coerced to "look the other way." For example, just a few years prior to the publication of *Poisoning for Profit*, an article in the *New York Times* described how organized criminal groups in New York were "illegally dumping vast quantities of dangerous chemicals" by "flushing them into sewer systems, pouring them into garbage landfills, dumping them into waterways, mixing them into heating oil, stacking them in warehouses and burying them in unmarked pits" (Blumenthal & Franklin, 1983).

As recently as 2013, the FBI indicted 32 organized crime figures from three New York area crime families for plotting to "control the commercial waste disposal industry" (Federal Bureau of Investigation, 2013) in the city. The pervasiveness of organized crime's illegal control and disposal of hazardous and toxic wastes and law enforcement's efforts to combat it was aptly summarized by the Manhattan U.S. attorney in a press release: "Organized crime still wraps its tentacles around industries it has fed off for decades, but law enforcement continues to pry loose its grip" (Federal Bureau of Investigation, 2013).

Poaching and Illegal Wildlife Trafficking

On the night of July 1, 2015, American dentist and big-game hunter Walter Palmer lay in the brush on private land abutting the Hwange Game Reserve in Zimbabwe. Nearby was Theo Bronkhorst, a safari guide who Palmer paid $50,000 to help him "bag" an African lion (Dorian et al., 2015). Using a dead elephant carcass as bait, the duo succeeded in drawing Cecil, a 13-year-old black-maned male lion outside of Hwange's protected park boundaries (Dorian et al., 2015; Figure 10.3). When Cecil approached the dead elephant, Palmer and Bronkhorst illuminated him with a high-powered spotlight, temporarily blinding him. Palmer then fired an arrow, which seriously injured, but did not immediately kill, Cecil, who then fled. Early the next day, July 2, Palmer and Bronkhorst tracked the badly bleeding and weakened Cecil and killed him. They then posed for pictures with his body before cutting off his head and skinning him.

Cecil was one of Hwange's most popular and photographed lions, and his death became international news and was shared extensively via social media. Cecil was also part of a long-running Oxford University research study and was outfitted with a GPS tracking collar, which eventually helped the research team and park rangers discover his body. A joint investigation by Hwange's authorities and the Zimbabwean government commenced and uncovered how Cecil was illegally killed, as well as the fact that Mr. Palmer and Mr. Bronkhorst lacked legal hunting permits. Mr. Bronkhorst and the private landowner were arrested and charged with criminal **poaching** and other crimes (Dorian et al., 2015). Poaching is the illegal killing, or attempted taking, of any game—including fish, reptiles, birds, or animals (Hurteau, 2011). The American dentist, Mr. Palmer, who had already traveled back to the United States, received a significant amount of negative publicity but was never criminally charged (McLaughlin, 2015). In several interviews, he rationalized his actions by saying he "had no idea that the lion ... was a known, local favorite, was collared and part of a study until the end of the hunt," and he "relied on the expertise of local professional guides to ensure a legal hunt" (McLaughlin, 2015).

FIGURE 10.3   Cecil the Lion Was Majestic and a Star of the Hwange Game Reserve Until He Was Killed by Two White Poachers, Including American Dentist Walter Palmer

Illegal poaching is a serious global crime that contributes to issues like global biodiversity loss, wildlife endangerment and extinction, and the destabilization of local communities and nation-states. Illegal poaching also feeds the **global illegal wildlife trade**. That black market is massive, involving more than 30,000 distinct plant and animal species—many of which are rare, threatened, endangered, or on the verge of extinction—and the movement of hundreds of millions of species or products derived from them each year (Wyatt, 2013), including things like ivory, shark fins, exotic hardwoods (Corporate Crime Reporter, 2016) and more. Many trafficked animals and reptile species are sold into captivity in zoos, wildlife shows, or into the pet industry, as the recent hit Netflix show *The Tiger King* illustrated. Likewise, animal and plant by-products and derivatives are often sought after for use in traditional medicines (Traffic, 2015), foods, and in the manufacture of consumer products, including souvenirs and even musical instruments (Sheppard, 2012).

Wildlife trafficking is the term applied to the "entire journey of an endangered and/or protected animal, plant or derivative thereof, from being taken in the wild to arrival at their final destination" (Wyatt, 2013). Trafficking in wildlife is estimated to generate at least $10 billion in revenue each year, making it the third most lucrative illegal black market in the world, trailing only the illegal drug and weapon trades (Wyatt, 2013, p. 304). As a result, the global wildlife trade is increasingly run by sophisticated transnational organized criminal networks that also traffic in drugs, weapons, and people (World Wildlife Fund, n.d.). Within the illegal wildlife trade, actors and interests from the corporate, organized crime, and government worlds converge, making it one of the most dynamic areas of study within green criminology. Importantly, animals and plants are often pulled or extracted from communities and ecosystems within vulnerable places, often by the poor, disadvantaged local population because of the demand for these species and by-products in wealthier nations and communities. Just as with drugs and human trafficking, the net result is a further negative impact and destabilization of those already unstable, disorganized places.

The global wildlife trade is a major political, social, ecological, and economic problem, particularly because the trade threatens national security and because the illegal proceeds from the trade support organized criminal and terrorist groups and other illegal activities. As a result, 179 countries have ratified the **Convention on International Trade in Endangered Species (CITES)**, an international treaty designed to reduce and control the global trade in all wildlife and plants. Recent data indicate that CITES may be playing a limited but effective role in helping reduce the scale of the global wildlife trade (Convention on International Trade in Endangered Species of Wild Fauna and Flora, n.d.).

Green Crime Characteristics
Green Crime Offenders
Individuals, corporations/organizations, and governments can all be green crime offenders as the examples in this chapter highlight. The characteristics of offenders are thus as diverse as the entities themselves. As discussed in the next session in reference to victims, it is extremely challenging

for us to accurately quantify how many green crimes/harms occur and who is responsible. For example, in countless situations, it may be difficult or impossible to trace pollution to its root or originating source; we may not know that an animal has been illegally killed until parts of it, like elephant or rhino ivory tusks, show up in a marketplace or confiscated shipment.

We do know that some forms of green crime/harm are state-sanctioned or allowed to occur by government bodies. We also know that corporations routinely violate environmental laws and regulations, especially those concerning air quality/air pollution. And we know that transnational organized criminal groups are playing an ever-larger, more significant role in perpetrating certain forms of green crime/harm, from disposal of hazardous or e-waste to illegal wildlife trafficking. Beyond this knowledge, hard data on prosecutions or the true extent of offending is unknown, and official data likely severely underestimates the extent of the problem.

Green Crime Victims

Anyone can become a victim of a green crime or harm. Depending on your perspective, you can argue that all of us are or have been victims or victimized by air and water pollution, illegal disposal of waste, littering, poaching—activities that impact commonly shared and enjoyed resources. In the age of global climate change, victimization takes on an even larger, more significant scope.

As noted in other chapters in this book, our knowledge of crimes or harms is only as good as our ability to capture and analyze good data. If a crime isn't reported or prosecuted, it won't show up in official crime statistics. If a crime isn't prioritized by a government or agency, arrests and prosecutions may be much lower, giving a false impression of the extent or severity of the crime(s). If a person is victimized but doesn't report the victimization, we miss them in our assessments and analyses. How we choose to define a crime also impacts what qualifies as crime; too narrow a definition may leave out many victims and crime events. For that reason, criminologists studying green crimes, as well as crimes of the powerful, adopt a broader view of crime to include social or ecological harms. Thus, as with other forms of crime, especially those that challenge our abilities to capture and analyze good data (e.g., cybercrime), the "dark figure" of green crimes and harms is immense.

There are few reliable green crime victimization statistics. For example, there may be as many as 800,000 deaths per year from ambient air pollution, but that's just an estimate; the true number might be exponentially higher, or lower, depending on what you choose to include or not include (Croall, 2010). Adding to issues with identifying the extent of victimization is the fact that many people are revictimized repeatedly—from things like water pollution—should we count each victimization separately? And for issues like poaching or wildlife trafficking, how do we assess victimization when no one truly "owns" the animal or plant species? We do know that poor, low-income, politically marginalized, and/or voiceless people, often from developing nations, are more likely to become victims of many types of green crime and harms than their wealthier counterparts. Nevertheless, accurately assessing victimization is one of our greatest challenges.

Key Takeaways

Review the following list of bullet points for a quick overview of the key ideas and information in this chapter:

- Green criminology is an analysis of crimes and harms that impact the natural environment, ecosystems, plants, animals, and people.
- Green crimes and harms have strong connections to big concepts like power and inequality, as well as other major forms of crime like organized crime, state crime, human and drug trafficking, and more.
- There are many subtypes of green crime and harm, sharing many similarities. Notably, they tend to impact poor or disadvantaged and disorganized people, communities, and places more than wealthy ones.
- Our knowledge of who is a green crime offender and victim is extremely limited by a lack of comprehensive, reliable data. While we know some general characteristics of both offenders and victims, the true extent of green crime/harm commission and victimization is unknown.

Conclusion and Formal Summary Questions

In this chapter, we introduced you to green criminology and looked at some of the main subtypes of green crime/harm and major issues and challenges facing us as we try to get a better sense of the extent and severity of this crime category. It is vitally important that we continue to develop data on this crime type so that we can communicate effectively about it to the public and ensure appropriate safeguards and resources are devoted to the problem. We hope you continue to explore the subject and pay attention to the coverage and control (or lack thereof) that green crimes and harms receive in our modern world.

- *Can you define green criminology, green crime, and explain why we also include "harms" when we study this crime type?*
- *Can you explain how issues and concepts like environmentalism, environmental justice, environmental racism, and greenwashing overlap or intersect with the study of green crimes and harms?*
- *Can you explain how green crimes and harms intersect with other crime types and how "power" plays a key role in determining who is more likely to become a victim?*

E-Resources

1. Website for the Green Criminology Specialist Group: https://www.iucn.org/commissions/commission-environmental-economic-and-social-policy/our-work/green-criminology

2. *What Is Environmental Justice* video: https://www.nrdc.org/stories/what-is-environmental-justice
3. *The 10 Worst Environmental Disasters*: youtube.com/watch?v=PcLrH2eIOWI

References

Beirne, P., & South, N. (Eds.). (2007). *Issues in green criminology*. Willan.

Block, A. A., & Scarpitti, F. R. (1985). *Poisoning for profit: The mafia and toxic waste in America*. William Morrow and Company.

Blumenthal, R., & Franklin, B. A. (1983, June 5). Illegal dumping of toxins laid to organized crime. *New York Times*. https://www.nytimes.com/1983/06/05/nyregion/illegal-dumping-of-toxins-laid-to-organized-crime.html

Bullard, R. D. (1990). *Dumping in Dixie: Race, class, and environmental quality*. Westview Press.

Cleaner Air for London. (2015). *History of air pollution in London*. Greater London Authority. http://www.cleanerairforlondon.org.uk/londons-air/air-quality-data/trends-london/history-air-pollution-london

California Air Resources Board. (2016, October 21). *Determination of total methane emissions from the Aliso Canyon natural gas leak incident*. https://ww2.arb.ca.gov/sites/default/files/2020-07/aliso_canyon_methane_emissions-arb_final.pdf

CalRecycle. (2021). *What is e-waste?* https://www.calrecycle.ca.gov/electronics/whatisewaste/

Cart, J. (2015, February 11). High levels of benzene found in fracking waste water. *The Los Angeles Times*. https://www.latimes.com/local/california/la-me-fracking-20150211-story.html

Causes International. (n.d.). *E-waste facts*. https://www.causesinternational.com/ewaste/e-waste-facts/

Convention on International Trade in Endangered Species of Wild Fauna and Flora. (n.d.). *What is CITES?* https://cites.org/eng/disc/what.php

Corporate Crime Reporter. (2016, February 1). *Lumber Liquidators to pay more than $13 million for felony environmental crimes*. http://www.corporatecrimereporter.com/news/200/lumber-liquidators-to-pay-more-than-13-million-for-felony-environmental-crimes/

Croall, H. (2010). Economic crime and victimology a critical appraisal. *Journal International de Victimologie, 8*(2), 162–182.

Cutler, J. J., Parker, G. S., Rosen, S., Prenney, B., Healey, R., & Caldwell, G. G. (1986). Childhood leukemia in Woburn, Massachusetts. *Public Health Reports, 101*(2), 201–205.

Department of Justice. (2015). *Prosecution of federal pollution crimes*. Environmental and National Resources Division. https://www.justice.gov/enrd/prosecution-federal-pollution-crimes

Department of Justice. (2021). *Environmental crimes section*. https://www.justice.gov/enrd/environmental-crimes-section

Dillard-Wright, D. B. (2009). Thinking across species boundaries: General sociality and embodied meaning. *Society & Animals, 17*(1), 53–71. https://doi.org/10.1163/156853009X393765

Dorian, M., Putrino, L., Rakowski, C., & Valiente, A. (2015, August 13). *What happened in the harrowing hours before Cecil the Lion was killed*. ABC News. https://abcnews.go.com/International/happened-harrowing-hours-cecil-lion-killed/story?id=33044279

Environmental Protection Agency. (n.d.). *Air quality index (AQI) basics*. AirNow.gov. https://www.airnow.gov/aqi/aqi-basics/

Environmental Protection Agency. (2016). *Wastes—hazardous wastes*. http://www3.epa.gov/epawaste/hazard/

Federal Bureau of Investigation. (2013, January 16). *Thirty-two individuals charged in Manhattan federal court in connection with alleged organized crime scheme to control the commercial waste disposal industry*. New York Field Office. https://

archives.fbi.gov/archives/newyork/press-releases/2013/thirty-two-individuals-charged-in-manhattan-federal-court-in-connection-with-alleged-organized-crime-scheme-to-control-the-commercial-waste-disposal-industry

Geman, B., & National Journal. (2014, May 21). 10 years of pollution, $2 million in penalties. *The Atlantic*. https://www.theatlantic.com/politics/archive/2014/05/10-years-of-pollution-2-million-in-penalties/447102/

Goedeke, T. L. (2004). In the eye of the beholder: Changing social perceptions of the Florida Manatee. *Society & Animals, 12*(2), 99–116. https://doi.org/10.1163/1568530041446562

Harvard University. (n.d.). *Regulatory tracker*. Environmental & Energy Law Program. https://eelp.law.harvard.edu/portfolios/environmental-governance/regulatory-tracker/?fbclid=IwAR0IW_w-Khbt8NBc3fla-h0My0IvtOV0gnRYfc-wBh05fXcy3_sWxx0lPYo

Hurteau, D. (2011). What is poaching? Check out the poaching definition. *Field and Stream*. https://www.fieldandstream.com/blogs/whitetail-365/2011/05/so-just-what-poaching/

Jerolmack, C. (2008). How pigeons became rats: The cultural-spatial logic of problem animals. *Social Problems, 55*(1), 72–94. https://doi.org/10.1525/sp.2008.55.1.72

Jarrell, M. L. (2009). Environmental crime and injustice: Media coverage of a landmark environmental crime case. *Southwest Journal of Criminal Justice, 6*(1), 25–44.

Kates, G. (2014, July 14). Environmental crime: The prosecution gap. *The Crime Report*. https://thecrimereport.org/2014/07/14/2014-07-environmental-crime-the-prosecution-gap/

Kennedy, Jr., R. F. (2004). *Crimes against nature*. HarperCollins.

Lynch, M. J. (1990). The greening of criminology: A perspective on the 1990s. *Critical Criminology, 2*(3), 3–12.

Lynch, M. J., & Stretesky, P. B. (2014). *Exploring green criminology: Toward a green criminological revolution*. Ashgate Publishing.

Mackenzie, D. (2002, December 4). Fresh evidence on Bhopal disaster. *New Scientist*. https://www.newscientist.com/article/dn3140-fresh-evidence-on-bhopal-disaster/

Massey, R. (2004). *Environmental justice: Income, race, and health*. Global Development and Environment Institute, Tufts University.

Mata, R. (1994). Hazardous waste facilities and environmental equity: A proposed siting model. *Virginia Environmental Law Journal, 13*(3), 375–467. https://www.jstor.org/stable/24786873

McLaughlin, E. C. (2015, October 12). Zimbabwe won't press charges against Cecil the Lion's killer. CNN. https://www.cnn.com/2015/10/12/africa/zimbabwe-cecil-lion-walter-palmer-no-charges/index.html

National Geographic. (2015). *Air pollution*. http://environment.nationalgeographic.com/environment/global-warming/pollution-overview/

New York Times. (2016, January 21). Events that led to Flint's water crisis. http://www.nytimes.com/interactive/2016/01/21/us/flint-lead-water-timeline.html?_r=0

Seattle University School of Law. (n.d.). *Anderson v. W.R. Grace*. http://www.law.seattleu.edu/centers-and-institutes/films-for-justice-institute/lessons-from-woburn/about-the-case

Sheppard, K. (2012, August 7). Gibson guitars and Feds settle in illegal wood case. *Mother Jones*. https://www.motherjones.com/politics/2012/08/gibson-and-feds-settle-illegal-wood-case/

Taylor, A. (2014, December 2). Bhopal: The world's worst industrial disaster, 30 years later. *The Atlantic*. https://www.theatlantic.com/photo/2014/12/bhopal-the-worlds-worst-industrial-disaster-30-years-later/100864/

The World Counts. (n.d.). *Hazardous waste statistics.* http://www.theworldcounts.com/counters/waste_pollution_facts/hazardous_waste_statistics

Traffic. (2015, October 15). *Chinese TCM industry says no to illegal wildlife trade.* https://www.traffic.org/news/chinese-tcm-industry-says-no-to-illegal-wildlife-trade/

Wong, E. (2013, January 12). On a scale of 0 to 500, Beijing's air quality tops 'crazy bad' at 755. *The New York Times.* https://www.nytimes.com/2013/01/13/science/earth/beijing-air-pollution-off-the-charts.html?smid=url-share

World Health Organization. (2021, October 11). *Lead poisoning.* https://www.who.int/en/news-room/fact-sheets/detail/lead-poisoning-and-health

World Wildlife Fund. (n.d.). *Illegal wildlife trade.* https://www.worldwildlife.org/threats/illegal-wildlife-trade

Wyatt, T. (2013). Uncovering the significance of and motivation for wildlife trafficking. In N. South & A. Brisman (Eds.), *The international handbook of green criminology* (pp. 303–316). Routledge.

Figure Credits

IMG 10.1: Copyright © by Brian Jeffery Beggerly (CC BY 2.0) at https://commons.wikimedia.org/wiki/File:Beijing_Forbidden_City_Smog.jpg.

Fig. 10.1: Source: https://www.financialexpress.com/india-news/bhopal-gas-tragedy-33-years-after-disaster-city-still-cries-foul/958239/. Copyright © by Reuters.

Fig. 10.2: Copyright © by Rwanda Green Fund (CC BY-ND 2.0) at https://www.flickr.com/photos/127716409@N05/36359985743.

Fig. 10.3: Copyright © by Daughter#3 (CC BY-SA 2.0) at https://commons.wikimedia.org/wiki/File:Cecil_the_lion_at_Hwange_National_Park_(4516560206).jpg.

Crimes of Power: Organized and State Crime Profiles

MODULE 5

Chapter 11

Organized Crime

Key Terms

Organized crime
Money laundering
Globalization
Omerta
Political corruption
Extortion
Racketeer Influenced and Corrupt Organization Act (RICO)
Racketeering
Narcotics trafficking
Human trafficking
Weapons trafficking
Antiquities theft, fraud, and trafficking

Opening Questions

Before you begin the chapter, take a few minutes to reflect on the following questions:

1. What is the relationship between organized crime, government, and legitimate business?
2. How has globalization influenced the development of organized crime?
3. What are several major forms of organized crime?
4. How is organized crime exploiting the Internet to engage in criminal activity?

Chapter Headings

1. Chapter opener
2. What is organized crime?
    2.1. The organization of organized crime
3. The scope and scale of organized crime
    3.1. The Catch-22—Law enforcement action may create organized crime
    3.2. The RICO Act and American organized crime
4. Organized crime subtypes
    4.1. Narcotics manufacturing, trafficking, and distribution
    4.2. Weapons trafficking and distribution
    4.3. Human and organ trafficking
    4.4. Antiquities theft, fraud, and trafficking
5. Organized crime characteristics
6. Chapter summary

Chapter Objectives

After reading Chapter 11, students will be able to do the following:

- Define organized crime and its key characteristics
- Describe different illegal activities that organized crime groups engage in
- Understand the scope of organized crime and connections to other crime types
- Understand the connections between organized crime and other crimes of the powerful

True Crime

At 6'5" and 300 pounds, Richard Kuklinski was an intimidating person, all the more so because of his short fuse and penchant for using violence against others with little provocation. As a youth, Kuklinski displayed the hallmark tendencies of someone destined to a life of violence: he took revenge against a neighborhood bully, beating him to death and cutting off his fingers, and killed and mutilated animals. As an adult, Kuklinski connected with one of New York City's most notorious organized crime families: the Gambinos. What began as a business relationship with Kuklinski pirating and selling pornographic films for the Gambinos eventually transitioned into something much more.

Richard Kuklinski wasn't shy about discussing his murderous exploits (Ginsburg, 2001), on his own and on behalf of the Gambino crime family as one of their top hitmen during the 1970s and 1980s, a period during which he claimed to have killed over 100 people. Kuklinski said he killed people using a variety of methods—guns, knives, poison—often experimenting, learning, and improving over time. He sometimes kept the bodies of victims on ice, only disposing of them much later to throw investigators off-balance, earning him the nickname: "The Iceman." Throughout his life, Kuklinski maintained the outward appearance of normalcy, marrying and raising two daughters. In many ways, Kuklinski was the ultimate organized crime soldier: he killed when asked, helping his organized crime employers advance their criminal interests, consolidate power, and remove any threats to their existence.

What Is Organized Crime?

The control, organization, and distribution of illegal goods and services on a national and transnational (i.e., international) scale is what we refer to as **organized crime** (Siegel et al., 2003). Organized crime occurs virtually everywhere and has existed for as long as people have been living in communities with laws, rules, and prohibitions. Indeed, it is the very act of formally prohibiting, banning, outlawing, and criminalizing certain goods, products, or services that gives life to, and helps sustain, organized crime throughout the world.

The Organization of Organized Crime

The analogy of an invasive weed is apt for picturing organized crime—once it establishes itself in a certain place, its roots spread quickly, impacting everything else around it. Organized crime often extends its roots into legitimate businesses and politics, not only creating the appearance of legitimacy but also helping create a protective, insulating barrier against investigation and prosecution. Organized crime relies on the cooperation of a network of individuals who have a mutually beneficial relationship. Corrupt politicians, dishonest judges, deceitful bankers, crooked law enforcement officers, and a breakdown of the legal system protect, sustain, and facilitate organized criminal activities (Glenny, 2008).

Knowing who belongs to criminal networks and how they differ from one another helps us better understand organized crime and guides law enforcement strategies and policies to combat it. To say that organized crime occurs along a spectrum of sophistication, and involves a diverse array of groups and networks, still doesn't adequately capture just how many, and how unique, the world's organized crime groups are. Organized crime occurs at the local, regional, national, and transnational levels with groups sometimes arranging themselves based on shared religious or cultural beliefs, or ethnic, or racial backgrounds; others are simply conglomerations of individuals united by a desire to make a profit. To help you make sense of organized crime, we have developed five different typologies of organized criminal groups and crime networks based on their generalized structural and organizational characteristics (United Nations Office on Drugs and Crime, 2002; see Table 11.1).

TABLE 11.1   **ORGANIZED CRIME NETWORKS**

Type of Organized Crime Group Network	Operational Structure
Standard Hierarchy	<ul><li>clearly defined with a single leader</li><li>a specific name is often linked to a social or ethnic identity</li><li>strong system of internal discipline</li><li>operates within, and controls, a clearly defined territory</li><li>violence is embedded in most activities</li></ul>
Regional Hierarchy	<ul><li>operates under a single central leader, but its regional organizations have a degree of autonomy</li><li>often share an ethnic and social identity</li><li>operate under the control of the central group to engage in multiple activities and help spread their influence</li><li>internal discipline is high and violence is a part of most dealings</li></ul>
Clustered Hierarchy	<ul><li>consists of a set of criminal groups with an established system of coordinating and controlling illicit activities</li><li>a core group acts as the central or oversight body, with clusters branching off into autonomous groups, each with an identity of its own</li><li>clusters often control divided markets</li><li>the potential for competition between groups and disruption of activity is high, making clustered hierarchies rare</li></ul>
Core Group	<ul><li>a small, tight, structured group of individuals conduct a criminal enterprise</li><li>the distribution of power is flat, with activities divided evenly among core group members</li><li>internal discipline is maintained by virtue of the small number of members and limited number of criminal activities</li><li>core groups usually have very little social or ethnic identity</li></ul>

Criminal Network
- loosely connected networks of individuals
- engage in ongoing criminal transactions
- are often built around individuals with characteristics, skills, or connections
- criminal networks are characterized by shifting alliances, with members providing their services to different components and "middlemen" serving as the connecting link between them and the central figures through which most connections operate

Source: *Results of a Pilot Survey of Forty Selected Organized Criminal Groups in Sixteen Countries.* September 2002. Global Program Against Transnational Organized Crime, United Nations Office on Drugs and Crime.

In addition to differing in structure, criminal groups may change their characteristics and operations over time and according to supply and demand. This variability in turn influences the nature and characteristics of organized crime.

WHO DID IT? A CLOSER LOOK AT THE RELATIONSHIP BETWEEN DRUG CARTELS AND BANKS — BOX 11.1

In 2013, multinational Hong Kong and Shanghai Banking Corporation, better known as HSBC Bank, admitted that several of its bank branches in Mexico and in South America had willfully allowed Mexican and Colombian drug cartels to launder more than $881 million in illegal drug profits through their banks. The **money laundering** operation, designed to take profits from illegal activities and funnel them through legitimate businesses thereby "cleaning" the money, was so blatant some of the HSBC Bank branches modified their deposit windows to accept large boxes full of cash, as noted in Figure 11.1 (Burnett, 2014).

FIGURE 11.1 In Conducting Business, Drug Cartels Engage in Violence, Human Trafficking, and Money Laundering, the Proceeds From the Drug Trade Often Corrupt Other Legitimate Businesses, Especially Banks

Even though HSBC managers and executives knew the sums of cash being deposited were highly suspicious, they did nothing to report them. Instead, the bank willingly accepted the deposits, which, like all other funds entrusted to the bank, could be used to support legitimate financial and investment activities. For its

(Continued)

crimes, HSBC was fined $1.92 billion—a record amount at the time—but no executives were charged with crimes, and the bank was not shut down. Unfortunately, HSBC is only one in a long list of major banks that have, or continue, to operate despite getting caught engaging in illegal money laundering on behalf of criminal organizations and governments. Other banks implicated in similar illegal activities like money laundering recently include Credit Suisse, Barclays, and ING, among others.

The Scope and Scale of Organized Crime

Best estimates indicate that organized crime groups generate revenues totaling $900 billion or more per year (Global Research, 2012), though the true sum is much higher. This is equivalent to 2% of global gross domestic product each year (United Nations Office on Drugs and Crime, n.d.). As with other forms of crime (e.g., cybercrime, violent crime), there is a "dark figure"—the true amount of crime and its impacts—that is difficult or impossible to account for.

The United Nations takes the issue of organized crime seriously, devoting significant resources to understanding and combating the problem. As with cybercrime, organized crime has benefited from **globalization** (United Nations Office on Drugs and Crime, 2010), a term that speaks to the ways politics and culture are increasingly connected around the world, as well as the increasingly efficient flow of goods, services, and people across borders. Also tied closely to the continued growth of organized crime is the development of computing and cyber technologies, as well as cybercrime, which make engaging in some types of criminal conduct easier.

Collectively, widespread societal changes now make it easier for criminal groups and networks to communicate and collaborate to engage in illicit businesses over long distances. Globalization has reshaped the world's economy, leading to a tremendous growth in international trade, making it easier to transport illegal goods. Additionally, the demands of the world's economy have encouraged things like human trafficking (i.e., modern slavery) to occur, which is often facilitated by organized crime groups and networks.

Finally, globalization and the rise of advanced technologies have opened new criminal opportunities for organized crime groups to engage in, such as identity theft, fraud, and more, and have led many organized crime groups to evolve their structures, operating procedures, and methods of working with similar criminal networks.

The Catch-22—Law Enforcement Action May Create Organized Crime

Organized crime does not arise in a bubble. Organized crime is a response to cultural or societal organization and structure—factors external to the organized criminal groups often help bring those groups together, give them a purpose, and sustain them over time. Those factors may be the development of restrictive or prohibitive legislation, political unrest, civil struggle, and the decline of authoritarian government that can compromise the rule of law, making a society particularly vulnerable and paving the way for widespread corruption and crime.

At other times, the actions of law enforcement to reduce or stop organized crime can create other opportunities for it to evolve and spread. Like the game whack-a-mole, no sooner does law enforcement crack down in one area than organized crime pops up in another. The power, influence, and money that organized crime groups have to work with make it very easy for them to buy or otherwise compromise law enforcement and political officials as well.

For example, the war in Afghanistan began in 2001 when, in response to the September 11 terrorist attacks, the United States and Great Britain launched a military offensive to disband and overthrow the Taliban and al-Qaeda terrorist groups. This offensive marked the beginning of an ongoing counterinsurgency by Taliban forces to survive and rebuild. In the struggle between allied forces and the Taliban, several changes within the social, political, and economic structure took place. A decline in authoritarian rule, the transition to democracy, and a shift toward a market-based economy led to a power vacuum that shook the foundation of key government institutions. Moreover, in the aftermath of the conflict, the capacity of police to enforce the rule of law became severely compromised, as resources were hampered by civil struggle and attacks by Taliban forces. Organized criminal groups—including drug lords, terrorists, and corrupt government officials—took advantage of weak legal and political institutions, and their organized criminal activity flourished particularly around the Afghan opium trade.

Researchers have identified six trends that demonstrate the escalation of organized crime, some of which are tied to the actions of law enforcement (Shaw, 2005).

- A decline in the number of smaller criminal operators (individuals, loose networks, or small groups) and the appearance of a limited number of larger and more powerful ones.
- The identification by law enforcement officials of clear organized criminal groups as opposed to just the naming of individual "smugglers" or "traffickers."
- Evidence of close and mutually beneficial associations among government, business, and criminal enterprises, including elements of the state or business being held in criminal hands.
- The exclusion from criminal markets of new operators or groups and the forced exit of others.
- The emergence of responses to increasingly vigorous law enforcement, such as higher levels of secrecy in the operation of criminal markets.
- The development of well-organized mechanisms of criminal protection that is well understood and coordinated by key players in the criminal markets.

The weakened state institutions in post-conflict Afghanistan have made it fertile ground for the rapid growth of organized criminal networks, with their strong connections to corruption in law enforcement and government (Rubin, 2004).

The RICO Act and American Organized Crime

Until the 1970s, federal and state governments did very little in terms of developing strategies to combat organized crime. In 1970, however, Congress passed the *Organized Crime Control Act,* which created the **Racketeer Influenced and Corrupt Organization Act (RICO)**. The intention of the RICO Act was to limit and control organized criminal activities by creating new categories of offenses in **racketeering**, the organized operation of an illegal business by a structured group for the purpose of making a profit. Under RICO (Figure 11.2), being engaged in two or more activities prohibited by 24 federal statutes and eight state statutes—including such crimes as murder, kidnapping, arson, robbery, extortion, bribery, prostitution, and fraud—constitutes racketeering. The goal of RICO was to disband the core of organized criminal enterprise by making it illegal to:

- Use income derived from racketeering activity or the illegal collection of debt
- Acquire interest in a business or enterprise through a pattern of racketeering activity
- Conduct the affairs of an enterprise through a pattern of racketeering activity
- Conspire to commit any of the offenses listed above

An individual convicted of racketeering could be fined up to $25,000 and serve 20 years in prison. The accused could also forfeit to the federal government any and all property related to the racketeering violations. RICO paved the way for the investigation of organized crime by focusing attention on aggregate acts of criminal enterprise rather than individual or isolated incidents of crime (McFeeley, 2001).

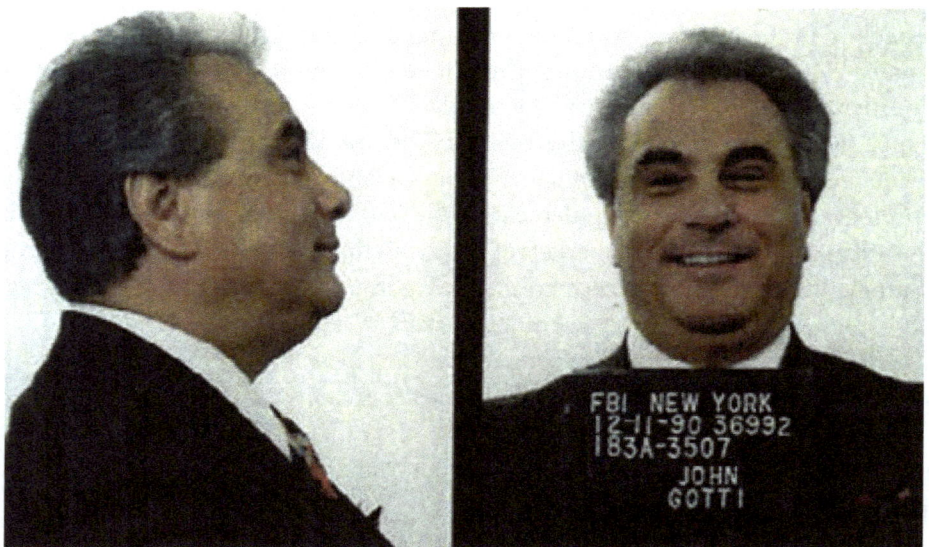

FIGURE 11.2   The RICO Act Has Been Used by Federal Prosecutors to Take Down Organized Crime Groups and Their Leaders, Including During the Early 1990s Trial of Mob Boss John Gotti

However, RICO laws have also been a great source of controversy. The application of RICO laws continues to stir up legal debates decades after their passage. For example, the ambiguity in the terms "enterprise" and "pattern of racketeering" has created issues and disagreement among lawyers, judges, and others. And while the original intention behind RICO was to target organized crime, a broad interpretation of the law would argue that it can be applied to all forms of white-collar crime and can also define an enterprise by reference to patterns of racketeering. This ambiguity has been the source of controversy in cases where legitimate businesses have been subject to forfeiture because of patterns of illegal activities by the owner in the course of its operation (Lambert, 2009).

THE REAL DEAL: THE ANATOMY OF THE NARCO-TRAFFICKING — BOX 11.2

On June 2, 2020, Mexican government officials froze the bank accounts of over 1,900 people and companies they believed were involved in laundering over $1.1 billion for a single Mexican drug cartel based in Jalisco, Mexico (Associated Press, 2020). There are at least four major drug cartels currently operating in Mexico, highlighting the immense scale and scope of the worldwide global drug trade, which is worth more than $700 billion per year (May, 2017). This example also underscores the immense power drug cartels can wield as they use their financial resources to buy off law enforcement and politicians, engage in political meddling, take over legitimate businesses, and more.

But how does narco-trafficking (the manufacturing and distribution of illegal drugs) work? First, the illegal drug trade begins with the creation of prohibitions (laws) that control or ban certain types of substances. For example, in the United States most illegal drugs are classified at the federal level as either Schedule I (e.g., heroin, marijuana) or Schedule II (e.g., cocaine) controlled substances. Classification and prohibition of these substances create a bottleneck on the demand side; organized crime (i.e., drug cartels) steps into the void to supply the demand for the prohibited substances. The drug trade then develops and runs much like any business. Suppliers obtain the raw materials to manufacture or refine illegal substances from growers or farmers (coca leaves for cocaine, opium poppy for heroin, marijuana buds, etc.). The raw materials are transformed into the finished product and distributed through various networks to wholesalers, who then supply retailers (including your local individual drug dealer). Money from drug sales then flows back through the chain to the groups or networks that control the supply. Most of the world's illegal drug trade is controlled by major criminal organizations, such as the drug cartels operating in Mexico, Colombia, Africa, the Middle East, and Asia.

Organized Crime Subtypes

In the history of crime, everything from sheep to people, wool, wine, gold, drugs, military weapons, books, and even ideas have been prohibited at some time. The paradox of prohibition, however, is that the commodity made illegal will continue to be in great demand by certain segments of the public. This demand will inevitably create the desire on the part of some groups to distribute the prohibited goods. Trafficking (moving) illegal goods, services, and people from places of supply to places of demand is the bread and butter of organized crime worldwide.

Narcotics Manufacturing, Trafficking, and Distribution

Organized crime generates in excess of $700 billion per year from the manufacture, distribution, and sale of illegal or banned substances. The three most widely used illegal substances (not including prescription pain pills) are marijuana, which is slowly evolving into a legal substance in the United States and generates nearly $100 billion from illegal sales (New Frontier Data, 2019); heroin, with sales north of $110 billion; and cocaine, which generates $130 billion (Worldometer, n.d.). Other drugs like methamphetamine, ecstasy, LSD, and more make up the balance. Cocaine is a good example of the tremendous revenue opportunities illegal drugs have. A kilogram (2.2 pounds) of cocaine sells wholesale for about $20,000 to $25,000 in the United States, $35,000 in Europe, $50,000 in China, and $100,000 in Australia (McDermott, 2018).

Law enforcement spends a lot of time and money enforcing drug prohibitions, especially in the United States, which has fought a multibillion-dollar "war on drugs" since the late 1970s. Police officers are often tasked with de facto duties as drug counselors as they enforce drug laws and deal with drug-related issues in our communities. Importantly, most law enforcement activity is directed at the lowest hanging fruit: the people who use illegal substances and are easiest to catch committing a crime. In 2018, there were about 1.65 million violations and arrests of individuals in the United States for violating drug laws with 86% of those arrests for possession of a controlled substance. Just 13% were for the higher level offenses of drug sales or manufacturing (McVay, 2021).

The global drug trade is dominated by transnational drug cartels (organized crime groups and networks) that control the production and distribution (i.e., the supply) of illegal drugs. These groups include the four current Mexican drug cartels that control the North American market: Sinaloa, Jalisco, Gulf, and Los Zetas. Other groups control the flow of illegal drugs into and through Europe, Africa, Oceania, Asia, and the Middle East.

Weapons Trafficking and Distribution

Weapons trafficking generates between $1.7 and $3.5 billion in revenue annually. This is also one of the most rarely discussed aspects of organized crime and one of the key areas where organized crime and legitimate government overlap. The Iran-Contra scandal in the 1980s highlighted the relationship between organized crime groups and the American government in a scheme where the United States illegally sold weapons to the Iranian government despite an arms embargo meant to keep them from obtaining weapons. Revenue from the illegal sales was then funneled, along with more weapons and training, to the Nicaraguan Contra rebels whom the United States was hoping would destabilize and overthrow a Nicaraguan government regime unfriendly to the United States (History.com Editors, 2020). In exchange, the U.S. government allowed drugs to continue flowing north into the United States.

The Bureau of Alcohol, Tobacco, and Firearms' (ATF) failed "project gunrunner" also deserves mention. Beginning in 2005, the ATF launched "gunrunner" as a way to track the flow of firearms to Mexican drug cartels, hopefully resulting in better intelligence on how those cartels operated so they could be targeted and dismantled by law enforcement (Department of Justice, 2010). There was some success with aspects of the project, but two ATF operations, "wide receiver" and "fast and furious", resulted in the loss of weapons, including assault-weapon-style rifles, which made their way from ATF sources into the hands of drug cartels. During the period from 2005 to 2010, when the project was ended, Mexico's cartels engaged in a heinous level of violence and murder, resulting in the deaths of thousands of Mexican citizens (Breslow, 2015).

Because weapons are durable, not consumable, goods, meaning once they're produced, they tend to stick around, arms trafficking occurs more frequently when conflicts arise around the world (United Nations Office on Drugs and Crime, 2020); when that happens, organized crime groups step in to fill the demand from rival drug cartels, rival political factions, rival ethnic or religious groups for firearms, explosives, and other weapons. It is difficult to know how many weapons are sold illegally around the world each year, but one estimate states that nearly 2,000 illegally sold firearms cross the U.S.-Mexico border each day (Gagne, 2015)!

Human and Organ Trafficking

Modern-day slavery exists in the United States and around the world. Vulnerable people, primarily women and children but also sometimes men, are trafficked each day from their country of origin into other nations to serve as laborers and sex workers. Worldwide, over 25 million people are enslaved in some form (Human Rights First, 2017). Much of this trade in human beings is facilitated by organized crime groups, which profit from the transportation and sale of human beings to the tune of $150 billion per year (May, 2017). Victims of human trafficking are also drawn from vulnerable populations, especially in Asia and Africa, though American citizens, especially women and children, are also victims of trafficking, in particular sex trafficking.

A separate, but related organized crime activity is the global trade in human organs. As detailed by Emily Lenning, there is a global market for human organs (Lenning, 2007). Organized crime groups help facilitate the collection and distribution of organs, sometimes while working closely with elements of legitimate government. In China, for example, the organs and skin of executed state prisoners are sometimes sold—without the consent of the prisoner or their family—into the lucrative black market (Lenning, 2007). The worldwide trade in human organs is estimated to bring in between $840 million and $1.7 billion each year from around 12,000 illegal transplants (May, 2017). As with human trafficking, demand from wealthy nations and among wealthier clientele fuels the exploitation of people from marginalized groups and nations who are victimized.

Much like with drug trafficking, the number of arrests—and who is actually held accountable each year—for human and organ trafficking is disturbing. There may only be around 10,000 convictions for human trafficking activities each year, with many of these targeting lower level players in the trafficking networks. Human trafficking is one of the fastest growing organized crime threats—indicating that current law enforcement actions and arrests are not impacting the ability of these groups to continue operating.

Antiquities Theft, Fraud, and Trafficking

Another major form of criminal enterprise that organized crime groups engage in involves the illegal theft and sale of cultural property. Cultural property includes things like artifacts from museums, tombs, and archaeological sites; art; written documents; and other items. This type of crime also covers the illegal forging of documents to give the appearance of legitimate ownership of stolen or looted cultural items. Worldwide, this organized criminal activity generates between $1.2–$1.6 billion in illicit revenue.

An investigation headed by the law enforcement agency Interpol and the World Customs Organization recently recovered 19,000 archaeological artifacts and artwork that had been stolen or illegally acquired via their joint campaign Operation Athena II. The investigation involved 103 countries and resulted in 100 arrests (Europol, 2020). This investigation revealed how the Internet is helping facilitate the movement of illegal goods and services, as it does for other forms of organized crime and criminal behavior. In this example, over 8,000 stolen antiquities were found for sale via online websites.

Organized Crime Characteristics

Organized crime and organized criminal groups exist in every country in the world.

In a 2002 study, the *United Nations Office on Drugs and Crime* surveyed 40 organized crime groups in 16 different countries. The following were identified as key characteristics of organized crime:

- Organized crime is the sustained and systematic coordination of illegal activities.
- Criminal activities revolve around the organization and provision of illegal goods and services for economic gain, such as drugs, gambling, pornography, prostitution, loan sharking (lending money to pay debts at illegal interest rates), human trafficking, and weapons trafficking.
- Most organized crime groups engage in one particular type of criminal activity, with a minority engaged in multiple types simultaneously.
- The majority of organized crime groups have a classical hierarchical structure with 20 to 50 members and participants.
- Violence, intimidation, corruption, and fraud are key elements in sustaining organized crime activities.

- The majority of crime groups operate in multiple countries.
- Organized crime activities penetrate the legitimate economy in order to launder illegal profits through legal businesses.

From this overview, we see that what makes organized crime a unique category of criminal behavior is the ability of ethnically diverse groups of individuals to both cooperate and compete for the control and distribution of goods and services in various geographic locations. It sounds like the operation of global corporations in the business industry. The only difference, however, is that the goods and services in demand are deemed illegal, and the illegitimate operation often involves the use of violence and coercion to negotiate transactions.

While it is true that the Italian Mafia (*La Cosa Nostra*) was once a very powerful organized criminal group in the United States, today there are dozens of organized crime groups operating in the United States. In fact, the FBI now organizes its organized crime investigations by world region and nationality/ethnicity, noting in bold letters on its organized crime website "it's not just the Mafia anymore" (Federal Bureau of Investigation, 2016). Currently operating in the United States are powerful, dangerous, and very wealthy organized crime groups from the Baltics and Europe (e.g., Russian Mafia), Asia (e.g., Japanese Yakuza, Chinese Triads), Central and South America (e.g., Mexico's Sinaloa Drug Cartel), Africa and more all operating at the same time (see Table 11.2). Increasingly, organized criminal groups, including the aforementioned, are extending, expanding, and diversifying their operations to multiple countries around the globe.

TABLE 11.2   THE WORLD'S MOST PROFITABLE ORGANIZED CRIME GROUPS (MATTHEWS, 2014)

Organized Crime Group	Nationality/Ethnicity	Estimated Annual Revenue (in USD $)
Solntsevskaya Bratva	Russia/Russian	8.5 billion
Yamaguchi Gumi (Yakuza)	Japan/Japanese	6.6 billion
Camorra	Naples, Italy/Italian	4.9 billion
'Ndrangheta	Calabria Region of Italy/Italian	4.5 billion
Sinaloa Cartel	Mexico/Mexican	3 billion

Other characteristics of organized crime include the requirement of engaging in the secretive, often rapid, movement of goods, money, people, drugs, weapons, and information across boards. Currently, organized criminal groups are becoming more involved in the commission of cybercrimes, particularly identity theft.

Finally, it is very common among organized crime groups to enforce and require strict adherence to a code of conduct. The codes, like the Italian Mafia's code of silence called **Omerta**, hardly differ from other subcultural codes of conduct. In fact, the Omerta code is like the blue wall of silence that governs the actions of police, including those who engage in corrupt activities.

In short, organized crime groups use formal and informal codes that dictate rules for members and help settle disputes, divide territories, and establish control of markets (Lyman & Potter, 2004). How exactly one becomes a member of organized crime differs with the groups. Some people are born into organized crime and enter the "family business" as part of their socialization. Others are recruited to participate. And some people are forced, or coerced, into participation with organized crime, often because of their role in some type of legitimate business or government that organized crime hopes to gain control or influence over. Such was the case in the 1950s when many American labor unions were infiltrated by major organized crime networks (Witwer, 2008).

Key Takeaways

Review the following list of bullet points for a quick overview of the key ideas and information in this chapter:

- Organized crime has a long history and is closely tied to the development and growth of human civilizations; organized crime is the catch-all term used to summarize the crimes carried out in a planned, organized, systematic way by gangs, groups, or networks spread across the globe.
- The types of crime occurring under the umbrella of organized crime include drug manufacturing and trafficking, human trafficking, wildlife trafficking, arms smuggling, cybercrime, illegal logging, political corruption, bribery, theft and cargo theft, pirating of software, music, and movies, and much, much more.
- Organized crime operates a massive global, black market economy for goods and services that are either prohibited, banned, controlled, or hard to come by. Organized crime is driven by global pressures and influences like consumer demand for drugs or electronics and other sociopolitical factors.

Conclusion and Formal Summary Questions

In this chapter, we learned about organized crime. We found out that organized crime is an ever-present, constantly evolving type of crime that has existed for as long as humans have been organized into communities and societies. Organized crime is, in fact, an umbrella category—a catch-all—for many different types of crime, including all manner of smuggling or trafficking operations (i.e., drugs, humans, wildlife, weapons), theft, pirating, or copyright/trademark infringement (i.e., stolen or bootlegged music and movies or knockoff Nikes), and so on. Organized crime is a response to human demand for goods and services; it is also deeply intertwined with the legitimate economy and the world of politics. Organized crime is involved in the political economy or at the least has some hand in political corruption or influence peddling in nearly every country in the world.

- *Organized crime is always evolving to keep pace with new opportunities and the demand for prohibited goods and services. Can you describe how organized crime is able to leverage connections to legitimate governments and businesses and technologies (i.e., the Internet) to continue growing?*
- *Many forms of cybercrime result in the victimization of marginalized peoples. Can you identify and describe the forms of crime that are likely to impact the groups?*
- *Using the example of narco-trafficking, can you describe in general terms the business (supply and demand) side of organized crime? What does this say for how we might go about controlling organized crime and/or reducing its impact/power?*

E-Resources

1. Crime Museum—Origins of Organized Crime: https://www.crimemuseum.org/crime-library/organized-crime/origins-of-organized-crime/
2. Richard Kuklinski—History of the Most Prolific Hitman in Mafia History: https://allthatsinteresting.com/richard-kuklinski-the-iceman
3. *The 10 Biggest Crime Organizations in the World*: https://www.youtube.com/watch?v=7OyeebSaVPY

References

Associated Press. (2020, June 2). *Mexico finds links to over $1 billion in cartel money*. https://apnews.com/article/mexico-caribbean-drug-cartels-organized-crime-crime-001dc8b5f00a9ace4c0b5fee2081ba01

Breslow, J. M. (2015, July 27). *The staggering death toll of Mexico's drug war*. Frontline. https://www.pbs.org/wgbh/frontline/article/the-staggering-death-toll-of-mexicos-drug-war/

Burnett, J. (2014, March 20). *Awash in cash, drug cartels rely on big banks to launder profits*. NPR. https://www.npr.org/sections/parallels/2014/03/20/291934724/awash-in-cash-drug-cartels-rely-on-big-banks-to-launder-profits

Department of Justice. (2010). *Review of ATF's project gunrunner*. Evaluation and Inspections Division, Office of the Inspector General. https://oig.justice.gov/reports/ATF/e1101.pdf

Europol. (2020, May 6). *101 arrested and 19,000 stolen artefacts recovered in international crackdown on art trafficking* [Press release]. https://www.europol.europa.eu/media-press/newsroom/news/101-arrested-and-19000-stolen-artefacts-recovered-in-international-crackdown-art-trafficking

Federal Bureau of Investigation. (2016). *Transnational organized crime*. https://www.fbi.gov/investigate/organized-crime

Gagne, D. (2015, January 22). *2,000 illegal weapons cross US-Mexico border per day: Report*. InSight Crime. https://insight-crime.org/news/analysis/2000-illegal-weapons-cross-us-mexico-border-every-day/

Ginsburg, A. (2001). *The Iceman confesses: Secrets of a mafia hitman* [Film]. Home Box Office. https://www.youtube.com/watch?v=ceERzARTMGs

Glenny, M. (2008). *McMafia: A journey through the global criminal underworld*. Knopf Publishers.

Global Research. (2012, July 20). *Turnover of global organized crime: $870 billion … a year*. https://www.globalresearch.ca/turnover-of-global-organized-crime-870-billion-a-year/31995?pdf=31995

History.com Editors. (2020, January 17). *Iran-Contra affair*. History.com. https://www.history.com/topics/1980s/iran-contra-affair

Human Rights First. (2017). *Human trafficking by the numbers* [Fact sheet]. https://www.humanrightsfirst.org/sites/default/files/TraffickingbytheNumbers.pdf

Lambert, K. A. (2009, October 8). *RICO class action controversy continues.* ABAnet.org.

Lenning, E. (2007). Execution for body parts: A case of state crime. *Contemporary Justice Review 10*(2), 173–191. https://doi.org/10.1080/10282580701372053

Lyman, M. D. & Potter, G. W. (2004). *Organized crime* (3rd ed.). Pearson Prentice Hall.

Matthews, C. (2014, September 14). Fortune 5: The biggest organized crime groups in the world. Fortune. https://fortune.com/2014/09/14/biggest-organized-crime-groups-in-the-world/

May, C. (2017). *Transnational crime and the developing world.* Global Financial Integrity. https://globalinitiative.net/wp-content/uploads/2017/12/GFI-Transnational-Crime-and-the-Developing-World-2017.pdf

McFeeley, R. (2001). Enterprise theory of investigation. *FBI Law Enforcement Bulletin, 70*(5), 19–26.

McVay, D. (2021, September 29). *Arrests and the criminal justice system.* Drug Policy Facts. https://www.drugpolicyfacts.org/chapter/crime_arrests#arrests

McDermott, J. (2018, March 15). *The 'invisibles': Columbia's new generation of drug traffickers.* InSight Crime. https://insight-crime.org/investigations/invisibles-colombias-new-generation-drug-traffickers/

New Frontier Data. (2019, April 18). *New study estimates the global cannabis market at over $340 billion USD* [Press release]. https://www.globenewswire.com/news-release/2019/04/18/1806583/0/en/New-Study-Estimates-the-Global-Cannabis-Market-at-Over-340-Billion-USD.html

Rubin, B. R. (2004, October 7). *Road to ruin: Afghanistan's booming opium industry.* Center for American Progress & Center on International Cooperation. New York University. https://cdn.americanprogress.org/wp-content/uploads/kf/ROADTORUIN.PDF

Shaw, M. (2005). Drug trafficking and the development of organized crime in post-Taliban Afghanistan. In D. Buddenberg & W. A. Byrd (Eds.), *Afghanistan's drug industry: Structure, functioning, dynamics, and implications for counter-narcotics policy* (pp. 189–214). United Nations Office on Drugs and Crime. https://www.unodc.org/pdf/afg/publications/afghanistan_drug_industry.pdf

Siegel, D., van de Bunt, H., & Zaitch, D. (Eds.). (2003). *Global organized crime: Trends and developments.* Kluwer Academic Publishers.

United Nations Office on Drugs and Crime. (n.d.). *Organized crime.* https://www.unodc.org/unodc/en/organized-crime/intro.html

United Nations Office on Drugs and Crime. (2002). *Results of a pilot survey of forty selected organized criminal groups in sixteen countries.* Global Program Against Transnational Organized Crime. https://www.unodc.org/pdf/crime/publications/Pilot_survey.pdf

United Nations Office on Drugs and Crime. (2010). *The globalization of crime: A transnational organized crime threat assessment.* https://www.unodc.org/documents/data-and-analysis/tocta/TOCTA_Report_2010_low_res.pdf

United Nations Office on Drugs and Crime. (2020). *Firearms trafficking.* UNODC Global Learning Platform. https://www.unodc.org/e4j/en/organized-crime/module-3/key-issues/firearms-trafficking.html

Witwer, D. (2008). *Corruption and reform in the Teamsters union.* University of Illinois Press.

Worldometer. (n.d.). *Spending on illegal drugs this year.* https://www.worldometers.info/drugs/

Figure Credits

Fig. 11.1: Source: https://commons.wikimedia.org/wiki/File:Moneycoronado.jpg.

Fig. 11.2: Source: https://commons.wikimedia.org/wiki/File:John_Gotti.jpg.

Chapter 12

State Crime

Key Terms

State crime
Commission
Omission
State-corporate crime
State-initiated corporate crime
State-facilitated corporate crime
Genocidal mentality
Dehumanization
Critical criminology
Risk-benefit analysis
Edwin Sutherland
White-collar crime
Corporate/organizational crime
False claims advertising
Price-fixing
Occupational crime
Embezzlement
Pilferage
Chiseling
Influence peddling
Bribery

Chapter Headings

1. Chapter opener
2. What is state crime?
   2.1. The difference between state crime and white-collar crime
   2.2. Characteristics of white-collar crimes
3. The scope and scale of state crime
4. State crime subtypes
5. State crime characteristics
6. Chapter summary questions

Chapter Objectives

After reading Chapter 12, students will be able to do the following:

- Define state crime and its key characteristics
- Describe different forms of state crime
- Understand the scope of state crime and connections to other crime types
- Understand the connections between state crime and other crimes of the powerful

Opening Questions

Before you begin the chapter, take a few minutes to reflect on the following questions:

1. What is the relationship between state crime, government, and legitimate business?
2. What are several major forms of state crime?
3. How do governments exploit their legitimate political power to engage in criminal activity?

True Crime

Soccer is no doubt one of the most popular sports in the world. Fans flock to the World Cup, and to bars and restaurants, to root for their teams and countries. It was a shock to many fans when, in May 2015, the FBI filed criminal indictments against 14 of the highest ranking officials from the *Federation Internationale de Football*, better known as FIFA, the governing body that both coordinates and promotes international professional soccer. FBI documents disclosed that those officials, in fact, the entire FIFA organization, had been engaging in corruption that was "rampant, systemic and deep-rooted" (Department of Justice, 2015) for as long as 24 years, perhaps longer. Myriad criminal charges were brought against this group, including racketeering, wire fraud, money laundering, and conspiracy, with some individuals allegedly involved in schemes in excess of $150 million (Department of Justice, 2015).

The case didn't end in May 2015, however. By December of the next year, 16 more FIFA officials had been indicted, bringing the total to 30 (O'Grady, 2015; The Independent, 2015). More details emerged of their criminal acts, which extended beyond the FIFA officials and organization and implicated the governments of FIFA member nations. Among the most high-profile allegations were that FIFA officials and FIFA member nation governments were engaging in game selling and that bribes were given out to allow Russia and Qatar to host upcoming World Cup tournaments. These allegations were extremely serious, as fairness and transparency in the sighting of games and allocation of World Cup tournaments are supposed to be paramount given the financial and revenue implications for those countries that are selected. Just consider that the World Cup draws more viewers—in person and on television—than any other sporting event in the world. Countries that host the games can make hundreds of millions of dollars in revenue as fans flood their country and buy hotel rooms, food, gifts, and more.

The FIFA corruption scandal, which grew to include a parallel investigation by Swiss authorities, is a prime example of a state-corporate crime—one of the subtypes of state crime we explore later in this chapter. Not surprisingly, as you will see again and again with this form of crime, the vast majority of those indicted and prosecuted cut deals that saw them forfeit some of their financial windfall from their criminal exploits but did not see them serve lengthy prison sentences.

What Is State Crime?

The crimes that attract the most media attention, occupy our imaginations, and cause us the greatest anxiety and fear are those of the street: murders, rapes, muggings, assaults, etc. There's a reason for that: those crimes are tangible; we may have personally been victimized or known someone who was victimized by them, and we are repeatedly exposed to stories, TV shows, and movies that depict them.

There is another level of crime and criminal behavior. We don't regularly think of government, or state officials, as criminals engaging in widespread criminal conduct. The study of state crime, however, shows that government officials can, and do, commit heinous criminal acts, including acts of violence, on a regular basis.

State crime is a term for the crimes committed by governments and their officials in carrying out their functions or duties and in pursuing goals and interests. Examples include genocide, war crimes, torture, corruption, and environmental harms of many varieties. State crime incorporates crimes committed or condoned by these entities and actors but not crimes committed against the state. For example, we are not talking here about treason or spying.

State governments, and state government actors, can engage in criminal conduct by breaking existing criminal laws. However, we do not limit our definition of state crime strictly to examples where a law is broken. The reason for this is because states create laws, and have the power to alter, enforce, and ignore them. So, we also examine harmful actions, or as Penny Green and Tony Ward put it, we "include all violations of human rights that are deviant in the sense that they infringe some socially recognized norm" (Green & Ward, 2004).

A great example of why it's important that we not limit our concept of state crime to only violations of existing laws is found in the systematic killing of Jews, homosexuals, gypsies, and other people deemed deviant or undesirable by the German Nazi political party during the late 1930s through the mid-1940s. The Nazi government was legitimate in that it was duly elected by the German people. Led by Adolf Hitler, this government then created laws enabling it to persecute Jews and others, culminating in one of the largest genocidal mass killing campaigns ever perpetrated during World War II. Yet, no state laws were broken. Indeed, during the Holocaust, many horrible acts were carried out *legally* and with the full support of the legitimate government (United States Memorial Holocaust Museum, 2020).

In sum, we study and draw attention to state crimes because often, the harmful acts of governments and government actors, be they violations of law or not, produce more death, destruction, and trauma than all other forms of crime combined.

The Difference Between State Crime and White-Collar Crime

State crime is distinct from white-collar crime, though as you will see later, the two forms can merge on occasion.

It used to be common to refer to people who worked in manufacturing or industry (e.g., manual labor jobs) as "blue-collar" workers because they often wore uniforms or coveralls that were blue or dark blue in color. Conversely, those who worked office jobs, or in management (e.g., nonmanufacturing or manual labor jobs) were called "white-collar" workers.

White-collar crime is one of the broadest categories of crime and is often committed by people with significant power, status, and/or prestige. Criminologist **Edwin Sutherland** referred to **white-collar crime** as the illegal acts of high-status, respectable individuals during their occupation (Sutherland, 1949). He noted that individuals may abuse their positions, including their access and authority, while working in business enterprises for their own personal gain, even breaking the law as they do so. We use the phrase *white-collar crime* to describe both the criminal acts of individuals occupying positions of power to benefit themselves and the criminal acts of individuals working to benefit the larger organization they work for. In comparison, "state crime" involves a government component; it refers to crimes committed by individuals, or groups of individuals acting within, or on behalf of a government, or crimes committed by the government itself.

Characteristics of White-Collar Crimes

White-collar crime is basically business, or work-related, crime. It can be committed by a single individual or a group of individuals. Typically, white-collar crimes involve deception, concealment, theft, and breach of trust (Shover & Hochstetler, 2006). Often, the motivation for committing a white-collar crime is to obtain money and/or gain privilege, status, or respect, or to avoid the loss of money and privilege, status and respect (Shover & Hochstetler, 2006). White-collar crimes are usually nonviolent, but their impacts on society and harms to victims are still quite serious. Victims include other individuals, consumers, clients, other corporations, and the general public.

White-collar crime can broadly be grouped into two subcategories: individual-occupational crime and corporate/organizational crime (Miethe et al., 2006). **Occupational crime** involves the illegal acts of individuals who seek to promote their *own* self-interests rather than the interest of the organization (Friedrichs, 2002). One example would be **embezzlement**—theft of money or property from a business by a legitimate employee. A trio of Pasadena, California, residents were convicted of embezzling $6 million in 2014 from the City of Pasadena over a more than 10-year period; two of the convicted were former city employees (Favot, 2014). The major difference between larceny, discussed in Chapter 7, and embezzlement is the manner in which the property is stolen: when a larceny is committed, the perpetrator did not have legal possession of the stolen money or goods; when embezzlement takes place, the perpetrator *does* have legal possession of the money or item but misappropriates it for his or her own benefit. The key difference between embezzlement and larceny-theft is who has a legal right to access the money or property. An employee can embezzle because they have a legal right to the money or property but take the property for their own benefit, whereas a non-employee has no legal right.

Pilferage is the systematic theft of fairly small amounts of company property over an extended period, for example, food, wine, or liquor, and is an even more common subtype of embezzlement. Pilferage can cost companies hundreds of thousands of dollars a year. Nevertheless, employees often steal from their employers, justifying their actions with a variety of rationales.

Corporate or organizational crime refers to the illegal acts of people who occupy positions of power within institutions and willfully and knowingly break the law to advance their interests and/or the interests of their organization (Clinard & Yeager, 2005). Examples include price-fixing, overbilling, money laundering, securities fraud, making false claims about products or services, and other forms of fraud (Burnett, 2014). Violations of workplace safety rules and laws—including violating the Occupational Safety and Health Act of 1970 (OSHA Act, 1970)—represent another common type of corporate crime with millions of violations reported each year.

The wholesome seeming Campbell's Soup Company got caught in the 1960s for engaging in **false claims advertising.** Partnering with a New York City ad firm to photograph and promote the company's soup, the ad firm executives confronted a dilemma: the soup didn't look very exciting in the bowl; all the vegetables and meat pieces settled to the bottom. The only thing the camera picked up was the still liquid on top. So thinking creatively, the ad team beefed up the soup by placing marbles at the bottom of the bowls—this gave the appearance of thicker, fuller, chunkier soup, with more vegetables and meat pieces in it, when in fact this was not the case (Scott, 2012). Campbell's eventually got sued in 1968 by the Federal Trade Commission for false claims advertising, under the reasoning that when customers saw the ads of the beefed-up soup, they would reasonably expect their soup at home to look similar!

More recently, Apple and several major book publishers were charged and found guilty of **price-fixing**—conspiring among each other to arbitrarily maintain a higher price for e-books (Department of Justice, 2016; Roberts, 2015). While it is a common practice for businesses to adjust prices to meet supply and demand, it is illegal for them to conspire internally, or with others, to set and control those prices in order to stifle competition.

Companies, and their employees, are sometimes willing to engage in harmful and criminal acts because they see the reward outweighing the risk. **Risk-benefit analysis** is commonly used by corporations and their legal teams to evaluate the risk/reward of certain actions. The Ford Pinto scandal of the 1970s is one example of that type of analysis put into practice, with Ford executives ultimately deciding that settling lawsuits with angry customers and/or their families would be cheaper than ordering large-scale repairs and redesigns of their faulty Ford Pinto gas tanks, which could leak and explode if the car was rear-ended even at low speeds. They made this decision knowing that people could be seriously injured or killed (and some people were) by driving the cars with the poorly designed tanks (Dold, 1985; Dole, 1980). Employers who willingly put consumers or their employees at risk do so because they are willing to incur fines, which are often less costly than correcting the causes of the problems or violations in the first place.

There is no shortage of white-collar crimes—either individual or organizational. Just remember they are distinct from state crimes. In the following section, we will discuss one area where state crimes and corporate crimes may merge, known as state-corporate crime.

The Scope and Scale of State Crime

As with cybercrime, green crimes, and other forms of crimes of the powerful, it is difficult, if not impossible, to accurately state the extent of the problem. State crime is particularly difficult because, as noted earlier, the state has the power to create and enforce laws; it also has the power to define what is or is not criminal. Rarely with a government work tirelessly to prosecute itself for its actions and will often find ways to justify its violation of its own principles or laws, or of international human rights principles or laws. That is why it is so important to understand this form of crime and call it out when and if it does occur (Chambliss & Moloney, 2014).

Nevertheless, we do know state crimes occur. Genocide is a horrible form of criminality, defined by the United Nations Genocide Convention in 1948 as "acts committed with intent to destroy, in whole or in part, a national, ethnic, racial or religious group" (United Nations General Assembly, 1948). This form of state crime has occurred repeatedly throughout history: Nazi Germany in World War II, Armenia in 1915–1917, Cambodia 1975–1979, Rwanda

1994, Darfur, Sudan 2003, Bosnia 1992–1995, etc. Collectively, just these few events have killed upward of 30 million human beings—with the vast majority innocent men, women, and children, not soldiers or combatants.

Measuring state crime is difficult; it often takes investigative journalists, whistleblowers, and others to draw attention to the illegal, harmful acts of governments, who then must raise awareness of the crimes and develop support among others that the event is worthy of being called a crime—either because it violates the law or is socially or environmentally harmful. This can be a long process, but as we have seen, it is not impossible to bring the crimes of governments to light and hold them—and the individual actors responsible—to justice.

> ### WHO DID IT? A CLOSER LOOK AT UNITED STATES' TREATMENT OF NATIVE AMERICAN TRIBES
> BOX 12.1
>
> Only in more recent history have the crimes and harmful acts perpetrated by European (White) settlers and, later, government officials against the Native American tribal groups of the United States begun to receive the attention they deserve; even still, there remains a glaring lack of awareness, acknowledgment, or effort to right past wrongs against Native Americans (see Table 12.1 for more detail on the atrocities committed against Native American tribes).
>
> Take for example the U.S. government's treatment of one tribe, the Navajo Nation in northeastern Arizona. The Hopi people first occupied land where Arizona, Utah, Colorado, and New Mexico meet, an area known today as the four corners. In 1934, the U.S. Congress set aside a large portion of land in Arizona for the Navajo and "other such Indians as may already be located thereon" (San Juan Southern Paiute Tribe, n.d.). This lit the fuse for potential conflict between the Navajo and the Hopi, who already had a village (called Moenkopi) in the area. To reduce conflict, Commissioner of Indian Affairs Robert Bennett instituted a ban on any development in the area in 1966. That ban created horrible living conditions for the Navajo and other Indians who could not build or repair their homes (even to fix leaking roofs or broken windows), take care of the roads, or ensure adequate schools or health facilities. Even though the Navajo Nation produces most of the energy for the southwest, the ban also meant no electric lines could reach homes in the Bennett Freeze area. There were also no gas lines for heat and no water lines for indoor plumbing or any type of sanitation. People either hauled in water fit for human consumption or drank from the same wells as their livestock, which were often contaminated by companies mining and processing uranium ore (Cole, 2010). Indians also unknowingly used sand and crushed rock from old uranium mines to make concrete slabs for floors and ovens, not knowing these materials were radioactive. Gastric cancer rates rose 50 percent during the 1990s among Navajo in two New Mexico counties with uranium sites and a sharp increase in breast, ovarian, and other cancers has been recorded among teenage girls from the reservation. Cancer rates 17 times the national average were found in the entire Navajo Nation (Pasternak, 2006).

FIGURE 12.1 Native Americans Have Been the Victims of Genocide and State-Sanctioned Violence by Both Direct and Indirect Means, Including the Destruction of Their Staple Food Source, the Bison, in the 1800s

President Obama lifted the Bennett Freeze in May 2009 (Navajo-Hopi Observer, 2009). But it will take decades and millions of dollars to build or repair infrastructure. Thankfully, thousands of tribal members are now eligible for federal compensation for health problems caused by uranium exposure. Despite passing laws that created third-world conditions within this country, which undoubtedly led directly to the suffering and deaths of many Native Americans, none of these government actions was illegal; in fact, they were 100% legal. Worse still few people know this story—or the countless others—that highlight the state crimes committed against the native peoples of North America. This is the crux of the state crime issue.

State Crime Subtypes

State-Corporate Crime

At times, the criminal conduct of governments aligns with the criminal conduct of other organizations, especially businesses. State-corporate crime is the study of "how the actions of corporations and governments intersect to produce crime and social harm" (Kramer et al., 2002). A state-corporate crime is a criminal or socially harmful act that results when one or more government institutions pursue a goal in direct cooperation with one or more corporations or businesses (Maakestad, 1987).

State-corporate crimes occur in two general forms.

State-initiated corporate crimes occur when "corporations, *employed by the government*, engage in criminal or deviant conduct, at the direction or with the approval of the government" (Kramer et al., 2002). One example is the 1986 NASA space shuttle Challenger disaster, which resulted in the deaths of several NASA astronauts, including New Hampshire schoolteacher Christa McAuliffe. Research has now shown that this preventable tragedy resulted from the manufacture and use of a defective O-ring seal in the space shuttle; despite warnings being raised over this issue, NASA officials pushed forward with the launch of the Challenger (Kramer, 1992).

In contrast, **state-facilitated corporate crime** occurs when "government regulatory institutions *fail to restrain* deviant or criminal business activities" (Kramer et al., 2002; Grogin, 1987). One example is the fire at the Imperial Food Products processing plant in Hamlet, North Carolina, in September 1991, which killed 25 plant workers and injured over 50 more. The fire caused significant death and injuries because Imperial Food Products locked several fire doors that could have helped workers evacuate; federal inspectors from the Occupational Safety and Health Administration and the U.S. Department of Agriculture knew about this illegal practice at the plant but did nothing to fix the issue prior to the fire, thus enabling the tragic outcome via their omission (or failure) to act (Aulette & Michalowski, 1993).

Abuse of Power and Corruption

The purpose of electing people to public office is so that they can represent the interests of their communities at the state or federal levels of government. Thus, elected and other government officials must use their positions, power, and status for the public good. Reaching public office and maintaining power, however, often leads some elected officials to cross ethical and legal boundaries and, in the worst instances, engage in criminal behaviors like corruption, bribery, and extortion. Commonly at play in these situations are political campaign financial contributions—made by corporations and individuals alike—which may be given, but with strings attached. This can create a dynamic where elected officials feel beholden to the contributors and then engage in conduct that advances or protects their interests. As criminologist Nubia Evertsson noted in her study of political corruption in Western Europe, "electoral donations are cloaked with legality" but may "facilitate corruption" (Evertsson, 2013).

Political corruption is the abuse of power by political or elected officials to maintain privilege and reap personal gain (Green & Ward, 2004). For example, former Nigerian national security advisor Sambo Dasuki engaged in serious political corruption when he abused his power and position by "awarding phantom" military contracts for supplies like "fighter jets, bombs and ammunition" in order to pocket over $2 billion (Onuah, 2015).

Influence peddling is a specific subtype of corruption that occurs when government or elected officials exploit their influence in exchange for favors, financial gain, or material advantages. Accepting large campaign contributions in exchange for the awarding of government contracts to specific contributors is one example of influence peddling. Using a public office to hire relatives and making expensive and lavish trips and purchases on government expense accounts are also examples.

Bribery occurs when a government official accepts a direct payment in exchange for official government action, such as gaining votes, sponsoring legislation, and appropriating government funds to private contractors (Wrage, 2007). A recent case in the African nation of Ghana illustrates both influence peddling and bribery in action, as 32 Ghanaian judges were caught on hidden cameras accepting bribes in exchange for handing out shorter prison sentences to criminals whose cases they were presiding over (Mark, 2015).

Lastly, **extortion** is when a government official uses their position of power and influence to force or coerce individuals into providing them with some type of financial reward or material gain. Withholding legislation, failing to renew a contract or issue a permit, and threatening to close down a business because of lack of compliance with financial demands are all examples of extortion. In April 2015, two former New Jersey state government officials and close associates of former New Jersey governor Chris Christie were indicted by the U.S. Department of Justice for engaging in a conspiracy to arbitrarily restrict the traffic lanes leading from New Jersey to the George Washington Bridge and into Manhattan. The purpose of the intentional traffic jam was to "exact political vengeance against a mayor" in a town where the traffic backups would be felt the most. That mayor didn't support Governor Christie during his reelection campaign (Zernike, 2016).

Crimes Against Humanity

One of the most challenging topics in criminological study is the large-scale, organized acts of violence and other criminal conduct committed by governments at the domestic and international levels, including genocide, the systematic killing or attempted destruction of a national, religious, ethnic, racial or political group. Crimes like genocide threaten the rule of law, peace, and stability as well as the fundamental human rights to which everyone should be entitled. Often, however, these horrific events occur under the guise of legality or during the fog of war and/or revolution.

Genocide has occurred around the world throughout most of human history. In fact, it was a point of pride among ancient rulers to eliminate an entire enemy, including civilians and children, in addition to soldiers. Genocide was not considered a crime until after World War II when the world became aware of the atrocities, including the Holocaust in Europe, perpetrated by Nazi and Japanese forces. The **1948 United Nations Convention on the Prevention and Punishment of the Crime of Genocide** officially made it a crime to "commit genocide, plan or conspire to commit genocide, incite or cause other people to commit genocide or be complicit or involved in any act of genocide" (United Nations General Assembly, 1948). This agreement among United Nations member nations created a potentially powerful new political reality by declaring, "States would no longer have the right to be left alone" to pursue internal conflicts as they saw fit. In other words, state sovereignty would no longer shield a country from the consequences of committing genocide within its borders.

THE ANATOMY OF GENOCIDE — BOX 12.2

Genocide has devastating and destructive consequences. Genocidal acts include torturing members of a targeted group, eliminating them through mass killings, imposing harsh conditions intended to bring about physical deterioration and eventual death (i.e., starvation), forced sterilization to prevent future births, and removing groups by forced transfer or migration. Look at the human impact just a small sampling of genocides has had (and note that all of these genocides occurred in the 20th century with the exception of one):

- The Armenian genocide of 1915, which killed more than one million people
- The Nazi Holocaust of World War II, which killed at least six million Jews, as well as around seven million Soviet and one million Polish non-Jewish citizens, and several hundred thousand gypsies, homosexuals, people with mental illness, and other so-called undesirables. In total, more than 13 million people—not including combat deaths of soldiers on either side of the struggle (United States Holocaust Memorial Museum, 2020). For comparison, only four U.S. states have more than 13 million residents. Another way to visualize the scale of death from this one event is to picture the entire modern-day populations of Wyoming; Vermont; Washington, D.C.; Alaska; North Dakota; South Dakota; Delaware; Rhode Island; Montana; Maine; New Hampshire; and Hawaii being wiped out within a brief 4- to 5-year period.
- The Cambodian/Khmer Rouge holocaust of the 1970s, which killed between 1.5 and two million people
- The Rwandan genocide of the early 1990s, which killed 500,000 to one million people
- The Bosnian genocide of the early and mid-1990s, which killed about 8,000 people
- The genocide in the Darfur region of Africa, which began in the early 2000s and killed approximately 500,000 people
- Genocidal acts are not relegated only to far-off or distant lands, however. We must also count the genocidal murder of Native American Indian peoples committed by the earliest European settlers and continuing into the late 1800s by the United States state-level and federal governments, which reduced the Native American population of the United States and Canada from over 10 million in the 15th century (i.e., 1400s) to fewer than 300,000 by 1900 (United to End Genocide, 2015).

How can these large-scale murderous events occur repeatedly within just 100 years? Dehumanization is a critical reason (Organization of African Unity, 2000). When one group, often because of hateful and misleading propaganda, begins to view another group as less than them or as undeserving of their respect or dignity, the dehumanization process is already well underway. This is exactly what happened during the Rwandan genocide between rival Hutu and Tutsi ethnic groups: in the years before the genocide, political debates, demonstrations and rallies, speeches by government officials, and broadcasts on radio stations filled the air with what official reports described as "vicious, pornographic, inflammatory rhetoric designed to demonize and dehumanize the Tutsi." The Tutsi became the enemy, seen as a threat to the very existence of Hutus. Tutsi men, women, and children became objects, not humans, making it easier for the Hutus to commit unthinkable acts of torture, rape, and murder against them.

Predictably, governments are reluctant to label genocides as such because, under the United Nations' rules, a genocide requires intervention. It was partly a fear of incurring such an obligation, as well as a desire to carefully guard its sovereign decision-making powers, that caused the United States to delay ratifying the United Nations convention against genocide for many decades. Governments thus resort to labeling genocides as "civil wars" or the even more vague term "ethnic conflicts"—none of which carry any legal obligation to intervene or stop the killing.

Characteristics of State Crime

State crimes can occur through **commission** (i.e., actually doing something) and **omission** (i.e., failing to do something). An example of a state crime of commission would be engaging in genocide, whereas an example of a state crime of omission might involve state officials willfully failing to act to prevent an outbreak of disease, resulting in the injuries and deaths of many people.

One commonality shared by state actors is that they possess an immense amount of power. Even in the most democratic of countries, like the United States or in Western Europe, the influence and control of the state extend to all spheres of social life: economy, culture, and media, etc. While citizens are represented through their elected leaders and there is at least some transparency, it is still those leaders who have the power to create laws, push for their enforcement or nonenforcement, and make decisions that can alter the lives of millions. In totalitarian, dictatorial, or despotic government regimes, control and power are even more complete and intense. Thus, another characteristic of state crimes is that they all represent a terrible abuse of government power.

Additionally, state crimes violate and exploit the public's trust that has been vested in the government and commonly inflict far greater social and economic costs upon the world's populations than do crimes like murder, assault theft, arson, robbery, treason, burglary, prostitution, drug use, etc. (Chambliss, 2000). Many people are hyperfocused on criminal homicides, especially serial murders. Yet, our yearly U.S. statistics show that despite a country with over 320 million people, only around 14,000 people are murdered in any given year in the United States; serial homicides account for less than 1% of that already small total.

State crimes also commonly exert a large financial consequence on society. For example, the 2008 economic recession, which resulted from the criminal activities of big corporations, banks, and inadequate government oversight, cost American citizens over $12.8 trillion (Puzzanghera, 2012), with many people losing their retirement funds and life savings. Prior to that, the 1980s Savings and Loan Fraud Scandal cost Americans between $300 and $500 billion. Researchers estimate the annual financial cost of all street crimes combined to be just $3.8 billion (Mohkiber, 2000). But if you compare that sum to the estimated financial costs (Mohkiber, 2000) of just a single type of crime engaged in by the powerful political, corporate, and state actors, you can see the financial harm is far greater:

- Annual losses from securities fraud = $15 billion per year

The hidden consequences of state crimes are also notable—the psychological, emotional, and cultural scars they inflict and leave in their wake—and cannot be justly equated with the effects stemming from other forms of crime or criminality (Chamblis & Moloney, 2014). Importantly, state crimes are more likely to impact the poor, the disenfranchised and disadvantaged, the voiceless and powerless than those with economic resources, or social and political capital and connections.

With respect to specific subtypes of state crime, like genocide, we know the following characteristics are often present: political and social environments that increase the likelihood of genocide occurring, such as when governments are (1) authoritarian, or (2) when countries are plagued by civil war, and (3) when political leaders are heavily engaged in corruption. Under these conditions, government officials may use genocide as a mechanism of achieving social control to eliminate threats to their rule, to spread fear among enemies and dissenters, to acquire wealth, to maintain status, or to implement a belief system or ideology. Further, genocide often requires that a "**genocidal mentality**" has been created. This mindset is often found to be present during acts of genocide. The genocidal mentality is one that dehumanizes potential victims. The Nazi's labeled Jews, homosexuals, and others "inferior" and concocted stories about how they were disrupting society and harming innocent people. Rwanda's Hutus called their Tutsi targets "cockroaches." Radio broadcasts imploring Hutus to "kill cockroaches" fostered mass killings. In modern society, media have made the process of disseminating the propaganda of dehumanization even easier. The establishment of institutions and organizations that justify and carry out the atrocities is a key component of the spread of genocide. From academia to the government to the military, the leadership mobilizes organizations in its power to destroy those defined as "others."

Finally, a characteristic of all state crimes, as with many other crimes of the powerful including white-collar crime, environmental crimes, organized crime, and more, is that they often go unnoticed and are under punished. As a result, the media and the public are less likely to hear about and care about the crimes of the powerful elites, organizations, and governments, and those entities are more likely to get away with their criminal and harmful acts.

Key Takeaways

Review the following list of bullet points for a quick overview of the key ideas and information in this chapter:

- State crime, like organized crime, is an umbrella category (many crimes fit within the idea of state crime), but state crime is focused on the criminal or harmful acts of governments or their representatives acting on behalf of the government.
- State crimes include things like genocide, or systematic environmental destruction, or many other types of crime; importantly, those who study state crimes also point to harmful acts that may not be "criminal" by definition, noting that governments will likely justify or not criminalize actions that cause serious harm but which they benefit from by engaging in.

- One of the key subtypes of state crime is state-corporate crime, where government and corporate interests come together to produce criminal or harmful outcomes.

Conclusion and Formal Summary Questions

In this chapter, we learned about state crime. We discovered that state crime, like organized crime, is an umbrella category that encompasses the crimes or harmful acts committed by governments, or their representatives on behalf of their government. Genocide, abuse of power, corruption, environmental destruction, and more all would qualify as state crimes. Governments may engage in cybercrime and may also turn a blind eye to the actions of organized crime groups if those groups' actions serve the interests or goals of the state. One of the most difficult aspects of state crime is in defining the actions of the state as criminal because often the state will justify its actions—or may even refuse to pass laws or sign treaties that prohibit its conduct (Barak, 2015). Further, policing or controlling the state is incredibly difficult—as is holding the government accountable for its wrong, criminal, or harmful actions.

- *State crime involves power, status, and politics. Can you describe how state crimes might intersect with the corporate world to produce crimes or harms in society?*
- *Genocide is one of the most harmful forms of state crime. Can you place genocide into context against other types of crime like murder or robbery and highlight the common characteristics and the role that power plays in enabling genocide to occur?*
- *State crime often harms the least powerful and most vulnerable people of the world. Can you discuss the types of physical, financial, and other harms that result from state crimes? What do you see as the pathways forward or solutions to address this crime type?*

E-Resources

1. International State Crime Initiative Website: http://statecrime.org/about-isci/about-state-crime/
2. *Rwanda—25 years after the Genocide:* https://www.youtube.com/watch?v=8lV1RubWD8Y
3. *The Path to Genocide:* https://www.youtube.com/watch?v=sRcNq4OYTvE

References

Aulette, J. R., & Michalowski, R. (1993). Fire in hamlet: A case study of a state corporate crime. In K. D. Tunnell (Ed.), *Political crime in contemporary America: A critical approach* (p. 171–206). Garland.

Barak, G. (2015). Introduction: On the invisibility and neutralization of the crimes of the powerful and their victims. In G. Barak (Ed.), *The Routledge international handbook of the crimes of the powerful* (pp. 1–35). Routledge.

Burnett, J. (2014, March 20). *Awash in cash, drug cartels rely on big banks to launder profits.* NPR. https://www.npr.org/sections/parallels/2014/03/20/291934724/awash-in-cash-drug-cartels-rely-on-big-banks-to-launder-profits

Chambliss, W. J. (2000). *Power, politics, and crime*. Westview Press.

Chambliss, W. J., & Moloney, C. J. (2014). *State crime: Critical concepts in criminology*. Routledge.

Cole, C. (2010, March 8). Closing coal plant a numbers game. *Arizona Daily Sun*. https://azdailysun.com/news/local/closing-coal-plant-a-numbers-game/article_4da48786-38c9-5fba-a8f7-209b3cf4604f.html

Clinard, M. B., & Yeager, P. C. (2005). *Corporate crime*. Transaction Publishers.

Department of Justice. (2015, May 27). *Nine FIFA officials and five corporate executives indicted for racketeering conspiracy and corruption* [Press release]. https://www.justice.gov/opa/pr/nine-fifa-officials-and-five-corporate-executives-indicted-racketeering-conspiracy-and

Department of Justice. (2016, March 7). *Supreme Court rejects Apple's request to review e-books antitrust conspiracy findings* [Press release]. https://www.justice.gov/opa/pr/supreme-court-rejects-apples-request-review-e-books-antitrust-conspiracy-findings

Dold, R. B. (1985, April 16). The charge: Murder by executive decision. *The Chicago Tribune*. https://www.chicagotribune.com/news/ct-xpm-1985-04-16-8501220235-story.html

Dole, C. E. (1980, March 14). Pinto verdict lets jury off the hook. *The Christian Science Monitor*. https://www.csmonitor.com/1980/0314/031435.html

Evertsson, N. (2013). Political corruption as a form of state crime: A case study on electoral donations. In W. J. Chambliss & C. J. Moloney (Eds.), *State crime* (pp. 283–300). Routledge.

Favot, S. (2014, December 31). Who are the Pasadena embezzlement suspects Danny Wooten, Melody Jenkins, Tyrone Collins? *Pasadena Star-News*. https://www.pasadenastarnews.com/2014/12/31/who-are-the-pasadena-embezzlement-suspects-danny-wooten-melody-jenkins-tyrone-collins/

Friedrichs, D. O. (2002). Occupational crime, occupational deviance, and workplace crime: Sorting out the difference. *Criminal Justice, 2*(3), 243–256. https://doi.org/10.1177/17488958020020030101

Green, P., & Ward, T. (2004). *State crime: Governments, violence, and corruption*. Pluto Press.

Grogin, J. P. (1986). Corporations can kill too: After film recovery, are individuals accountable for corporate crimes? *Loyola of Los Angeles Law Review, 19*(1411), 1411–1449.

Kramer, R. C. (1992). The space shuttle Challenger explosion: A case study of state-corporate crime. In K. Schlegel & D. Weisburd (Eds.), *White collar crime reconsidered* (pp. 212–241). Northeastern University Press.

Kramer, R. C., Michalowski, R. J., & Kauzlarich, D. (2002). The origins and development of the concept and theory of state-corporate crime. *Crime & Delinquency, 48*(2), 263–282. https://doi.org/10.1177/0011128702048002005

Maakestad, W. (1987). Redefining corporate crime. *Multinational Monitor, 8*(5). https://multinationalmonitor.org/hyper/issues/1987/05/clark.html#Multinationals

Mark, M. (2015, September 24). Ghana's top undercover journalist masters disguise to expose corruption. *The Guardian*. https://www.theguardian.com/world/2015/sep/24/anas-aremeya-anas-ghana-corruption

Miethe, T. D., McCorkle, R. C., & Listwan, S. J. (2006). *Crime profiles: The anatomy of dangerous persons, places, and situations* (3rd ed.). Roxbury Publishing Company.

Mohkiber, R. (2000). *Top 100 corporate criminals of the decade*. Corporate Crime Reporter. http://www.corporatecrimereporter.com/top100.html

Navajo-Hopi Observer. (2009, May 8). President Obama repeals 'Bennett Freeze' law. *Navajo-Hopi Observer*. https://www.nhonews.com/news/2009/may/08/president-obama-repeals-bennett-freeze-law/

Occupational Safety & Health Administration. (n.d.). *Commonly used statistics*. U.S. Department of Labor. https://www.osha.gov/data/commonstats

Onuah, F. (2015, November 18). *Nigeria's Buhari orders arrest of former security advisor for graft*. Reuters. https://www.reuters.com/article/nigeria-corruption-idUKL8N13D2RE20151118

Organization of African Unity. (2000, July 7). *Rwanda: The preventable genocide*. https://www.refworld.org/docid/4d1da8752.html

OSHA Act of 1970. Publ. L. No. 91-596, 84 Stat. 1590 (1970). https://www.osha.gov/laws-regs/oshact/completeoshact

Pasternak, J. (2006, November 19). A peril that dwelt among the Navajos. *Los Angeles Times*. https://www.latimes.com/news/la-na-navajo19nov19-story.html

Puzzanghera, J. (2012, September 12). Financial crisis, recession cost U.S. $12.8 trillion, report says. *Los Angeles Times*.

Roberts, J. J. (2015, June 30). Apple conspired with book publishers, appeals court confirms. *Fortune Magazine*. https://fortune.com/2015/06/30/apple-conspired-with-book-publishers-appeals-court-confirms/

San Juan Southern Paiute Tribe. (n.d.). *About the tribe*. https://www.sanjuanpaiute-nsn.gov/about

Scott, L. M. (2012). Shooting marbles: Another look at the landmark Campbell Soup deceptive advertising case. *Advertising & Society Review, 12*(4). https://doi.org/10.1353/asr.2012.0004

Shover, N., & Hochstetler, A. (2006). *Choosing white-collar crime*. Cambridge University Press.

Sutherland, E. H. (1949). *White collar crime*. Dryden Press.

The Independent. (2015, June 3). FIFA corruption timeline: The events that led up to the resignation of President Sepp Blatter. https://www.independent.co.uk/sport/football/international/fifa-corruption-timeline-the-events-that-led-up-to-the-resignation-of-president-sepp-blatter-10294646.html

O'Grady, S. (2015, December 29). The worst corruption scandals of 2015. *Foreign Policy*.

United Nations General Assembly. (1948, December 9). *Convention on the punishment and prevention of the crime of genocide*.

United States Holocaust Memorial Museum. (2020, December 8). Documenting numbers of victims of the Holocaust and Nazi persecution. In *Holocaust Encyclopedia*. https://encyclopedia.ushmm.org/content/en/article/documenting-numbers-of-victims-of-the-holocaust-and-nazi-persecution

United to End Genocide. (2015). *Atrocities against Native Americans*. http://endgenocide.org/learn/past-genocides/native-americans/

Wrage, A. A. (2007). *Bribery and extortion: Undermining business, governments, and security*. Praeger Security International.

Zernike, K. (2016, November 4). Two ex-Christie allies are convicted in George Washington Bridge case. *New York Times*. https://www.nytimes.com/2016/11/05/nyregion/bridgegate-conviction.html

Figure Credits

Fig. 12.1: Source: https://www.tsln.com/news/a-unique-study-of-bison-populations/.

Printed in the USA
CPSIA information can be obtained
at www.ICGtesting.com
LVHW061756110524
779861LV00014BA/44